Contents

IATEFL 2013

Liverpool Conference Selections

47th International Conference
Liverpool
8–12 April 2013

Edited by Tania Pattison

Editorial Committee: Siân Morgan, Sandie Mourão, Amos Paran

Published by IATEFL
2–3 The Foundry
Seager Road
Faversham
Kent ME13 7FD

Copyright for whole volume © IATEFL 2014

Copyright for individual reports/papers remains
vested in the contributors, to whom applications for
rights to reproduce should be made.

First published 2014

British Library Cataloguing in Publication Data
Education
Tania Pattison (Ed.)
   IATEFL 2013 Liverpool Conference Selections

ISBN 978-1-901095-53-1

For a complete list of IATEFL publications, please
write to the above address, or visit the IATEFL
website at www.iatefl.org

Cover photographs © 2013, Mike Hogan, York.
Copy-edited by Simon Murison-Bowie, Oxford.
Designed and typeset by Keith Rigley, Charlbury.
Printed in Britain by Berforts Information Press, Eynsham.

Editor's introduction

Liverpool is a city of superlatives: it is the home of the UK's largest cathedral, the country's most famous horse race, some of the biggest names in British popular music, and one of England's most successful football teams. It is fitting, therefore, that in 2013 Liverpool was the scene of another superlative: the largest IATEFL conference to date was held in the city. In April 2013, a record 2,633 delegates from around the world had a ticket to ride to the hometown of Lennon and McCartney for the 47th Annual International IATEFL Conference and Exhibition—and Liverpool did not disappoint.

Liverpool has undergone a transformation in the last few years, not least in the Albert Dock area, now home to the Arena and Convention Centre (ACC) and nearby Jurys Inn. This was IATEFL's home for four days of conference sessions (five, if we include the pre-conference events); delegates could choose from over 600 talks, workshops, publishers' demonstrations, SIG events, and more. As always, the accompanying Exhibition enabled us to explore new materials from over 50 exhibitors, while the Jobs Market matched job seekers with potential employers. IATEFL 2013 also saw the launch of a new Special Interest Group, the Materials Writing SIG, known as MaW SIG.

Fundraising continued to play a vital role in Liverpool, with badges sold to raise funds for the Wider Membership Individual Scheme, which allows IATEFL to sponsor memberships for ELT professionals in less-developed parts of the world.

For those unable to attend the conference in person, the British Council once again sponsored IATEFL Online, which allowed 'virtual' delegates from around the world to watch recordings of sessions and interviews. IATEFL remains grateful to the British Council for their support of this venture.

Liverpool was European Capital of Culture in 2008, and the culture of Merseyside was much in evidence at the conference. Highlights included Liverpool poet Roger McGough's closing plenary; the annual Macmillan party, held at the famous Cavern Club; and walking tours of the city's landmarks, as well as longer trips to nearby Chester and Port Sunlight. There was truly something to interest everyone here, from the historian to the music fan to the art lover.

The 103 contributions presented in this volume are remarkable in their diversity and innovation. Needless to say, those involved in technology in ELT never fail to impress with their innovative approaches to language education; this year, there is a focus on the use of technology *outside* as well as inside the classroom, in the form of mobile learning. But pushing the boundaries goes further than modes of delivery. In these pages, we find topics rarely addressed: for example, the use of gay-themed literature in ELT [5.7]; the tragedy of learner suicide [4.7]; and the question of whether religion belongs in the classroom [4.11]. Readers are encouraged to take risks, to experiment, to 'do something you don't want to do, every day' [12.4]. There is also no shortage of controversial topics in this issue. Do laptops in schools make a difference [7.8]? Is teacher talking time underrated [4.4]? Is current ELT discourse dangerously reminiscent of Orwell's *Nineteen Eighty-Four* [12.2]? Many of these papers will leave readers pondering the issues they raise, long after the volume has been closed and placed on the bookshelves.

This year, some changes were made at the conference. Symposia were suspended for 2013, hence no Symposium reports; still in place, however—and included in this volume of *Conference Selections*—were the *ELT Journal*/IATEFL Debate, in which Scott Thornbury squared off against Catherine Walter [5.2]; as well as plenaries from IATEFL Patron David Crystal [**Prologue**], Susan Barduhn [**3.1**], Deniz Kurtoğlu Eken [**12.1**] and Jun Liu [**Epilogue**]; and signature events from Pearson [**11.5**], the British Council [**3.2**] and the A. S. Hornby Scholars [**2.1**].

As always, I enjoyed reading each and every paper I received for this volume of *Conference Selections*, and I am grateful to all writers for submitting their work for consideration. *Conference Selections* is a refereed publication, and my job would not be possible without the hard work of Editorial Committee members Amos Paran, Siân Morgan and Sandie Mourão. Sadly, this year we say goodbye to Siân and Sandie, both of whom are stepping down after four years of much-appreciated service to *Conference Selections*. I am enormously grateful for their time and dedication, and I thank them for their invaluable input. I am also grateful for the talents of our copy-editor Simon Murison-Bowie and our designer and typesetter Keith Rigley, and for the advice provided by IATEFL President Carol Read.

As *Conference Selections* 2013 goes to press, many of us are making plans to travel to the north of England for IATEFL 2014. From 2–5 April we will be back in a well-loved destination, the Harrogate International Conference Centre in the beautiful spa town of Harrogate, Yorkshire.

I look forward to seeing many of you there!

Tania Pattison
Editor, IATEFL *Conference Selections*
cseditor@iatefl.org

Prologue

This issue opens—as the conference did—with a paper by IATEFL's Patron, **David Crystal**. The paper presents an analysis of the use of syntactic blends, as exemplified by the words of Liverpool's own Paul McCartney; implications for ELT are discussed.

Plenary: The world in which we live in: Beatles, blends and blogs

David Crystal *University of Bangor, UK*

I take my title from the opening lines of Paul McCartney's theme song for the 1973 James Bond movie *Live and Let Die*. It was performed by Wings, the band he created after the Beatles broke up.

> When you were young and your heart was an open book
> You used to say live and let live
> (You know you did, you know you did, you know you did)
> But if this ever-changing world in which we live in
> Makes you give in and cry
> Say live and let die.

It's the fourth line I want to draw your attention to. People don't notice the double preposition while they are listening to the music. Only sad linguists do that. But when they see it, they immediately say this is not a grammatical sentence. It ought to be either 'this ever-changing world in which we live' or 'this ever-changing world which we live in'. Not both. What is going on?

The point has attracted some discussion by Beatles fans. A couple of years ago there was a lively debate about whether the line was actually '... world in which we're livin', with the final -*g* dropped, as often happens in rapid colloquial speech, and which is commonly heard in the Liverpool accent. But this seemed unlikely. The version I've quoted is the one we read in the published sheet music. And when Paul himself was asked to comment, he said he couldn't recall which it was originally, but he thought the published version 'wronger but cuter'!

I assume by 'cuter' Paul meant the artistic shape of the line in its context. The end-placed preposition is echoed by the phrasal verb in the next line, 'makes you *give in* and cry'. The fourth line has an iambic rhythm which requires an 'in' before 'which'. And the tune demands an unstressed syllable at the line end. Imagine how it would sound if the line ended on 'live', with an elongated vowel, 'li-ive'. The tune needs a lyric with two prepositions. When music calls, grammar bends.

Linguists have no problem dealing with such sentences. We call them blends. A blend is a conflation of two independent entities. They can be words, as in the case of 'brunch', 'heliport', 'motorcade', 'Internet', and many more. And they can be syntactic constructions, as here—the end-placed versus the mid-placed preposition. But there's a big difference between lexical and syntactic blends. Many lexical blends quickly become part of Standard English: they get into the dictionary. Syntactic blends don't get into grammars. You'll never see 'in which we live in' in an English grammar. Which is why grammar books are no help at all when it comes to understanding how syntactic blends operate.

The point to note is that blends are very frequent, especially in speech. Paul McCartney is by no means alone. Not so long ago I heard someone say 'I don't know to which hotel I'm going to'. And the blend can even be seen in writing, as in these extracts from websites:

- For which party will you be voting for in the March 9 election?
- Mentors can help you with your marriage, too. After all, we all have marriage role models, couples to which we look up to and aspire to be like.
- From which country does a Lexus come from?

There's no musical justification in these cases, so what is going on here?

Syntactic blends arise when people are uncertain about which construction to use—so they use them both. It's an unconscious process, which operates at the speed of thought. So the interesting question is why there is uncertainty. In the case of the two prepositions, it arises from the choice between formal and informal usage, which has long attracted prescriptive discontent. We can say both the formal 'This is the man to whom I was speaking' and the informal 'This is the man I was speaking to'. Native speakers are often uncertain about the distinction because, in the prescriptive tradition which dominated schools since the 18th century, teachers tried to eliminate the informal version by imposing the rule 'Never end a sentence with a preposition'. It was never an authentic rule, of course, for end-placed prepositions can be found in the language from Anglo-Saxon times and are frequently found in, for instance, Shakespeare. But the rule appealed to classically minded pedants and it became a standard shibboleth for over 200 years. It would hardly ever be taught nowadays, thanks to decades of scorn poured upon it by writers and orators—notably Winston Churchill, in his famous remark that this was a rule 'up with which he would not put'. But it has left a legacy of doubt in the minds of many, who feel that putting a preposition at the end of a sentence is somehow wrong. So they bring the preposition forward, thinking that this is a more correct usage. But then the natural pattern of the language takes over, prompting them to keep the preposition where it most easily falls, immediately following its verb. They realise they need a preposition at the end to make the sentence sound natural. So they put one in, forgetting that they have used one already. This is especially likely when the preposition is monosyllabic and the phrasal verb has a highly predictable collocation, such as we see in 'live in', 'go to', 'vote for', and 'look up to'.

The double preposition also occurs especially when there is some length between the first and second use. Compare the following examples. We are less likely to encounter the first one because the two prepositions are very close to each other:

- For which candidate will you vote for?

We are a bit more likely to encounter the next one, because there is more to process:

- For which of the five candidates are you going to be voting for?

And we will certainly hear examples like the following—this one on a BBC news channel recently:

- For which of the five candidates in the forthcoming by-election will the people of Eastleigh be voting for?

I shall return to the question of length later.

Now, if it were simply a matter of double prepositions, the point would hardly be worth a keynote lecture. But blending can take place between *any* two (or more) closely related constructions. The Beatles songs illustrate several more. In *Bad Boy* we hear:

> A bad little kid moved into my neighborhood.
> He won't do nothing right just in sitting down and look so good

Standard English requires 'looking', but the extra syllable won't work, so we end up with a blend of 'sitting down and looking' and the creole-like 'he ... look so good'. And in *Boys* we hear:

> I been told when a boy kiss a girl,
> Take a trip around the world,

Here the 'when' construction, which requires 'kisses', is blended with some other one, such as 'should a boy kiss a girl' to get the required metre.

When we leave music behind, and begin to listen to everyday conversation, we find blended constructions all the time, as people begin a sentence and, in the middle, change their minds as to how it should end. What we have is technically described as an *anacoluthon*, defined (for example, by the *OED*) as 'a construction lacking grammatical sequence'. They appear in lecturing too. You won't hear any examples in lectures that have been carefully written down, like this one, but when lecturers speak spontaneously, you'll hear lots—though you probably won't notice them, as you are paying more attention to *what* is being said than to *how* it is being said. I take the examples from a recent DVD of my own spontaneously delivered lectures (Crystal 2009). The first two are from a lecture on the future of English:

- ... where English has some status as the language of the press or of broadcasting, or the Church, or the government, or what it might be, the law courts ...

'Or what it might be'. The two constructions blended here are a question and a statement.

- And within ... how long do you think? ... Within how long did it take for an American English to start to grow?

'Within how long'. This time the blend constructions are two questions. The direct question to the audience interrupts the flow of thought, and a blend is the result.

The third example is from a lecture on language death, where the lecturer is role playing a dialogue between a young person and his parents. The youth is asking them why they no longer speak his ancestral language, and they are blaming *their* parents:

- 'We don't speak it?' 'Why don't we speak it?' 'Well, cos I was never taught it.' 'Why weren't I taught it?'

'Why weren't I taught it?' The rhetorical build-up is first-person plural, 'we ... we... we ...', but the parent switches to the first person, 'I'. The response conflates two constructions: 'Why weren't we taught it?' (continuing the rhetorical pattern) or perhaps 'Why weren't you taught it?' (responding to the parent's use of 'I'), and 'Why wasn't I taught it?' (which is how the dialogue began in the first place). In the enthusiasm of the role play, these alternatives blend.

The fourth example comes from a talk on language and the Internet:

• So this is the dynamic character of the screen is something which makes written language very very different from anything we've had in the past.

Here the blend is between two subject–verb–complement constructions: 'The dynamic character of the screen is something which makes written language different' and 'This is the dynamic character of the screen, which makes written language different'. The alternatives convey the same information but with different emphasis. The first choice is a straightforward SVC construction. The second one works like a cleft sentence, in which a bit of information is brought to the front of a sentence and given special emphasis: 'It's the dynamic character of the screen which ...'. Clearly the lecturer was uncertain as to where he wanted the emphasis to fall in the sentence as he began to process it, and a blend was the result.

These are all examples from speech. It's much more difficult to encounter examples in the traditional domain of the written language. Blends rarely appear in public writing because we notice them when we reread our text prior to publication—or, if *we* don't, someone else does, such as an editor or copy-editor—and the anomaly is eliminated by rephrasing. You have to remember that Standard English is, first and foremost, what you read in the public domain, and to appear there a piece of writing has to pass through a number of filters, whether it is a book, a magazine, a newspaper, a billboard, a brochure, or a notice on a wall. The checks are carried out by editors, sub-editors, copy-editors, proof-readers and printers, whose job is to ensure that a use of written language is clear and consistent, and that it reflects the house style of the publisher. If you have written anything for public consumption, you will know about house style, and how your submission is edited by others before it appears in print. It is a practice which has steadily grown since the 15th century, and it is standard procedure today.

But not on the Internet. In blogs, social networking sites, web page forums and personal websites there is little or no external editorial influence. We see our writing there in its most naked form, in passages of continuous prose (often of considerable length), but presented in a screen typeface that can be as elegant as in any paper publication. The style might be totally spontaneous and conversational, but the visual impact is one of care and revision. Indeed, we can—if we wish and have the time—revise our posts so that they conform exactly to what we believe to be Standard English; but the evidence is that most people do not, especially in interactive contexts where emotions are running high (as is so often the case on the Internet). As a result, blends of the kind I am illustrating are increasingly to be found.

I spent just a few minutes randomly dipping into the top 100 UK blogs, as established by the Branded website, and saw several examples on the opening pages. Here is one, from the number 5 site:

Although MajesticSEO have already entered into the browser extension market with their release of their Google Chrome extension, the news that their release on Monday will open up their services to Mozilla Firefox browser users, giving them even quicker access to the information that they receive while using the tool.

We need a finite verb after 'users' to make this sentence grammatical. It has to be 'gives them' or 'is giving them' or 'will give them', or the like. The problem here is that, by using a very long subject ('the news ... users', 17 words), by the time the writer gets to the verb he has forgotten how the sentence is going. He evidently thinks that the sentence began at 'Their release on Monday will open ...', where a non-finite 'giving' would be acceptable. Here, what is semantically most important in his mind (the news of the release) has taken priority over grammatical construction.

It's the length of constructions that tends to get in the way and cause blends. Once a construction goes beyond the easy limits of working memory capacity, problems arise. You may recall George Miller's 'magic number seven, plus or minus two'—a 'law' that has been repeatedly explored in psychology, with varying results depending on the kind of data being manipulated. For words (as opposed to digits), the number of chunks we can easily process is much lower than seven, perhaps as small as four. But whatever the lowest level is, it's evident that 17 words is wildly beyond our comfortable working memory. Even if we ignore the grammatical words and focus on just the items with lexical content, we are dealing with nine chunks:

the news—their release—on Monday—will open up—their services—to Mozilla—Firefox—browser—users [giving them even quicker access]

This is an awful lot to remember. No wonder the writer loses his way. He can't recall where he has been, and is anxious to push on to his main point, which is 'quicker access'.

Poorly constructed sentences of this kind have attracted stylistic complaints for generations. Fowler's *Dictionary of Modern English Usage* is full of examples attacking them. How is one to avoid them? Reading text aloud is one way, which can help in the case of blends in short sentences. But it doesn't help in the case of long ones. It's not really possible to read a 50-word sentence aloud so as to retain its meaning. The only possible solution is to rephrase, or rewrite in shorter sentences. And in doing so, we must take on board one of the basic principles governing listening and reading comprehension: that comprehension is governed by the distribution of weight throughout a sentence.

English is a language where end-weight is normal. In everyday speech, speakers tend to place the most important information towards the end of the sentence, and not towards the beginning. Specifically, the weight occurs after the main verb and not before it. Take the piece of informal conversation presented in Table 1 (overleaf)—from the first recording in *Advanced Conversational English* (Crystal and Davy 1976)—ignoring non-fluencies. Note what happens before and after the verb:

The vast majority of subjects in everyday conversation are like this—a single pronoun or a short noun phrase of just two or three words. If I continued this example for another 100 clauses, you wouldn't see anything different. All the length is concentrated after the main verb. Occasionally a bit of extra length is added before the

Pre-verb	Verb	Post-verb
I	think	
it probably	is	the money for what you get, you know
I	was reading	in the paper this morning, a chap
he	's	a director of a big company in Birmingham
who	was	the world's number one football fan
he	used to spend	about a thousand a year watching football, you know
he	's watched	football in every league ground in England, all 92, and
he	's been	to America to watch West Bromwich playing in America
he	's been	to the last two or three World Cup tournaments, and
he	goes	to all the matches away, you know, European cup matches, and everything that
English teams	are playing in	
he	's	all over the world watching it, you see
this year, he	's watched	22 games so far this year
which	is	about 50 per cent of his normal, and
even he	's getting browned off ...	

Table 1: Sample of informal conversation

verb in the form of a short emphatic adverbial (as in 'probably', 'this year', 'even'). But long subjects and long opening adverbial clauses are definitely out. Making these clause elements lengthy immediately affects listening comprehension, as can be easily demonstrated. Which of the following two sentences do you find easier to process?

- It was nice of John and Mary to visit us the other day.
- For John and Mary to visit us the other day was nice.

The answer is obvious. So note the potential problem, then, when we encounter an exercise like that in Figure 1, in an ELT coursebook (Broughton 1969: 48), which I took at random from my shelves. It is part of a lesson on relative clauses.

Exercise 4

Finish these sentences, for example, *Salesmen who sell books at your door are a nuisance. The books they sell are often expensive.*

Salesmen who sell books at your door	are a nuisance.
The books they sell	are often expensive.
People who buy expensive clothes	go shopping at ——.
The clothes they buy	are ——.
Men who drink and then drive	——.
The passengers they carry	——.

Figure 1: Textbook exercise on relative clauses

The pattern is a complete reversal of what we encounter in everyday speech.

Now, I'm not of course saying that such exercises are of no value. All I'm saying is that teachers need to be aware that, by putting so much weight before the verb, they are making such sentences more difficult to process than they need to be, so that it would be wise to leave them until later in a course. In the earlier stages of teaching relative clauses, it would be sensible to keep the subjects short and introduce the relatives after the verb. So:

• I don't like salesmen who sell books at the door.
• It's often expensive to buy the books they sell.

And so on. You can do better than this. I am no materials writer. But I hope you see that these constructions are much easier to process, and the exposure to relative clauses is still there.

You can perhaps now see why my blogging examples caused their writers such difficulty. They begin with lengthy constructions which take up so much processing power that the sentence breaks down as it switches from subordinate to main clause.

Although MajesticSEO have already entered into the browser extension market with their release of their Google Chrome extension, [the news that] their release on Monday	will open up their services ...

The writers are no longer in control. Notice that there's no ambiguity in sentences that contain blends, because the semantic content remains clear in their minds. It is simply that the grammar has not kept pace with the thought.

I said earlier that syntactic blends don't get into grammars. *Could* a blend ever become part of Standard English? I don't see why not, actually, but it would take a lot of usage to get one established, and it would have to get past the eagle eyes of the copy editors. One possible candidate is seen in this next example from book where something did get through (Sambin 2008: 28):

The means by which one can solve the definitional equations are some very simple properties, which one should better specify in advance, and these are the properties of *and* and of *yields*.

'Should better'. The blend here is between two modal constructions which both mean 'ought to' ('had better' and 'should'), and a third construction where the 'better' is an adverbial modifying a following verb. I've heard this usage in regional dialects ('you should better go', 'you should better'), but it hasn't yet established itself as Standard English. I've also heard it quite a lot from learners of English as a foreign language, so it's probably already being claimed as a feature of English as a lingua franca.

Which brings me back to ELT. You have come across blends before, I have no doubt, in your students' writing. Learners' writing often displays blends, especially when they're attempting to use more advanced syntactic constructions. Sentences start in one way and finish in another. Getting them to read through their work before giving it in can help, or getting them to read the problem sentence aloud—but it won't solve all problems, as in some cases there's a genuine lack of awareness as to what the problem is. In such cases, it will be necessary to tease apart the contributing structures, to show what went wrong, in the way I've done with my examples.

Here's an example from a piece of writing by a 15 year old: 'Does it not worry you that the man to whom you will marry might be cruel to you?' The extra 'to' could be here for either (or both) of two reasons: the student could have been uncertain about how to use the 'whom' construction, or she was planning to write 'the man to whom you will be married', and changed her mind halfway through. It is very important to appreciate that errors such as these are signs of growth, not carelessness. To condemn a blend in a complex construction may lead to the student avoiding the construction altogether and staying with safer, simpler expressions. It's far better to spend a little bit of time analysing the sources of the blend. This points the way forward.

It's also important to know the contexts in which blends are likely to occur. Blends tend to be more common when there is pressure on the speaker or writer. The pressure might be simply a rush to complete a piece of written work, or having to say something in front of a class. That is why we often hear them in settings where the speaker is having to process language at speed, such as a sports commentary. As emotions rise, blends increase. Any family row will have lots of them, as the participants get their grammar tangled up as they strive to make a point! They are a natural consequence of the dynamics of a speech situation. Accordingly, they are nothing to feel guilty about. Of course, in writing one tries to eliminate them, as readers are more likely to notice them there, and they will be condemned as 'careless', 'lazy', or 'sloppy'. We don't want that. But speech is a very different scenario.

Now I'm not suggesting for one moment that you begin to teach blends. But I think you need to be prepared to encounter them, for they are frequent in everyday speech, and you need to know how to disentangle them. On the other hand, I don't think you need to throw yourself into the River Mersey if you realise you have just used one yourself. This is the world in which we live in.

davidcrystal2@gmail.com

References

Broughton, G. 1969. *Success with English*, Coursebook 2. London: Penguin.

Crystal, D. 2009. *The Future of Language*. Abingdon: Routledge.

Crystal, D. and D. Davy. 1976. *Advanced Conversational English*. London: Longman.

Sambin, G. 2008. 'Two applications of dynamic constructivism: Brouwer's continuity principle and choice sequences in formal topology' in M. van Atten *et al.* (eds.). *One Hundred Years of Intuitionism, 1907–2007*. Nancy: Poincaré Archives Publication.

1 Conference highlights

In this chapter, five delegates from around the world share their thoughts on what made IATEFL 2013 memorable for them. All come from diverse backgrounds and career paths. For **Partha Sarathi Misra**, winning a scholarship to attend the conference from India represented the fulfilment of a dream; he describes the atmosphere of passion and professionalism he encountered. **Jana Jilkova** attended the conference on behalf of the Association of Teacher Educators in the Czech Republic; she comments here on the difference IATEFL makes to ELT professionals around the world. **Nicola Perry**, attending from the UK, shares her secret for dealing with the unfortunate reality that many 'must-see' sessions are often scheduled at the same time. **Diana Metzner** travelled to IATEFL from Germany as a publisher's representative; she describes the key role played by the publishers' Exhibition in providing information to delegates. Finally, **Moundir Al Amrani**, who came to Liverpool from Morocco, describes the joy of meeting and being inspired by the authors of an admired coursebook.

■ My dream of attending the IATEFL Conference became a reality when I reached Liverpool this year as a recipient of the IATEFL Ray Tongue Scholarship. On the first morning, I reached the venue quite early as I had expected a huge crowd at the registration desk. To my utter surprise, I got my registration kit in five minutes. What a friendly and relaxed atmosphere! Was it an academic meeting, or a family reunion, I wondered.

The day long SIG PCE was highly stimulating. I was glad to share my concern for ESP in an EFL context with teachers from various parts of the world.

As a new IATEFL conference participant, I made a point of attending the talks in the 'How to …' series every day. Susan Barduhn told us how to 'jigsaw' our conference experience; Alison Schwetlick outlined how to write for IATEFL *Voices*; and Tania Pattison provided much-needed guidance on how to prepare our reports for *Conference Selections*. The precision of the talks made a permanent impression on our minds, and their talks showed us the way. Really great!

My interaction with the delegates gave me the impression that younger delegates outnumbered those who were older. Presenters in the early stages of their careers spoke so passionately and professionally! Their passion for teaching English as a global language and their commitment to professional development reverberated through their papers presented in the sessions I attended. David Crystal's plenary session on the language of the Beatles, Deniz Kurtoğlu Eken's plenary session on the weather in ELT and Jun Liu's plenary session on ELT tomorrow also brought out the youthful spirit of the conference.

English in the digital world was a recurrent theme in the conference. Presentations on topics such as the implications of digital media for the development of infants, designing materials for mobile learning, one-to-one learning, how to create a machinima, and the information superhighway for networked teachers were appreciated by the delegates who thronged the halls where these topics were presented and debated. There was hardly a vacant seat in those halls, and I have never seen such animated discussions!

Partha Sarathi Misra *India*

partha.misra@azimpremjifoundation.org

■ When Vanessa Esteves started her presentation about critical thinking with the command 'Give me a wave if you've seen a friend today', a forest of hands went up. For the fourth day a crowd of educators flooded the streets of Liverpool around the conference centre on the banks of the Mersey. Over 2,500 participants followed talks, actively took part in workshops and in their free time shared their general and personal experience of ELT; they looked for ways to support their students in acquiring foreign languages, made contacts and enjoyed themselves.

Both 'big names' and unknown experts added their own fragments to the mosaic of ELT. How often do we get a chance to see a class in Libya? We saw students in simple rooms with bare white plaster walls. They had lots of questions for the teacher; they wanted to understand English and its rules because they believed that then they would be able to use it. The Libyan work shows the enormous power of motivation and responsiveness to student needs. These Libyan students made significant progress through a learner-centred approach.

Variety was typical. A lively debate took place on the topic 'Published course materials don't reflect the lives or needs of learners'. In the end, it was clear that the opinions of the debaters were as varied as the needs of teachers and students.

IATEFL makes a difference. Supporting people who aren't working in optimal conditions is the goal of sponsorship and scholarships. Pre-conference meetings of the representatives of teachers' associations are also traditionally supported. This year the meetings focused on determining needs and ideas for the support of a wide range of members. Results of the various discussions will be used in setting further strategies for work together.

Personally, my biggest highlight was constant wonder at how much potential is hidden in ELT teachers, and how IATEFL contributes to its use. It does make a difference.

Jana Jilkova *Czech Republic*

jajilkova@gmail.com

■ There was just too much choice! Every time I decided on one presentation to go to, there were two or three or four others that looked equally interesting and useful at the same time. I had heard about an idea for 'jigsawing' with other delegates. Eventually, I had a chance to try it out.

Here's how it worked: Michael Harrison posted on the IATEFL Facebook page that he would like some feedback from Ken Wilson's session because he didn't want to miss Jamie Keddie's. I saw Jamie last year and really wanted to hear what Ken had to say. So Michael and I arranged to meet in the coffee break after the sessions to exchange notes.

Ken was an entertaining speaker and his session was very interactive. We were up on our feet a lot as his talk was designed to show us how to get learners to listen to each other. However, I also noticed that with the extra responsibility of reporting back to Michael, I became involved even more and wrote lots of notes—something I'm not usually very good at.

It was good to meet Michael because we often exchange comments on the IATEFL Facebook page. We reported on what we had learnt and discussed how we might use the activities in our very different teaching contexts. This immediate, verbal and collaborative reflection process really helps to bring the session out of the seminar room and into the 'real' world. Not only does describing and hearing about the activities help you to remember them more clearly but getting someone else's reaction to them encourages the discovery of even more ways they could be adapted and used in different contexts.

I really like this jigsaw idea. Not only can you experience more presentations close-up but the sharing and reflection add value, too. I highly recommend this to participants at future conferences.

Nicola Perry *UK*
Nicolaperry57@hotmail.com

■ 'Caution: your luggage may put on weight at Liverpool!' Of course there was no notice to this effect printed in the conference programme, but I (like others, I expect) did end up taking home at least 10 extra kilos' worth of brochures, books and papers: tangible proof of the wealth of information and inspiration gleaned from those jam-packed days.

In fact, much of my time was spent 'downstairs', on duty at the *telc–language tests* stand. For me the Exhibition epitomises IATEFL's annual event in the way it holds a unique appeal for very different attendees. One visitor to our stand could be a recently qualified teacher from a low-income country on the lookout for little tokens to take home as well as for information on our products; the next visitor might be the senior representative of a big British publishing house sounding me out on our assessment criteria. I found this variety and immediacy typical not only of the Exhibition but of IATEFL Liverpool as a whole.

Many delegates look forward to visiting stands and browsing new teaching resources, and they are excited if the author or the project manager is on hand to answer specific queries. As elsewhere, there is no alternative to personal contact! Of course, it also adds to the enjoyment if you can leave a stand with free promotional brochures or discounted books; and those little presents for your colleagues and students back home will involve them vicariously in the Liverpool experience.

This type of conference always has attractive and unique social events; on Wednesday, for example, I found it impossible to choose between the two big publishers' parties—so I went to both! But the more informal, spontaneous gatherings were equally enjoyable and valuable networking opportunities … more proof that face-to-face interaction has not yet been ousted by virtual communication.

For the handful of sessions I could attend, I deliberately chose smaller ones show-casing personal experience from young colleagues. Nicky Francis and Helen Ashton/ Sarah Shepherd were particularly inspiring. I plan to watch the 'big names' sessions online or read their papers in *Selections*, thus maximising the benefits gained from those 10 kilos of Liverpool material.

Diana Metzner *Germany*

diana.metzner@gmx.de

■ My experience of IATEFL 2013 in Liverpool is memorable in different ways, and although there is a lot to say about it, I would like to share my appreciation and admiration of one specific session. I did not realise how enjoyable and informative this session would be until I was there attending it. This was the session entitled 'How to write a cutting edge course for your students', given by Peter Moor and Sarah Cunningham. Although the title was changed to 'How to be a cutting edge author', the presentation was still as interesting as I had expected it to be—but I had not real-ized that I was about to learn from the writers of a bestseller I have always admired. It was silly of me not to have realised this from the beginning, but the moment I was there, I understood it was a gift from IATEFL.

The session went on as expected and it offered a lot of information and tips on the arduous task of writing a successful course and being an author. There were other presentations about related topics that I did not want to miss, especially given that I came to the conference with the objective of learning as much as possible. Honestly, I had always had mixed views of writing materials, and I had thought it was a world where only certain people could survive; but all this turned out to be a misconcep-tion as I learnt more from the various sessions. I discovered materials writing was a world for teachers, because they are the ones close enough to understand the needs of students better than anyone else does.

After attending this conference, I realised how much I love my job. My career perspective and my idea of being part of the ELT family grew bigger. I met colleagues from all over the world, and it was great to see that we all share close ideas no mat-ter where we teach. I am looking forward, I hope, to attending the next conference.

Moundir Al Amrani *Morocco*

almoundir@gmail.com

2 Becoming an effective English teacher

The title of this chapter is taken from the first paper, the A. S. Hornby Scholars' report on teacher training in various contexts. Convenor **Martin Wedell** summarises the key issues in initial teacher training and INSET in transitional parts of the world. The next group of papers address some of the 'big picture' issues in teacher training. **Mark Daubney** reports on the anxiety experienced by trainee teachers; **Clare Fielder** explores the need to set goals and communicate these to students; **Barbara Buxton** discusses the language trainee teachers should be encouraged to teach and use in their teaching practice; and **Lynn Williams Leppich** describes the identification of suitable tasks for teaching practice. We then turn our attention to two specific teacher-training projects, carried out in China and reported by **Liping Zhou and Keith O'Hare** and in Brazil, reported by **Andreia Fernandes**. Both projects aim to train primary-school teachers to adopt a more communicative approach in their teaching. The final paper in this chapter is by **Briony Beaven** and relates research into trainers' perceptions of their own professional growth and development.

2.1 The Hornby Scholars' panel presentation: Becoming an effective English teacher: who, what and where helps it happen?

Convenor: **Martin Wedell** *University of Leeds, UK, with The A. S. Hornby Scholars at IATEFL 2013*

> **Shiva Kushwaha** *India;* **Hasantha Kuruppu** *Sri Lanka;*
> **Suman Laudari** *Nepal;* **Ali Zwair** *Iraq;* **Maria do Carmo Bazante** *Brazil;*
> **Zohra Fatima** *Pakistan;* **Thi Quynh Le Tran** *Vietnam;* **Samira Hazari** *Iran;*
> **Hintsa Addis** *Ethiopia;* **Dini Handayani** *Indonesia;*
> **Bernardo Cruz-Bello** *Mexico;* **Claudia Spatero** *Argentina*

Introduction

The worldwide spread of English in recent decades and the many national curriculum reforms that have attempted to introduce more 'communicative' approaches into English classrooms have increased the need for pre- and in-service training for English teachers. Substantial financial and human resources have been expended on numerous 'projects' that have attempted to provide such (mostly in-service) provision. In their presentation Hornby scholars from Nepal, India, Pakistan, Sri Lanka, Brazil, Argentina, Ethiopia, Iran, Indonesia, Iraq, Mexico and Vietnam focused on their personal experiences of participating in and providing teacher training and development initiatives. They tried to draw conclusions about what provision (in terms of content and process), provided by whom (formal or informal 'trainers') and situated where (in terms of distance from the actual classroom setting) was most likely to be successful in developing 'effective' teachers. The presentation had three main parts, each of which is discussed below.

What does an 'effective' English teacher need to learn/know/be able to do?

One way of deciding what is expected of an 'effective' English teacher in a particular context is through looking at what curriculum documents expect learners of English to achieve. For example, the Brazilian English curriculum hopes that learners will do the following:

- learn and use the modern foreign languages as an instrument to access information from other cultures and social groups
- understand how certain expressions might be interpreted according to social aspect and/or cultural reasons.

'Effective' Brazilian English teachers thus need a high level of personal language proficiency, an in-depth knowledge of their own and English-speaking cultures, and the pedagogical understandings and skills needed to help their learners achieve the above aims. In Vietnam the curriculum states:

> By 2020 most Vietnamese students graduating from secondary, vocational schools, colleges and universities will be able to use a foreign language confidently in their daily communication, their study and work in an integrated, multi-cultural and multi-lingual environment.

Again high levels of personal language proficiency and an extensive understanding of how second language pedagogy can help learners to develop their abilities to use English seem to be the minimum requirements for an 'effective' teacher in Vietnam.

In many English teaching contexts these expectations of English teachers challenge existing educational norms and practices. In many cases, there is a longstanding and deeply held view of teaching as a mostly one-way process of transmitting a set body of knowledge (about English) to learners; it is a considerable professional and personal challenge to make the transition from this view to one of teaching language as a process of learning through interaction and shared social participation in classroom activities. The developing understanding of how teachers learn (Freeman 2009; Johnson 2009; Korthhagen 2011; Malderez and Wedell 2007) suggests that, for most of us, making such a transition is an ongoing process, needing support over time. What form(s) can such support realistically take?

What support will help teachers to become effective?

The Scholars divided possible forms of support into formal (usually government funded and staffed, sometimes with help from external agencies) and informal (provided by teachers for teachers, with more or less guidance and assistance from teachers' associations or unions). We will discuss each in turn.

Formal initial teacher training (ITT)

Ideally all English teachers everywhere would have access to a thorough initial teacher education. The Scholars agreed that a thorough training needed to be long enough to

- enable teachers to feel competent and confident in their own language ability;
- help teachers to understand ideas regarding language teaching and learning (for example, socio-cultural theory, scaffolding, student centredness, students' developmental and cognitive stages, individual differences); and
- provide teachers with a complete understanding of the main features of their teaching context, developed through opportunities to observe and practise teaching in real classrooms, and to reflect on and discuss the experiences of doing so.

In the Scholars' contexts, ITT programmes last for between two weeks and four years. This suggests that many such programmes do not include the above. Reasons offered included

- lack of funding;
- insufficient understanding of (some of) the above ideas among teacher educators; and
- the inflexibility of existing ITT curricula, where long-established areas in generic education studies (such as the history of education) or in theoretical language-related areas (such as linguistics or semantics) continue to take up much of the training time.

Informal in-service training (INSET)

Many national English curriculum reform initiatives include in-service training programmes. Scholars believed that these should provide

- input to help teachers understand the thinking behind whatever changes are being proposed; and
- opportunities for teachers to develop their practical knowledge of what the changes imply for classroom teaching in their context, through supported practice over time.

Three principles of 'good' INSET were highlighted. Firstly, INSET needs to start from where the trainees are (Wright and Bolitho 2007) and to be clearly linked to the contexts in which they work. Trainers in Mexico and Iran observed trainees' classrooms before designing their training programmes, while in Ethiopia, Vietnam, Iran and Nepal trainers made efforts to link the new ideas closely to trainees' teaching contexts and to the materials that they used. Secondly, if training is to engage trainees, the training process needs as far as possible to model the principles and techniques that it is hoping to introduce (Woodward 2004) and to provide opportunities for experiential learning. Finally, training cannot develop effective teachers if it is just a one-off event; it needs to provide ongoing support over time. This rarely happens, although one Scholar's experience of INSET in Vietnam did include trainers supporting teachers in their schools through mentoring classroom teaching and in materials development for some time after the formal INSET ended.

Informal support

Given the very large numbers of English teachers who need training (especially in the many countries that have introduced English as part of the primary curriculum), the availability of formal training is always likely to be limited. The final part of the presentation, therefore, considered the many ways in which teachers are able to offer each other informal support, with or without the guidance of a teachers' association or union.

Teachers' associations can help provide teachers with opportunities for supported development of their practice in their own settings. Examples from Nepal, India, Sri Lanka and Iraq showed how this might be done through organising localised training, workshops, conferences and seminars (sometimes with support from external agencies such as universities and the British Council). Technology can also be utilised to provide online versions of the above, and/or online forums where teachers can discuss local teaching issues. Scholars from Iran and Iraq reported on the success of weekly or monthly meetings for secondary and primary school teachers within a local area, where they can discuss problems, share experiences, distribute resources and evaluate and develop exam papers. In Ethiopia, English Open Days for teachers from different parts of the capital city provide training sessions and workshops. The opportunity for teachers to regularly share and reflect on their classroom experiences has had very positive influences on many teachers' practice. In Nepal the development of a local ELT journal with locally authored and peer-reviewed papers discussing contextually relevant issues has provided another means of raising English teachers' awareness of teaching issues and possible responses to these.

Conclusion

There is a worldwide need for English teachers who can effectively help their learners to achieve curriculum goals. These increasingly emphasise the need to use learner-centred pedagogies to develop learners' communication skills. We have outlined some ideas about how formal and informal initiatives might support teachers.

Many formal programmes are still not planned or designed to adequately address teachers' needs, perhaps because many teacher educators do not fully understand what such needs are. This suggests that if formal teacher training is to become more effective, teacher educators themselves may need to be provided with trainer training to become better able to, for example,

- understand the main professional and personal challenges of becoming a communicative/learner-centred teacher in their context;
- understand the processes that support teacher learning, and what these imply for their own training skills; and
- develop criteria for designing training content and processes appropriate for teachers and their classroom contexts.

Financial and logistical constraints suggest that, in most countries, nationally organised programmes to help English teachers become more 'effective' will rarely be able to do more than provide the first stage of support for teachers' ongoing learning processes. It would, therefore, seem wise for the formal system to enthusiastically acknowledge the economic and professional benefits of encouraging teachers to develop and maintain their own, ongoing, informal support systems.

Teachers in any local area know the problems, needs and requirements of their context fully. They share similar emotions and feelings and can motivate and encourage each other to reflect on their daily professional classroom experiences. Regular opportunities to meet and discuss practice with colleagues can help teachers develop the professional awareness and confidence which are prerequisites for beginning to make personal decisions, and so to become ever more able to effectively support English learners in their own classrooms.

M.Wedell@education.leeds.ac.uk

References

Freeman, D. 2009. 'The scope of second language teacher education' in A. Burns and J. C. Richards (eds.). *The Cambridge Guide to Second Language Teacher Education*. Cambridge: Cambridge University Press

Johnson, K. E. 2009. *Second Language Teacher Education: A Sociocultural Perspective*. New York: Routledge.

Korthagen, F. A. J. 2011. 'Making teacher education relevant to practice: the pedagogy of realistic teacher education'. *Orbis Scholei* 5/2: 31–50.

Malderez, A. and M. Wedell. 2007. *Teaching Teachers: Processes and Practices*. London: Continuum.

Woodward, T. 2004. *Ways of Working with Teachers*. Broadstairs: Tessa Woodward Publications.

Wright, A. and R. Bolitho. 2007. *Trainer Development*. (Retrieved from http://www.lulu.com/shop/tony-wright-and-rod-bolitho/trainer-development/paperback/product-800868.html)

2.2 Good, bad or just plain ugly: on trainee teachers' anxiety

Mark Daubney *Leiria Polytechnic Institute, Portugal*

The relevance of anxiety

Language anxiety is acknowledged by many in teaching and research circles as a key psychological factor in language acquisition and classroom interaction. It is defined as a tension or apprehension that arises in second language contexts and is, therefore, seen as a situation-specific type of anxiety (MacIntyre 1999). It is likely to resonate with teachers, who probably recognise in their students some of the multiple signs of anxiety: a reluctance to speak, stuttering contributions, sensitivity to others' opinions, and shaking and blushing, to mention but a few.

It is no surprise, then, that anxiety has been seen as a negative influence to be reduced or eliminated from the classroom.

Key findings and characteristics of anxiety research

Research into anxiety has reinforced this notion of anxiety as something to be eliminated. Key findings point up important considerations: anxious learners are likely to speak less, have lower motivation and reach lower levels of academic achievement. Again, these findings are likely to resonate with educators. Yet much anxiety research has been carried out with lower-level learners in the North American context, and much of the research reveals a continuing over-reliance on the use of questionnaires and self-reports to first 'measure' anxiety, and then to carry out interviews with learners to further explore the sources of anxiety. Somewhat puzzlingly, researchers have avoided studying anxiety in the classroom itself, the very place where anxiety is said to arise.

Motivation and methodology for a PhD study

One of the key reasons, therefore, for carrying out my PhD study on anxiety was to study this emotion in the classroom itself. A second reason was to study trainee teachers as opposed to learners in the more traditional sense. My previous research (Daubney 2004) focused on anxiety experienced by future TEFL teachers in their language classes. These were highly motivated, proficient language learners who experienced anxiety, so it seemed a logical step to then carry out a longitudinal study of trainees on their practicum, a pressurised and stressful period little explored in anxiety research.

Furthermore, trainee teachers are often situated on the slippery frontier that differentiates teacher from student. As Horwitz (1996: 367) says, 'It is one thing to say you speak a language; it is quite another to be a teacher of that language.'

The subjects of this study were three Portuguese trainee teachers. A range of data was collected, including video-recordings of their lessons; audio-recordings of the post-observation conferences; a video-recorded semi-structured interview conducted halfway through the practicum; a video-recording of the final meeting between the mentors and the trainees; and video-recordings of stimulated recall protocols carried out by the researcher with each trainee at the end of the practicum.

The main research questions were 'What are the signs of trainee anxiety in the classroom?' and 'What are the influences on trainee anxiety?'

Findings

Of the three trainees—Sandra, Odete and Renata (pseudonyms)—anxiety was found to be particularly evident in Sandra and Odete. However, Sandra's experience of anxiety can be characterised as facilitating. Constantly praised for her dynamic lessons, Sandra had a constant desire to give better classes but found it difficult to accept mentor criticism. Nevertheless, she remained motivated and positive about her practicum. Odete's experience of anxiety was debilitating, a sense of disappointment and disillusionment quickly replacing her initial high hopes. A sign of—and a strategy to overcome—anxiety was her over-planning in order to avoid uncertainty in the classroom.

Principal signs of anxiety included the following:

• nominating good pupils to answer questions;
• using Portuguese for instructions and to ensure pupil understanding;
• using animated behaviour, both verbal and kinetic;
• being defensive about pupil laughter; and
• focusing on the next phase of class rather than exploring pupil answers.

The key contexts and circumstances influencing their anxiety, and helping to explain the above signs, were:

- the pervasive sense of being evaluated;
- how feedback was delivered by their mentors; and
- the need to complete the lesson plan in given time limit.

However, the key influence was the tension between their desired self-image and the image that was co-constructed with mentors and colleagues. In other words, anxiety arose when they were not 'living up' to their desired self-image.

In sum, anxiety in this context appears to interact with the desire to excel, an emotion that arises in the confluence of a multitude of factors. Longitudinal research, therefore, is likely to identify aspects of language anxiety that previous research may have overlooked.

mark.daubney@ipleiria.pt

References

Daubney, M. 2004. *Language Anxiety in Oral Communication in the Classroom: a Case Study of Future Teachers of English*. Unpublished Master's thesis. Aveiro: University of Aveiro, Portugal.

Horwitz, E. K. 1996. 'Even teachers get the blues: Recognizing and alleviating language teachers' feelings of foreign language anxiety'. *Foreign Language Annals* 29/3: 365–72.

MacIntyre, P. D. 1999. 'Language anxiety: a review of the research for language teachers' in D. J. Young (ed.). *Affect in Foreign Language and Second Language Learning: A Practical Guide to Creating a Low-anxiety Classroom Atmosphere*. Boston: McGraw-Hill.

2.3 Teacher training versus reality: are detailed objectives necessary in lesson planning?

Clare Fielder *University of Trier, Germany*

This presentation was based on action research prompted by frustrations trainee teachers reported at having to compose long and detailed lesson plans, whereas qualified teachers rarely include such detail in lesson planning. The topic was motivated by considerations following my article *Stating and Explaining Course, Lesson and Activity Objectives* (Fielder 2011). The overarching questions were: (a) should teachers produce detailed explanations of aims as part of their lesson planning; and (b) should these aims be communicated to learners?

Background and research

Literature on the topic seems to highlight the idea that stating aims is an integral part of lesson planning (for example, Woodward 2001; Bailey 1996). To assess the practical benefits and possible drawbacks of including details of aims in lesson plans and communicating these to learners, I compiled a developmental record including lesson plans with explicit explanations of the aims of individual activities and the lesson as a whole, my reflections on activities, and students' feedback on lessons (using a sentence completion task adapted from Woodward 2001).

Findings on lesson planning

Firstly, my developmental record identified several benefits of including aims in lesson planning. These points seem generally applicable to diverse teaching contexts and include the fact that formulating aims clearly helps teachers memorise what is planned for a lesson; this means they express things clearly and avoid confusing learners with jumbled messages. Furthermore, having formulated the aims of a lesson, teachers can better evaluate materials and activities by measuring their effectiveness and contribution to the set aims. Equally, the long-term value of the trained skills/language is also considered more openly. Finally, planning with detailed aims underlines links between the lessons of a course, preventing teachers from teaching self-contained lessons which do not necessarily move students forward in their learning.

Nonetheless, a couple of drawbacks to such detailed planning probably explain why so many teachers neglect stating their aims so explicitly. Planning in this manner can be time-consuming. This time may also be wasted if the course goals require modification, and inflexibility may ensue if teachers stick slavishly to plans they have made too far in advance. However, the benefits clearly outweigh these problems, and so it seems that stating the aims of a course, lesson or activity, and the relationship between these, is very valuable in lesson planning. Nevertheless, the act of thinking about aims is perhaps more important than the actual form the planning takes or when it is done.

Findings on communicating aims

Regarding the second question, my reflections and students' feedback provided interesting insight. Firstly, communicating aims appears to empower students in their learning, in that they can decide which parts of the lesson to concentrate on most; it can thus foster learner autonomy. It also increases learners' receptivity to the teacher and course/lesson content, which in turn often strengthens students' motivation to participate, especially in tasks they might otherwise have seen little value in. Moreover, providing explanations of aims can enable learners to 'file' acquired language and knowledge logically in memory, in 'chunks' or patterns within their previous knowledge. Finally, my students reported a heightened sense of achievement, as they could measure their accomplishments against the set aims. In combination, these benefits of communicating aims are likely to lead to better overall performance on assessments and more effective learning progress.

My presentation included suggested strategies for communicating aims, such as displaying lists, reading or paraphrasing these to learners, giving examples of activities to achieve aims, or asking learners to brainstorm ideas of aims to compare with the teacher's ideas. Individual activities can also be introduced with brief explanations of their aims within the course/lesson goal(s), or by presenting 'menus' of activities and their contribution to the course/lesson aims. Students' feedback indicates, though, that different strategies are appropriate for different groups and levels. Brainstorming, for example, is effective with advanced learners, who often find reading lists dull. My intermediate learners preferred 'menus'.

Conclusion

My presentation answered both questions with 'yes'. Firstly, asking trainees to produce detailed explanations of course/lesson aims provides training in the essential task of considering short- and long-term objectives, which all teachers should include in their lesson planning, even if no written plan is made. Secondly, it is recommended that teachers communicate aims to learners, though how this is done will depend on the teaching context.

fielder@uni-trier.de

References

Bailey, K. M. 1996. 'The best laid plans: teachers' in-class decisions to depart from their lesson plans' in K. M. Bailey and D. Nunan (eds.). *Voices from the Language Classroom.* Cambridge: Cambridge University Press.

Fielder, C. 2011. 'Stating and explaining course, lesson and activity objectives'. *Teacher Development*, Summer 2011: 22–5.

Woodward, T. 2001. *Planning Lessons and Courses: Designing sequences of work for the language classroom.* Cambridge: Cambridge University Press.

2.4 Get real

Barbara Buxton *Freelance, Milton Keynes and Birmingham, UK*

I have become increasingly concerned about the actual language that teachers are selecting as suitable teaching content for today's learners, and the seeming lack of understanding of true communicative language. So much effort is being expended by teachers teaching language that has very little use in the real world.

I looked at examples of the language selected for teaching by teachers on pre-service (for example, CELTA) and in-service courses (for example, DELTA), and examined why so many lessons are unproductive and ineffective for learners because teachers fail to focus on real communication. I investigated the following:

- Teaching language for language's sake, without reference to the learners' needs. Often there is a focus on esoteric and idiomatic language that is not relevant. Some teaching that I have seen is self-indulgent and teaching for the amusement of the teacher, for example, the choice of idioms like 'spick and span' and the ubiquitous 'raining cats and dogs', neither of which I have ever used. Trainees sometimes need to be reminded that teaching English is *not* a branch of the entertainment industry.
- 'Structure speak'. Why are grammar lessons valued so much more highly than other lessons, particularly on CELTA courses? In a DELTA lesson the candidate was observed teaching 'My arm was bitten by a shark' as an example of the passive—hard to think of a real-life context. Why are skills lessons relegated to a subordinate position? Why do trainees have to 'prove themselves' by showing that they can do a lesson devoted to the present perfect continuous? The system of fixed, pre-set teaching practice (TP) points is largely instrumental in this.
- The meta-language teachers feel the need to employ, which has no relevance outside the classroom (for example, 'make these sentences negative' or 'put it in the passive'). One of the trainees' persistent preoccupations—and indeed even terrors—is with not knowing what the present perfect continuous or the second conditional is.

They need to know what it *conveys* more than they need to know what it is called. As trainers we are at fault here because we present trainees with long expositions of language using meta-language, presenting it as a science in itself.

I then looked at strategies we can employ to train teachers to plan for and teach the language learners need for genuine communication (Beth Grant's 'Notion to Noise' paradigm).

- Carry out a tutor-led needs analysis of the learners with the trainees participating. A ranking task followed by a discussion of the context and priorities for the learners can form the basis of TP points.
- Establish the real context. In pre-service and even in in-service situations, teachers have great difficulty differentiating between the *setting* (illustrating where the action takes place) and the real *context* (illustrating what the action means). Trainees need a lot of help with this, too.
- Carry out lesson preparation with the tutor, especially on pre-service courses (and this must not be skimped or relegated to five minutes after TP feedback). This needs to focus a bit less on how and more on *what*, with a framework for the lesson already in place. The discussion can centre on the actual choice of language to be taught for recognition and for active use; it should always come back to how useful that language will be for learners. Will they actually want or need to use this? A good task is to ask learners to keep a record of when and where they heard/saw or used language items they were taught in the classroom—a sort of 'I spy' task which can be fun and instructive for the trainee teacher as well.
- Provide positive and appropriate models of teaching for the trainees to observe. Trainees must see the practical application of what the trainers are doing before being asked to understand pedagogic principles behind it.

On courses where this has happened, the positive feedback from trainees and learners is overwhelming. The progress of the learners is inspiring for the trainees, and the trainees' confidence is enormously boosted by the success of their lessons because they realise they are truly and realistically empowering their learners.

barbara@barbarabuxton.orangehome.co.uk

2.5 TASKs: transferring applied skills and knowledge in secondary teacher education

Lynn Williams Leppich *University of Applied Sciences and Arts Northwestern Switzerland*

What materials can we supply to help trainees focus their classroom work better? How can we create more transparent and substantive links between the various training areas? What instrument can we provide to support coaches who are observing and evaluating trainees?

These are some of the questions we have been considering within the scope of a small-scale research project in our department over the last 18 months. At our institution aspiring teachers of English at upper secondary level participate in seminars in educational science and subject methodology. They hone their teaching skills in a range of placements where they are coached by experienced teachers of English at local state secondary schools. Trainees are encouraged to reflect on their progress in coaching and reflection seminars and undertake an action research project in an area of their choosing.

As a lecturer in the department for English teaching and learning, one of my main interests is the interface between subject methodology and teaching practice. In placements trainees are assessed according to one of three standardised competence grids (one for each placement level), which are generally applicable to all subjects, so I set out to create a transparent and feasible set of tasks specifically for English. Trainees and practice coaches would then be better able to situate those competences, and we as lecturers could successfully promote transfer between seminars and placements. Tasks would 'provide a framework for meaningful discussion by providing an explicit outcome or goal.' (Willis and Willis 2007: 12).

I began by carefully analysing the assessment grids, extracting key competencies and relating these to English teaching pedagogy. One important consideration in formulating the tasks was 'striking a balance between specific and general goals' (Van den Branden 2006: 29). Tasks which are too closely defined are not flexible enough for the placements, while those which are too freely formulated can be hard to interpret. In addition to the tasks, my head of department and I developed a number of model outcomes, including brief theoretical background and suggestions for further reading, and distributed these to interested students.

The current version of the task list consists of eight to ten tasks per placement level. Trainees are required to choose one or two of these to work on during the course of their 8–14-lesson teaching placements. Reflecting on the challenges and opportunities presented forms an essential part of the trainee's learning process.

In two feedback questionnaires over the course of a year, students commented on their work with the list. Around a third of trainees reported that they chose their task(s) only after deciding on the content and learning objectives for their placements. This was somewhat surprising for us, though we do in fact see an advantage here: apart from acknowledging that each placement brings with it certain frameworks and limitations (such as curricular requirements), this approach also encourages trainees to examine their teaching practice situation, identify the focal points and relate this back to the task list—thus also to the competences defined in the assessment grids.

Trainee feedback so far has been essentially positive. As one trainee commented, using the task list 'really helped to select a focus for the placement'. The general feedback highlights some interesting points. Trainees would like more explicit reference to be made to the task list in our methodology seminars. We will certainly adopt this approach as it will lead to a better understanding of our requirements and a greater degree of transparency. Another valuable suggestion involves trainees reporting back on their placement task in the plenary.

The most important insight we gained from the student feedback was the importance of modelling what we want students to do. Consequently we have reformulated the assignments students work on in seminars. A typical assignment now explicitly emulates the tasks and will read: 'Choose a literary text suitable for the classroom. Design a pre-, while- and post-reading task and explain the rationale behind your choices.' Members of my audience at IATEFL Liverpool concurred that the reflection aspect is of vital importance for a trainee teacher.

Other plans for the project include developing a standardised template for students to document their work with the tasks. As well as providing a useful support for students, this will help us compare students' various experiences. We also intend to establish a database of teaching materials developed in response to the task list. After all, our trainees can be justly proud of their work and we would like to showcase it for future generations of trainees and practice coaches.

References

lynn.williams@fhnw.ch

Willis, D. and J. Willis. 2007. *Doing Task-based Teaching.* Cambridge: Cambridge University Press.

Van den Branden, K. (ed.). 2006. *Task-Based Language Education: From Theory to Practice.* Cambridge: Cambridge University Press.

2.6 A collaborative approach to running teacher training projects in China

Liping Zhou *Chongqing Education University, China and*
Keith O'Hare *British Council, Taipei, Taiwan*

Introduction

This talk presented a comparative study of two teacher trainer development projects run in Chongqing, China in the last ten years, with a view to sharing the 'good practice' of the collaborative approach to running the projects.

Context

Traditionally, English teaching in China has focused on how to help students pass exams. Questions in these exams tend to be of a discrete point and passive nature, so classroom practice has tended to rely on the grammar translation method, prioritising memorisation and rote learning. The Chinese New Curriculum reforms that began in 2001 see the transformation of teachers' beliefs as the prerequisite to the transformation of teaching practices from traditional teacher-centred approaches to more progressive student-centred approaches. The policy stream was concerned with the quality of education.

The first project: Chongqing 2001

Chongqing is a municipality directly under the jurisdiction of the central government of China; it is the largest municipality in the world with around 30 million people and 60,000 English teachers. Based on the government policies which emerged around 1999, the Chongqing Education Commission decided to set up a teacher training project for English teachers in the city. A diverse approach was taken in selecting trainees and forming training groups; these included frontline primary school teachers, teacher researchers and university teachers.

The collaborative approach adopted in 2002 was developed by UK suppliers under the guidelines of the documents drafted by the Chongqing Education Commission and the British Council Chongqing, without any local contribution. The teacher researchers and frontline teachers did not take the initiative to participate in the training but were appointed and assigned by local education authorities.

The training programme was drafted by UK trainers after one month of ethnographic fieldwork in different districts of Chongqing. A survey was conducted by UK trainers to find out what trainees needed most before the training started. The final programme is shown in Figure 2.6.1.

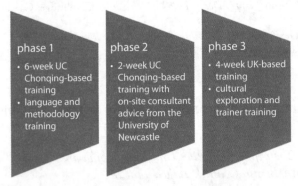

Figure 2.6.1: The 2001 training programme

The positive outcomes and the weaker aspects of the project were identified in the project evaluation report (Griffiths 2004), as seen in Figure 2.6.2.

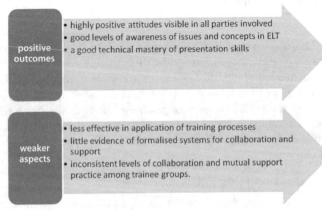

Figure 2.6.2: Evaluation of the programme

According to the report, the first programme lacked a reflective phase. The trainees did not thoroughly digest or experiment with what they had learnt in the UK before acting as trainers. A collaborative working style was not truly established among the trainees because there was no time scheduled for them to work together. They had to prepare separately for the cascade training after their UK-based training. Therefore, teaching theory and practice was not integrated as university teachers focused more on the understanding of the teaching theories, frontline teachers paid more attention to practice, and teacher researchers shifted their roles.

The second project: Chongqing 2011

This project followed several government policies in the 2000s and was based on UK–China collaboration, focussing on the needs of rural schools and the need to enhance systems of continuing professional development for teachers and trainers.

Trainees were selected more rigorously than for the first project, but the profile of trainees was similar. The design of this project was somewhat different from the first, as can be seen in Figure 2.6.3; differences included longer training time in the UK and more support for trainees when they were preparing to train other teachers.

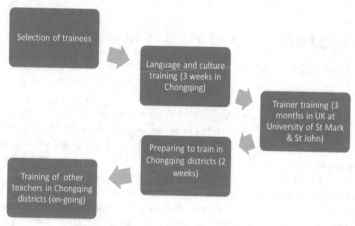

Figure 2.6.3: The 2011 training programme

Comparisons

Three main features appear when we compare the two projects. Firstly, collaborative approaches became more deeply embedded in this second project. Collaboration existed administratively among decision-making bodies, as seen by all three parties establishing the project goals together. It also existed instructionally in the course design stage, and academically among trainees. The latter was seen especially in the use of the local social network site QQ to share ideas, lesson plans and other resources when trainees were training other teachers in five geographically disperse districts of Chongqing.

Secondly, the education community, including the education authorities, teachers and trainers, had grown in experience in managing such large-scale projects. This was seen, for example, in the setting up of feedback cycles to monitor and improve training at regular intervals. There were weekly planning meetings in the project design stage and during training in the UK. There were weekly reflection and feedback sessions.

Finally, there was a move from 'transmission' approaches to 'reflective' ones. This is seen by many stakeholders as being the most important feature because it adheres strongly to the aspirations of the National Curriculum upon which the project is based. Training and teaching models moved from transmission of knowledge towards experiential learning. In training, trainees moved from a 'watch and repeat' model towards a 'try out, process, reflect, share and own' model. They became more reflective and independent, and better able to evaluate and make decisions for themselves on what skills, materials and techniques they needed to bring to their teaching and training in the Chinese context.

belinda0229@126.com

Reference

Griffiths, M. 2004. *Chongqing Primary ELT Project Report on Evaluation Consultancy.* Chongqing, China: British Council Chongqing.

2.7 Training English teachers at public schools in Brazil

Andreia Fernandes *Freelance, Rio de Janeiro, Brazil*

Background

One remarkable aspect of training teachers who deal with large groups of young learners from the first up to the fifth grade at public schools is the fact that professionals from different parts of the world are interested in the topic. Different questions about the programme implementation and the results achieved so far were asked during the presentation.

English was first taught at public primary schools in Rio de Janeiro, Brazil, in 2010; however, it is not yet part of the national curriculum. The main goal of the English programme is to help students achieve communicative competence, especially as the city will host two international events—the World Cup in 2014 and the Olympic Games in 2016—in which the ability to communicate in English will be of paramount importance.

In 2010, 800 English teachers were involved in the English programme; by 2013 the number had increased to 1,864. In order to take part, teachers have to take both a written and an oral test. They teach monolingual groups of students, whose ages range from six to ten and whose mother tongue is Portuguese. In the first three grades, the classes last 50 minutes once a week and in the fourth and fifth grades there are two 50-minute classes per week.

In my session I demonstrated not only the challenges teachers and trainers have faced but also the strategies used to help teachers improve professionally and make the foreign language learning process a rewarding experience for students. As Foord (2009: 9) states, 'dealing with all the challenges at work can be development itself'.

All teachers took a 20-hour initial training programme in 2010. All the sessions were conducted in English, and the main goal was to make teachers familiar with the learning process of teaching a foreign language to young learners. After that, every year there are two training sessions lasting four hours each; class observation is carried out throughout the year. It has been observed that these training sessions are the only opportunities teachers have to get to know each other and share experiences. It is important for teachers to feel they are not anonymous members of the educational system.

Teachers' challenges

Firstly, a great number of teachers lacked experience in teaching young learners; therefore, one of the first topics addressed in the training programme was primary school teaching, and how language learning occurs in early childhood. Secondly, overcrowded classes and discipline is a source of discouragement for many teachers; thus, classroom management is a theme discussed in every training session. Thirdly, teachers found it challenging to motivate students and make them use English to communicate with their peers. Class observation takes place throughout the year and the results of the data collected are shared among teachers during training meetings. Finally, it was noted during class observations that a lack of school material and technological equipment made it harder for some teachers to do their job properly. How to make pedagogical adjustments based on the reality present in different classrooms is a topic that has been extensively debated.

Trainers' challenges

One topic that deserves close attention is the choice of appropriate theoretical background that will offer teachers a solid basis for making their classes meaningful to young learners. Another challenging aspect is the fact that the trainer needs to be accepted by the trainees for improvement to take place; otherwise, teachers may see both training sessions and class observation as a heavy burden instead of a valuable source of professional development. Moreover, it is essential that the trainer help teachers believe that they are able to make young learners, a great number of them from poor areas, learn a foreign language successfully. For that, the trainer has to support teachers effectively and provide them with the pedagogical tools that will make the English learning process a memorable experience; this will help students have a better chance of achieving higher educational levels and securing a better position in a competitive job market.

Summing up

At the beginning of the training programme, a considerable number of teachers felt demotivated and thought the work they had done was not effective. Today, three years later, it is time for teachers and trainers to evaluate the programme; this is the next step. Nonetheless, despite the challenges and difficulties faced, it has been gratifying to see how much our young learners have produced when it comes to communicating in a foreign language.

andreia.lof@gmail.com

Reference

Foord, D. 2009. *The Developing Teacher: Practical Activities for Professional Development.* Peaslake: Delta Publishing.

2.8 Learning and growing as a teacher educator

Briony Beaven *Freelance, Munich, Germany*

Background

ELT teacher educators work on many types of course including, but not limited to, school-teacher training, CELTA/DELTA courses, one-off workshops, publisher-sponsored training and TEFL tasters. Courses take place in many settings, for example, universities, private language schools, cultural institutes, state schools and adult education institutes. Teacher educators may be salaried, but are often freelance, a status which sometimes leads to their being itinerant with no permanent occupational community.

My previous research (Beaven 2009) highlighted difficulties teachers have in moving from teaching to teacher training, one such difficulty being the lack of statutory professional preparation for becoming a teacher educator. New entrants to the field often feel further cast adrift by the poorly defined knowledge base and absence of an agreed skills set for teacher educators. This is unlike becoming a teacher, a job usually preceded in most contexts by some form of pre-service training. Uncertainty about the demands of teacher education work and a diversity of contexts and duties made for a rocky, hesitant and problematic start to teacher educators' careers.

Yet many teachers strive to become teacher educators and what is more, those who succeed in doing so appear keen to stay in the job. In view of my earlier research this surprised me, but I suspected that the opportunities for growth and learning provided by the field might be relevant. So I conducted a preliminary investigation based on three questions:

1 What do ELT teacher educators think they learn through their work?
2 How do they feel they are different in mind, morale and behaviour after a period of time working as a teacher educator? Is there a link between professional and personal development, and if so, is it a problem or a benefit of the job?
3 What counts as worthwhile learning and development for teacher educators?

The survey

A questionnaire was sent to an opportunity sample of 48 teacher educators, of whom 30 responded. They had different levels of experience, included both freelance and salaried trainers, worked with in-service and/or pre-service teachers, and worked in a wide range of contexts with varied goals. The sample was too small to allow for the creation of sub-groups so typicality and transferability are not ensured. Purposeful selection of sample groups, and larger sample groups, would be desirable in future research on this topic.

Results

Key findings were that the great majority of the respondents
- learn new professional skills; and,
- find their learning useful in all areas of their lives;

and for many that
- professional and personal lives are intertwined.

The professional skills fell into three categories: technical skills, trainee-centred skills and general professional growth. The most frequently mentioned technical skills were the extension of teacher educators' repertoire of training activities and the ability to use loop input (Woodward 2003). Examples of becoming more trainee-centred were: learning to take account of different trainee contexts, introducing differentiated levels of challenge, leading trainees to 'question' rather than giving information, and—a recurrent theme—leaving space and time for trainees. General professional growth involved becoming more tentative, flexible and affirmative, and less judgmental.

Twenty-nine of the 30 respondents considered that their work leads to personal as well as professional growth. From 13 areas of personal growth, including, for instance, validation of identity, greater confidence and better organisational skills, the respondents selected the ones that applied to them. It was notable that most chose from six to eleven areas of personal growth as relevant, suggesting considerable transfer of skills from the professional to the personal domain.

For 12 respondents some separation of the personal and professional was relatively easy, though even for them there were connections between the two spheres. For the 18 for whom separation of personal and professional was more difficult, 11, about a third of all respondents, found the links beneficial. They seemed to echo Marturano (2012: 2): 'There is no work-life balance. We have one life. What's most important is that you be awake for it'.

Conclusion

It appears that my respondents value highly the opportunities for professional and personal development and learning available to teacher educators. In spite of negative features of the job mentioned by many respondents, such as poor pay, insecurity and losing touch with teaching learners of English, not one of the 30 wanted to give up being a teacher educator. Cited attractions of the job were the multiple opportunities to develop life skills, the diversity of people, contexts, experiences, and the 'wonderful professional family' of 'people you really like and enjoy working with'.

brionybeaven@t-online.de

References

Beaven, B. 2009. 'Becoming an ELT teacher trainer'. *The Teacher Trainer* 23/3: 11–15.

Marturano, J. 2012. 'The mind business'. *Financial Times Life & Arts* 25/26.8.12: 1–2.

Woodward, T. 2003. 'Key concepts in ELT: loop input'. *English Language Teaching Journal* 57/3: 301–3.

3 Identity, imperialism and the role of the EFL teacher

What is the role of EFL programmes, and what is the relationship between EFL providers and the host community? **Susan Barduhn**'s plenary paper, which opens this chapter, provides a unique perspective on this question, positioning English as a 'drug' with English teachers as its 'dealers'. Is this 'drug' a cure, in that it provides access to economic success and equality, or is it a poison, in the form of linguistic imperialism? The topic of linguistic imperialism, and the question of whether it continues to thrive, is also addressed in the following paper, based on the British Council Signature Event on this topic and reported by **Esther Hay**. In the next two papers, **Hywel Coleman and Aïché Bâ** present the results of British Council-supported research into language use in Francophone West Africa, and **Anne Wiseman** reports on the effects of a British Council teacher development project in Bulgaria. The themes of imperialism and identity are furthered in the next paper by **Miri Tashma-Baum**, which deals with attitudes towards English seen among trainee English teachers in Israel. Next, **Maike Grau** questions what teaching culture entails and reports on a study carried out with trainee teachers. In the final paper of this chapter, we move away from theoretical issues and into classroom activities; the activities presented by **Alexandra Reynolds** are designed to encourage students to think about their own identity as language learners.

3.1 Plenary: Language dealing

Susan Barduhn *SIT Graduate Institute, Brattleboro, Vt., USA*

A few years ago I did some research on the cultural identity of expatriate teachers of English around the world; one respondent declared that if English were a drug, expatriate teachers would be the dealers. Bill Johnston of Indiana University has written about the moral dimension of English language teaching, and in particular once drew provocative parallels between EFL teachers and medieval knights errant (Johnston 1999). In this paper I will explore these metaphors and argue that the phenomenon of expatriate English teachers could be considered a historical, cultural movement. I will then consider a new drug: Mandarin as a Foreign Language, and consider the effects that Chinese expatriate teachers might have as language dealers.

The 'drug'

Following on from the statement, 'If English were a drug, expatriate teachers would be the dealers', it might be useful to consider other questions, such as: Is a dealer an exploiter of the drug? What is the drug here? Is it language?

There are different ways to conceive of 'drug' here. Medicine is also a drug, and medicine has both properties in itself of poison and cure. In reference to language as poison, what comes to mind are English imperialism and the death of indigenous languages. In terms of cure, there is the view that English is not the property of the native speakers, that it is what people around the world are demanding, that it provides access to education, and that it can serve as an anti-exploitation tool. O'Dowd says, 'For successful global cooperation, a common language is required (2012: 10). My aim in this paper is not to lead you to one belief, but to ask to remain aware of these different views about English as you continue reading.

Let's now question whether the drug we are referring to is actually language. If we think of drug as an 'it', one way to think of this is to look at Hawkins' (1974) famous triangle (Figure 3.1.1):

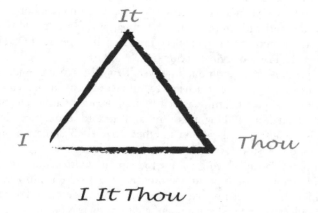

Figure 3.1.1: Hawkins' triangle

If the 'it' is indeed language, there are different views about who then the 'I' might be: Imperialists looking for power? Capitalists looking for markets? Big Business looking for profits? If my point is not to judge the spread of English but to look at the spreaders, let the 'I' in this paper be teachers and the 'thou' be students and other teachers, not governments; as for the 'it', allow one of my students to speak:

> English is merely a tool. Why our students need that tool and what they will do with the tool once they have it is a question whose answer changes from individual to individual. However, the end goal is usually not the tool itself. As teachers, we need to keep that in mind. We are not teaching medicine so our students can cure the sick. We are not teaching engineering so our students can build up their world. We are not teaching agriculture so our students can feed their people. We are teaching English. We are giving our students a tool to help them learn medicine, engineering and agriculture. There is an old adage, 'give a man a fish and he eats for a day; teach a man to fish and he eats for a lifetime'. The IT of the Great Triangle is not the fish or even learning how to fish. The IT of the Great Triangle is the fishing rod. The IT is the tool of English (Buboltz 2012: 2).

Jay Walker, the founder of Priceline, in his 2009 TED talk, might have been thinking of this image when he stated that the world is *pulling* English, which he calls the language of problem solving.

But what if the drug is not language? Could it instead be values? Or culture? Canagarajah (1999) has said that ELT methodology can be seen as both a carrier of cultural values and as an export product. If it is methodology, how does the poison/cure metaphor work when we're talking about pedagogy? To consider this, let us move on to the 'spreaders' of this pedagogy and consider Johnston's metaphor using parallels between EFL teachers and medieval knights errant (1999).

Postmodernity

In his 1999 article *The Expatriate Teacher as Postmodern Paladin*, Johnston defines 'paladin' as any determined advocate or defender of a noble cause; he compares medieval knights errant to expatriate teachers of English by stating that both are concerned with marginality and with those traditionally marginalised in social or other ways. Both focus on encounters that take place in marginal or border territory. In short, Johnston views ELT as a marginal occupation.

It is the postmodern condition, however, that distinguishes medieval knights errant from expatriate English teachers. To fully comprehend this concept, it may be useful to first define modernity, which typically refers to a movement away from medievalism, feudalism and agrarianism, and toward capitalism, industrialism, Marxism, existentialism, secularisation and the formal establishment of social science. It is not a period of history *per se*. It's a paradigm shift.

The example of dance, which I will use to help differentiate modernism and postmodernism, is actually about postmodernity but will serve our purpose. Hargreaves (1994) distinguishes between postmodernity and postmodernism. Postmodernism is an aesthetic, cultural and intellectual phenomenon, whereas postmodernity is a social condition. In many ways postmodernism is a subset of postmodernity.

My husband's early career was as a postmodern dancer, and classical ballet has been a hobby of mine all my life, so we have had many discussions about dance. Classical ballet is bound by strict rules. Modern ballet took those rules and broke or altered them. I have come to understand that postmodern dance doesn't deal with the same rules at all but re-conceptualised what dance was entirely, including that dance is something that has to take place on a stage. (One of my husband's most acclaimed performances took place in a tree.)

As stated above, postmodernism has to do with aesthetics, not a social condition. This paper is about postmodernity, which can involve change for change's sake, and a failure of grand narratives. Postmodernity helps to explain the disruptive nature of globalisation. As Hannerz put it, 'There is now a world culture, but we had better make sure that we understand what it means. It is marked by *an organization of diversity* rather than by a replication of uniformity' (1990: 237).

Appadurai (1990) has helpfully come up with a way to organise the diversity of globalisation into five dimensions of cultural flow:

- *Mediascapes* are the flow of culture through forms of communication. This means that the reproduction of a range of social institutions, like dress, or home building, becomes more subject to global influences.

- *Ideoscapes* describe ideological messages relating to modern life in various differing political systems.
- *Technoscapes* refer to how mass production is becoming globally integrated to supply mass consumption, on a global basis.
- *Financescapes* refer to economic flow, as in the 24-hour dealings of a global economy.

And the one which most concerns the ideas in this paper is:

- *Ethnoscapes*, which refer to how people choose or are forced by economic need to travel the world to find work and income (Appadurai 1990: 295–310).

Appadurai's scapes also relate to the spread of Chinese as a world language.

The knight errant metaphor

With this understanding of the definition I am using for postmodernity, we can return to the knight errant metaphor. The original paladins were the knightly champions attending Charlemagne. Preferable to staying at home was errantry, crossing the sea in quest of adventures and fame. The knight's goal was both spiritual (self-realisation, self-discovery, to serve others) and earthly (material gain, the acquisition of a good name for oneself).

Let's play with the postmodern paladin metaphor, the knight errant. It's about those who choose to work outside their own country. The paladin [and perhaps English language teachers as well?] is characterised by:

- nobility: a wish to educate, to share knowledge, expertise and skills; and
- the restless traveller, one who is driven not only to do good deeds but to wander the earth in the process, never settling and in constant motion.

Victoria Lindsay-Towner's PhD (2011) was a study of the Black Flag Café, a forum for people who travel to dangerous places. She created a framework to identify five benefits which participants obtain from travelling to dangerous places: flow, self-actualisation, improvement to self-esteem, the achievement and/or maintenance of status, and familiarity with death. While this framework has been developed for tourists who travel to dangerous places, undertaking danger tourism, there were similarities with my own research below on expatriate teachers.

There is a Sanskrit word, *Antevasin*, which means 'one who lives at the borders'. Apparently it originally referred to people who chose to leave the safety of their homes and venture out to the edge of the forest where the spirits dwelt, in order to uncover the answers to the sacred in their lives. In *Eat, Pray, Love*, Elizabeth Gilbert describes it as 'living on that shimmering line between your old thinking and your new understanding' (2007: 203).

As stated above, one reason the medieval knight errant doesn't fit has to do with postmodernity. The knights knew exactly what they believed in, why they were venturing forward, and how they expected to benefit. *And they intended to go home.*

The 'dealers'

Some researchers behave as if English were being spread by governments, by nasty imperialistic forces. It was actually humble, mostly young, expatriate teachers being paid a pittance. What motivates them? Warren Merkel, my student who came up with the 'language dealer' image on which this paper is based, recently emailed this statement about privilege to me:

> I never forget how lucky I am, how wonderful my job is and that it quite possibly wouldn't exist for me if some language other than English dominated the scene right now. After all, how many Finns, for example, can travel the world teaching Finnish, regardless of their level of education? (personal correspondence 2013).

I turn now to my own research, which was motivated by these questions: Why do those of us in the ELT profession not only go to live in other countries, but continue moving on to new ones? What has been our influence on the spread of English and on trends in teacher training? I was fortunate to receive over 200 responses from Americans, Britons and seven other nationalities to such questions. The respondents needed to have lived outside their country of origin for at least six years and in at least two different countries. My starting point was looking at cultural identity.

Cultural identity

I wanted to explore the cultural identity of itinerant expatriate teachers. Who are we? Are we cultural marginals? Do we have an identity group? It is helpful to contrast perceptual groups with identity groups. Perceptual groups consist of groups of individuals who perceive aspects of the external world in a similar manner yet do not communicate these perceptions among themselves. Once they do communicate these common perspectives, they become an identity group. This distinction helps explain how individuals may see the world from a perspective of gender, religion, marital status or race, yet until they communicate their shared perspective, they do not necessarily identify with others of this particular group. We identify with others who think as we do.

Our identification with others, however, is only part of the role of groups in identity. The other part is outside our control and depends on others. Based on their perceptions, others in the culture assign persons to groups. Observable features such as skin colour, appearance, age, gender, dress, mannerisms, accent, vocabulary, possessions or even locale all serve as means of classifying persons as members of particular groups. In a word, we are labelled by others.

The avowed and ascribed dimensions of identity turn around two distinct perceptions: how individual members of the culture perceive and identity *themselves*, and how *other* members of the culture perceive and identity these individuals. These two perceptions do not necessarily coincide. For example, because of their skin colour, certain persons may be perceived by others as black, brown or white, whereas they might not consider themselves in these terms. In my own case, during the many years I lived in the UK, Britons never ceased to think of me as American, even as Americans came to see me as 'other', not quite American. My avowed identity—how I saw myself—was internationalised, yet American-conditioned; my ascribed identity—how others saw me—depended on who was doing the looking.

Janet Bennett (1993) describes cultural identity in terms of individuals' relationships among identity groups, in particular, in relationship to dominant groups. She uses the notion of marginality to describe the rapport that persons of non-dominant communities have with dominant communities, suggesting that there are two essential responses, *encapsulated marginality* and *constructive marginality*. Encapsulated marginals are persons who allow the dominant groups to *ascribe* their identity. Constructive marginals are persons with *avowed* identities with a relativistic outlook, not dependent on particular group affiliations, who are capable of moving among all communities. Bennett's analysis is useful in considering how group affiliations affect a person's identity, particularly in situations that may be oppressive or diminishing to a person (Moran 2001: 103).

Table 3.1.1 shows a few comparators for these two types of marginal:

Encapsulated marginal	Constructive marginal
• No recognised reference group	• Marginal reference group [other expats]
• Conscious of self	• Conscious of choice
• Troubled by ambiguity	• Intrigued by complexity
• Never 'at home'	• Never not 'at home'

Table 3.1.1: *Encapsulated versus constructive marginals* (Bennett 1993)

Overview of the research

Survey One: quantitative

My starting point was wondering if all expat itinerant teachers fall into the constructive marginal category. There were two surveys. The first was quantitative, and over 200 expat teachers responded (native and non-native speakers of English). I asked what motivated them to go to live in each country, and I instructed them to choose all that applied from 19 options. These were: personal development, culture, adventure, foreign language, professional development, career advancement, economic reasons, romantic involvement or complications, family, attracted to change or risk, travel, religion, politics, idealism, service, Peace Corps, love of teaching, running away from something, looking for greener pastures. Table 3.1.2 shows the top three for each year:

Country 1	Travel, adventure, Peace Corps
Country 2	Professional development, culture, love of teaching
Country 3	Love of teaching, professional development, career advancement
Country 4	Career advancement, economic reasons, professional development
Country 5	Professional development, career advancement, economic reasons
Country 6	Family, attracted to change and risk, professional development
Country 7	Love of teaching, professional development, attracted to change and risk
Country 8	Looking for greener pastures, attracted to change and risk, personal development

Table 3.1.2: What motivated teachers to go and live in each country?

Look closely at how often 'professional development' appears.

I asked who the respondents' closest friends were in each country, and the majority answer was other expatriate language teachers. I asked about language learning and discovered that the respondents tended to reach a very high level in the language of their first foreign country, but that this happened rarely in subsequent countries. When asked what the primary reason was (or would be) for returning to their country of origin, one reason stood out: family.

In describing personality and skills, the top eight, in order, were:

1 I am curious.
2 I am self-reliant.
3 I have a willingness to communicate.
4 I like helping others.
5 I have empathy.
6 I am perceptive.
7 I am self-motivated.
8 I have a strong sense of self.

The lowest rated were:

• I am able to let go.
• I am able to manage stress.
• I am able to access supports.

Neilson, in his 2009 study *Travellers' Tales: The Expatriate English Language Teacher in the New Global Culture* found that half of his respondents reported that seeking the experience of being 'othered' was part of the motivation for going overseas.

Survey Two: qualitative

Some facts:

• The majority of respondents were from the UK and USA, but there was also one from each of Pakistan, India, Uzbekistan, Romania, South Africa, Australia and Canada.
• The range of years living abroad was 6 to 45, with 15 the average.
• The number of countries lived in was four (it was two for the quantitative survey); these countries were mostly in Europe and Asia.
• When asked, 'Do you still live outside your country of origin?' 65.7 per cent said yes.
• One third of respondents were in the 30–39 age range; the next most common age range was 40–49.
• The majority (57.1 per cent) were men!

Qualitative questions

The eight qualitative questions had to do with attitudes and reflections on the teaching of English and its place in the globalising world. I include here a few interesting responses or tendencies:

1 In what ways has your attitude changed towards your country of origin since living overseas?

- Most stated they have become more tolerant. Due to maturity? Different lenses?

2 In what ways have your attitudes changed towards the teaching of English since working abroad (methodology, perceived needs of students, wider attitudes as to the role of English, etc.)?
- Focus on students, according to context and their needs—not just 'student-centred as a trend.
- Expats have developed their teaching through experiencing different contexts and content (ESP, EAL, YL, TT), whereas non-expats may teach in the same context their whole career.

3 In what ways do you feel that your presence has made an impact on people in countries where you have taught?
- An ambassador for my country—I've helped dispel stereotypes, expand my students' world view.
- Helped students get scholarships, pass tests, advance their careers.

4 In what ways do you feel the cultures of the countries where you have lived have had an impact on you?
- They become part of you, like rings on a tree.
- Stretched me, expanded my humanity/tolerance.

5 What is your perception of the role of English in the world today? Is it culture-bound or truly international?
- Strong views on both.

6 In what ways do you think expatriate teachers of English have had an influence on the spread of English around the world?
- Expat teachers have created a huge community of teachers round the world.
- Serving a need more than creating it.
- Well-travelled expat teachers make learning more interesting and are likely to be tolerant.
- We teach future leaders.
- All those young teachers willing to travel the world make English more attainable for the masses.

7 In what ways do you think expatriate teachers of English have had an influence on trends in teacher training around the world?
- Professional teacher organisations.
- Expat teachers bring knowledge of multiple contexts into teaching.
- Expats are happy living abroad—they bring their low stress into their teaching.

8 What have you done for your own professional development since you started teaching English?
- LOTS!!!

In the next section I consider differences between expat teachers of English and another world language: Chinese.

More 'dealers': teachers of Mandarin/Putonghua.

One respondent to my survey wrote, 'Imagine if Chinese or Arabic were the language of the world now and expats from countries that speak those languages went all over the world to teach. I'm sure their forms of teacher training would be very different.' I wondered if this might be true, and I also asked myself other questions: Are Chinese language teachers a community of practice? Is Chinese language teaching a marginal occupation? Do Chinese language teachers have a cultural identity? Are Chinese language teachers medieval knights errant?

To get at these questions, I duplicated the qualitative Survey Two instrument I had done with English language teaching expats, simply changing 'English' to 'Chinese'. I include here a few responses which were unique or significantly different from that of the English teacher expats, but *the majority of responses were not markedly different*. Expat teachers of both English and Mandarin in my research focused on their students and their learning rather than a fixed methodology, and both groups were actively involved in their own professional development.

- I am more critical of my country of origin, but at the same time I love it more.
- China needs reform in teaching methodologies. But I have no power towards this.
- I try to adopt EFL teaching method in teaching Chinese as my learners are all English speakers.
- I have accepted a lot of Western (UK) cultures: equality, fairness, tolerance, openness, quality-oriented, etc.
- Mandarin is like Japanese in the 1980s and early 1990s. As long as China's economy keeps growing, it will become and remain important as a world language.
- I think in many cases expat teachers of Mandarin are the one and only channel through which people can access Chinese culture.
- Expat teachers understand the local culture better than teachers of Chinese in China. They perceive the students' needs better, and there is less miscommunication between them and their students. However, the teachers of Chinese in China are catching up soon.
- Teacher training is a much neglected area in Chinese language teaching. I don't think expat teachers receive much training on teaching Chinese, especially on the Chinese language proper. A lack of good knowledge of the language being taught is a huge concern among Chinese teachers. It cannot be remedied by whatever fancy teaching methods.

Through this study I became aware of the very extensive quantity of opportunities for conferences, seminars, websites, workshops and reading, all in Chinese language teaching (CLT). One expat teacher of Mandarin wrote that she receives about 20 conference news alerts a year. There is a wealth of websites and journals and institutes and teachers' organisations for CLT. The Chinese Language Teachers' Association (CLTA) is 50 years old—older than IATEFL and TESOL. The Overseas Volunteer Chinese Teachers' Program has parallels with the US Peace Corps. The Confucius Institute, begun in 2004 and with language institutes at universities all over the world, is not unlike the British Council (although they do not claim to be independent of the government). The *Vancouver Sun* in 2008 wrote:

> There are deeply divided views about the Confucius Institute in Vancouver. Some say it's a goodwill gesture by Beijing to teach Chinese language and culture, while others believe it's part of a plot by an emerging superpower to infiltrate and influence foreign citizens of their governments.

It seems that it is not only teachers of English who are accused of being imperialists through the spread of language! And yet it also appears that expat language teachers make their own decisions, and Mandarin, like English, is being spread by the spreaders more than by governments.

So what?

I return to my original questions: Is a dealer an exploiter of the drug? What is the drug here? Is it language? If not, is it pedagogy? Is it values? Is it culture? Here's a new question: could the drug be personal and professional development?

I also asked if the phenomenon of expatriate English teachers could be considered a historical, cultural movement. Julian Edge (1996) has written about the professional values we espouse as 'people-who-teach', and he uses the expression 'TESOL culture' to mean a set of shared values that include as central: diversity, inquiry, cooperation and respect. I believe these can be said of the expat Chinese language teacher community as well. Prabhu (1990) wrote:

> Perhaps the best method varies from one teacher to another, but only in the sense that it is best for each teacher to operate with his or her own sense of plausibility at any given time. There may be some truth to each method, but only in so far as each method may operate as one or another teacher's sense of plausibility, promoting the most learning that can be promoted by that teacher (1990: 175).

I close here by linking those two ideas: shared values and method, with an excerpt from another student paper:

> Teaching in Chinese universities is similar but for one point, which in a certain way may be seen as an argument for the way they handle foreign teachers. In my four years of teaching in China, I taught in a number of different settings, and not one of them provided, let alone mandated, a textbook. A program with no curriculum, no objectives, no oversight, and no textbook invites any number of possible outcomes. *Ex falso quodlibet*, as it were. But in the messy scribbling on the blank slate could occasionally be discerned an elegant innovation and even the occasional flourish. The act of evaluating the mélange of styles and techniques was itself a not unproductive challenge. I consider that most of my development as a teacher up to this point happened amid this chaos, and one of the best sources of impetus and inspiration was the casual dialogues with my colleagues. Of these colleagues, the one who had the most significant influence on my development was John [...], a 63 year-old rotund Australian poet, vagabond, stock market adventurer, world traveler, Zen Buddhist, and English teacher.
>
> After a long commute back from a late class, John and I would sit outside the small convenience store on the corner on plastic stools or beer cases, watching the passers-by and drinking and talking late into the night. A common theme was our classes. The nature of the program forced us to be creative, to develop our own

curricula and materials, and this made us feel invested in the work and we spoke of it with passion. We shared our stories of what worked and what didn't. John seemed to me a kind of revolutionary, a free-thinker. His lessons were experiential, student-centered, and grounded in real world events that had immediacy for students (migrant workers, modern women, etc.). He used authentic materials, input-flooding, and grammaring, but neither he nor I knew any of these terms. I could see that what he was doing was great, and I borrowed and adapted it for my own classes. There was feedback as well. I would describe what I was doing, and he would casually latch on to points that resonated and talk about them with enthusiasm. I learned a lot from these exchanges, from the act of narrating my lessons and hearing what resonated with him. And I think I was more receptive, with a lower affective filter, in these personal and informal discussions (Lee 2012).

This reminds me so much of the lives of many expat teachers—we grow in the company of other teachers because we do not have complicated daily lives to return to at the end of a teaching day (or evening).

My final question is this: What is it that we are we dealing? I don't think it is the same answer for everyone. But my advice for teacher education programs is that (in addition to everything else we want to cover) we need to delve deeply into social and cultural identity theory and experiential learning so that whatever it is that we are dealing, we are doing it with *awareness*.

susan.barduhn@sit.edu

References

Appadurai, A. 1990. 'Disjuncture and difference in the global cultural economy' in M. Featherstone (ed.). *Global culture: Nationalism, Globalization and Modernity*. London: Sage.

Bennett, J. 1993. 'Cultural marginality: Identity issues in intercultural training' in R. M. Paige (ed.). *Education for the Intercultural Experience*. Yarmouth, ME: Intercultural Press.

Buboltz. B. 2012. 'Approaches Final Paper'. Unpublished paper submitted as coursework for SIT Graduate Institute, Brattleboro, Vt.

Canagarajah, S. 1999. *Resisting Linguistic Imperialism in English Teaching*. Oxford: Oxford University Press.

Edge, J. 1996. 'Cross-cultural paradoxes in a profession of values'. *TESOL Quarterly* 30/1: 9–30.

Gilbert, E. 2007. *Eat, Pray, Love*. Penguin.

Hargreaves, A. 1994. *Changing Teachers, Changing Times: Teachers' Work and Culture in the Postmodern Age*. New York: Continuum.

Hawkins, D. 1974. *The Informed Vision: Essays on Learning and Human Nature*. New York: Agathorn Press.

Hannerz, U. 1990. 'Cosmopolitans and locals in world culture'. *Theory, Culture and Society* 7: 237–51.

Johnston, B. 1999. 'The expatriate teacher as postmodern paladin'. *Research in the Teaching of English* 34/2: 255–89.

Lee, T. 2012. 'Becoming a Teacher Educator Final Paper'. Unpublished paper submitted as coursework for SIT Graduate Institute, Brattleboro, Vt.

Lindsay-Towner, V. 2011. 'A Virtual Ethnography of the Black Flag Café: A Forum for People who Travel to Dangerous Places'. Unpublished PhD, Bournemouth University.

Moran, P. 2001. *Teaching Culture: Perspectives in Practice*. Boston: Heinle & Heinle.

Neilson, R. 2009. *Travellers' Tales: The Expatriate English Language Teacher in the New Global Culture*. Newcastle-upon-Tyne: Cambridge Scholars' Publishing.

O'Dowd, R. 2012. 'English at work: an analysis of case reports about English language training for the 21st century workforce'. The International Research Foundation for English Language Education. (Retrieved on 25 August 2013 from http://www.academia.edu/3002767/English_at_Work_An_Analysis_of_Case_Reports_about_English_Language_Training_for_the_21st-century_Workforce)

Prabhu, N. 1990. 'There is no best method—Why?' *TESOL Quarterly* 24: 175.

Vancouver Sun 2008. 'Has BCIT sold out to Chinese propaganda?' 2 April 2008.

Walker, J. 2009. 'The World's English Mania'. TED Talk. (Retrieved on 25 August 2013 from http://www.ted.com/talks/jay_walker_on_the_world_s_english_mania.html)

3.2 British Council Signature Event: Linguistic imperialism: still alive and kicking?

Esther Hay *British Council, Manchester, UK*

Chair: Anne Burns *Aston University, UK*

Panellists: Becky R. K. Ndjoze-Ojo *Former Deputy Minister of Education, Namibia,* **Sarah Ogbay** *University of Asmara, Eritrea,* **Robert Phillipson** *Copenhagen Business School, Netherlands and* **Danny Whitehead** *British Council, Indonesia*

In her opening remarks **Anne Burns** referred to linguistic imperialism as an 'enduring and challenging debate' on a 'complex and multi-faceted topic'. The session explored different related themes, drawing on the views of the expert panel and contributions from the audience.

Robert Phillipson argued that our role is to assess how far our activities open or close doors and assess where inequalities and injustice play a role in societies influenced by class, gender, ethnicity and language. Education in post-independence countries showed English-medium teaching using inappropriate books, and delivered by monolingual teachers lacking expertise in teaching and knowledge of other languages. Speakers of certain languages benefit more than others due to the way resources are allocated in education, attitudes to languages, or a focus on élites. The way in which English is used is problematic and has implications for teacher training. We need to challenge key ELT tenets such as monolingualism, native speakers, early start, maximum exposure and the subtractive fallacy, and to connect macro-level trends with micro-level classroom practice to form a multidisciplinary approach. ELT expertise is being exported as though it is universally relevant. It may keep linguistic imperialism alive if it is commercially or politically motivated and not well grounded on a local cultural, educational or linguistic basis.

Becky Ndoze-Ojo agreed that English is linked to linguistic imperialism and has an impact on local languages. If English is a global language, we need to look at how it can be best used to create hope for the speakers of 6,000 other languages, especially in Africa where multilingualism is the norm, not an option. New directions have to go beyond current thinking, question the relevance of the native speaker, and recognise different forms of English, particularly in Africa and Asia. English is what it is, but could be made to function better in multilingual education. The British Council is conscious of research into language policy, multilingual education and the impact of English on other languages. These issues were discussed at the Juba Language Education Conference in South Sudan and covered in the British Council publication that arose from that event (McIlwraith 2013).

Sarah Ogbay proposed that linguistic English imperialism is dying. Continuing to focus on linguistic imperialism can make it appear as if we are patronising the societies in which English is being taught. Learners of English have their own communities, identity and culture; when they are learning English they are not empty vessels. Culture and language are intertwined; we cannot teach English without reference to culture. The teachers are not to be held responsible for linguistic imperialism. The spread of English does not undermine the local language *if* the language policy looks after and supports the local language(s) of the people. If the policy says local languages are not important and not to be developed, then it *is* linguistic imperialism as English is being imposed. We should look at individual/social needs and economic factors. English is the engine in globalisation but there is competition from India and China, so Chinese may become the next international language.

Danny Whitehead suggested that linguistic imperialism provides a valid framework for analysing ELT but is being subdued and strangled. English has great value for individuals and potential for social good. All stakeholders (policy makers, organisations and teachers) face challenges to ensure that the benefits and opportunities are passed on to individuals/groups and mitigate the risks and negative consequences of the spread of English. Research shows children learn best in a language that they understand. Policy makers should educate stakeholders, advocate a policy of multilingual education based on the mother tongue, and integrate English language teaching in a way that supports this policy while protecting linguistic equality and human rights. Organisations should engage in better risk analysis and planning for assessing English language activity and advocate English as part of multilingual education rather than the medium of instruction. Teachers should develop critical practice, audit materials/methods for cultural/contextual bias and assess their impact on learners. They should also respect learners' languages/identities, use them as resources in class and be multilingual role models.

General discussion

The following points were raised:

- One legacy of linguistic imperialism is the lack of development and limitations of local languages. These are used at home but are not academic languages. How can we develop them to become a means of instruction and be applicable to 'higher thinking'? Many organisations put money into higher education in English rather than into multilingual education. If multilingual education is desirable, will the USA/UK put money into education in languages other than English and look at how to teach and learn in other languages better? This includes providing support for other languages in the UK (for example, Welsh and Gaelic) in primary schools and to immigrants.

- What language should be used as the means of instruction? It was noted that countries may have different national languages but have taken a policy decision to use English or another 'official' language. The selection of an official language may be related to economic, political, religious or social issues, rather than arising from what people want/need. English may be used for unity or to prevent conflict by not favouring one group (or language) over others. Alternatively the imposition of English may be seen as a political decision by a ruling group. It was suggested there is a need to 'domesticate' English in some countries and own it.

- Education policy and the role of policy makers are key factors in how far a language policy supports learners' needs and education outcomes. Policy makers choose the language of instruction, but children speak local languages and need that foundation to build on. English language policy might mean that they are taught from the beginning in a language they don't understand. Understanding your environment, and basic concepts, begins with your native language and so you take that with you to school. However, if students are taught through their mother tongue, they may speak the language but not know how to read and write in it. Also, we have to look at the number of local languages and what practical support can be provided for minority languages compared to English.

- The difficulties of putting a policy into practice were also raised. There may not be sufficient resources to translate books into local languages or enough experienced/qualified teachers. Poor policies and poor teaching exist but are not necessarily a result of intervention by the USA/UK. Rather than seeing it as English vs. local language, as an 'either/or' situation, we should be thinking of it terms of 'and'. The challenge for organisations like the British Council is to argue for English while supporting multilingual education and assisting the delivery of English teaching and the development of research.

- The question of who should teach English provoked a lively debate on native- vs. non-native speaker teachers. Some learners prefer a native speaker, but the latter may not know the context of the learners (for example, large mixed-ability classes) or do not have experience of living/teaching abroad. Not speaking the local language makes it difficult to manage large mixed-ability classes and check understanding.

- Expectations and perceptions were explored further. Some institutions advertise for native speakers only and employ them despite lack of experience or qualifications. Is there still a perception that being a native speaker makes a person a better teacher? Do we expect them to be white, western, and with a particular accent? We need to challenge this as there are different varieties of English and regional accents; we also need to question perceptions with regard to these variations. Native speakers from other ethnic backgrounds, and non-native speakers, may experience racism. This is now being addressed in some areas to stress near-native speaker competence rather than a particular ethnicity or native language.

- The monolingual native speaker model is now changing into a more bilingual or multi-lingual teacher. With the globalisation of English and an increase in mobility and diversity, more teaching is delivered by non-native speakers and multilingual teachers. Assessment of teachers should be made on the basis of qualifications and qualities. Can they deliver what is required of them in the classroom? This should be the fundamental question, rather than what native language(s) they speak.

This debate stimulated some rich and timely discussions on linguistic imperialism, past and present, and provided interesting and insightful observations on the issues and challenges in different contexts, and how to take this forward.

Esther.Hay@britishcouncil.org

Reference

McIlwraith, H. (ed.). 2013. *Multilingual Education in Africa: Lessons from the Juba Language-in-Education Conference.* London: British Council. (Retrieved from http://www. teachingenglish.org.uk/publications/multilingual-education-africa-lessons-juba-language-education-conference)

3.3 The English language in Francophone West Africa

Hywel Coleman *University of Leeds, UK and* **Aïché Bâ** *Lycée Massa Makan Diabaté, Mali*

Background

The Francophone West Africa (FWA) region covers eight countries: Benin, Burkina Faso, Côte d'Ivoire, Guinea, Mali, Mauritania, Senegal and Togo. It covers an area larger than India but has a population of just 92 million, the same as the Philippines. All the countries in the region use French as an official language.

FWA has received relatively little attention from the international language education community. Therefore, in 2011 the British Council commissioned a survey which aimed to answer these and other questions:

- What roles do English and other languages play in the region?
- Who teaches English in state secondary schools?
- What happens in English lessons in state secondary schools?
- What do learners actually learn?

The study was carried out by a team of 14 English teachers from the region. Aïché Bâ was a member of the team and Hywel Coleman coordinated the study. Across the region, more than 9,000 people (pupils, teachers, teacher educators, Ministry of Education officials and ordinary working people) were consulted. Some of the most striking findings of the study are summarised here.

What roles do English and other languages play?

- Almost 200 African languages are spoken in FWA. For the majority of people, they are the languages of everyday life, but in most education systems they are not taught and are not used in classrooms.
- French is the language of government, the universities and most schools. However, there are no reliable figures for how many people speak the language.
- Arabic is used by many people for devotional purposes.

- Chinese is beginning to attract attention as a language of trade.
- English has important, though limited, roles in several very specific domains: industrial operations involving multinational companies; regional economic cooperation organisations; international development agencies; studying abroad; international peacekeeping missions. Also, surprisingly, nearly a third of market traders claim that they need English for buying and selling goods outside FWA.

Who teaches English in state secondary schools?

Nearly 11,000 people in the region are involved in English teaching, as teachers, pedagogic advisers, inspectors, university lecturers and teacher educators. Each country has its own teacher preparation requirements; consequently, the amount of training that secondary school English teachers receive varies greatly from one country to another.

What happens in English lessons in state secondary schools?

We looked at time, class size and teaching/learning styles.

The time allocated in the school timetable for English varies from country to country. For example, some pupils in Mali receive only 375 class hours of English throughout their time in secondary school, whereas some pupils in Senegal are allotted 1,080 hours for studying English.

Class size also varies from place to place. The smallest class we observed had just 14 pupils in it while the largest had 136 pupils; the average across the region was 56. But we also found that on average 18.5 per cent of registered pupils were absent from observed lessons.

Although curriculum time and class size varied from country to country, there were many similarities in the teaching and learning styles found throughout the region. Generally speaking, teachers are the busiest people in the classroom. Learners usually work alone, copying down what the teacher writes on the board and responding individually to questions from the teacher. Learners are also often expected to join in choral chanting. In many classes, learners spend considerable amounts of time just watching and listening while others speak or perform tasks. Interaction between learners was almost never seen.

What do learners actually learn?

A country-by-country sample of pupils in their second year of studying English was asked to carry out an integrated reading and writing task in English. The short passages which they produced enabled us to identify what learners were able to do and what problems they were experiencing. We found wide variation in the pupils' writing, but this variation is not related to their age or whether they lived in urban or rural areas. Instead, variation seems to be associated with factors such as the number of hours allocated for English, whether teachers have studied at university and whether the child lives near the border with an Anglophone country.

What happens next?

The research reported here is only a beginning and more detailed studies are needed. But we hope that what has been found will encourage discussion in schools, teacher preparation institutions and Ministries of Education. The complete findings will appear in a book to be published by the British Council later in 2013.

h.coleman@leeds.ac.uk

ba.chou@yahoo.fr

3.4 Other people's lives: the long-term impact of English projects

Anne Wiseman *British Council, Lisbon, Portugal*

Background

In this talk I presented the initial findings of a study which looks at the long-term impact of an English project on a group of educators' lives. To date there has been very little focus on the long-term impact or results of development projects; this was highlighted in panel discussion at IATEFL 2012 around the British Council publication *The Management of Change* (Tribble 2012). The Independent Commission for Aid Impact also notes in its 2010 work plan:

> ... the impact of aid programmes can often be fully assessed *only* [my italics] long after the programme has been completed. Programme evaluations, however, usually take place during or shortly after the programme in order to be able to provide timely conclusions. This can present challenges as longer-term impacts may not yet be apparent (2010).

The project I focused on was one of many British Council teacher development/ training projects which were set up in Eastern and Central Europe in the early 1990s. The project was based in Bulgaria and established teams of trainer trainers across the country. It was monitored throughout, and evaluation questionnaires were administered to gauge the level of impact of the project. However, it is only after a number of years that we can really asses the full impact of this project on the education system and the people involved in it.

I chose to focus on the impact of the project on *the people* involved for a number of reasons. Systemic change (often identified as the long-term outcome of a project) does not happen in isolation, and the main contributors to the change are the people working within the project. However, project designers rarely consider what impact the project will have on people's own lives at the initial design stage. I also wanted to follow up comments often made by participants during the life of the project, to the effect that the project 'changed their lives'; a study such as this could gauge to what extent the project *had* actually changed people's lives.

Methodology

The use of personal narrative and histories as a research tool enables the researcher to look in depth at people's lives and how various events have affected them. The research is in its initial stage and the findings below are from three unstructured interviews focussing on narrative histories.

Initial findings

The findings fall into three main areas: career development, social and emotional outcomes; and pedagogic beliefs and values.

Career development

Findings so far show that the impact on participants' career development is two pronged: the project certainly helped them move forward and gain better jobs, often in universities. On the other hand, passionate involvement and commitment to the project and its aims sometimes meant people got left behind on the academic career ladder.

Social and emotional outcomes

Interviewees to date have all said how much more confidence they gained from the project and, eventually, how it gave them more 'status' amongst their peers; this in turn gave them more confidence to develop their thinking and ideas further. This links in to the third area below.

Pedagogic beliefs and values

All interviewees indicated that one key outcome of the project for them was a change in pedagogic beliefs and values. The move from a focus on linguistic teaching to pedagogy, discussions on the nature of teaching and learning, and the questioning of long-held beliefs all contributed to their change of thinking—or, in some cases, awoke long-held but unvoiced beliefs. In turn, as they became more influential, the project participants did manage to effect change within their educational system. In the words of one interviewee, 'Methodology was underestimated then. But we did contribute to changing that.'

Conclusions

Project evaluators/designers can underestimate or do not measure the effects projects have on people's lives for a number of reasons: the impact is very difficult to measure; it is qualitative, not quantitative, and so can appear fuzzy and be difficult to report; and in monetary terms there are no clear returns.

However, the research is showing that there *are* legacy outcomes such as a strong network of professionals who contribute to the country's development and build on the pedagogical foundations established in the project.

This research is ongoing and further updates can be obtained from the author.

anne.wiseman@britshcouncil.org

References

Independent Commission for Aid Impact. (Retrieved from http://icai.independent.gov.uk/)

Tribble, C. 2012. *The Management of Change*. London: British Council Publications.

3.5 'A matter of love': English, identity and the formation of the student-teacher

Miri Tashma-Baum *Givat-Washington Academic College of Education, Israel*

Introduction

My talk presents the results of a research project I conducted, aimed at exploring the meanings with which Israeli ELT students invest the English language and the culture they associate with it. It shows that the primary value of English in the eyes of these students is as a source of self-enrichment and a tool for self-expression. In other words, in keeping with other research on this topic, the motivation of the student-teachers was intrinsic rather than instrumental. Additionally, I found that the enthusiastic adoption of facets of English into the students' identities did not result in a concomitant sense of the inferiority of their native culture, but rather in a richer identity, woven of strands of both the native and the imported language and culture. These findings have interesting practical implications.

The research

The research project, a qualitative, phenomenological one, was based on 19 in-depth semi-structured interviews with ELT students from relatively disadvantaged socio-economic backgrounds, belonging to two teacher's colleges in outlying regions. They were asked to speak about the place and meaning of English in their lives. The analysis of the interviews was carried out according to the principles of categorical analysis.

The results: love and self-identity

Strikingly, while none of the students had any familial connection with English, they all mentioned the word 'love' in connection with the language numerous times, particularly in connection with English-language music and cinema. Seventeen out of the nineteen presented this love as the sole reason for choosing the profession of English teaching. While English was perceived differently by different student-teachers—some focusing more on linguistic elements, some on cultural ones, and a third group on its communicative possibilities—the contribution of English to both the formation and the expression of the student's self-identity was seen as central.

The late-modern self

From a critical post-colonialist perspective, this phenomenon may seem the sad, inevitable result of the linguistic imperialism of English (Phillipson 1992), carrying with it a concomitant sense of inferiority or 'self-marginalisation' (Kumaravadivelu 206: 22). However, my study argues that the psychological and cultural dangers which these critics warn against are averted in the case of my student-teachers, as a result of their continuing commitment, often attested to during the interviews, to other sources of self-identification, most clearly, Jewish cultural practices. The result is not a rejection of one identity in favour of another, but rather the development of a more complex, empowered identity.

This finding is in keeping with recent SLA research on language and identity, influenced by sociological theories of identity construction in the late modern world, with its previously unimaginable array of cultural possibilities and potential sources for identification (Giddens 1991). Viewed within this context, the students' love of English is thus less a sign of self-marginalisation and more a deliberate attempt at widening their range of possible identity models.

Implications for teaching and teacher training

Finally, it is worth considering what pedagogical lessons regarding more effective L2 teaching can be learnt from the experience of the interviewees. Strikingly, most of the student-teachers did not regard the English classroom as their primary source of L2 learning and of their love for the language; rather, this derived from their continued exposure to the English-language media. When asked to envision their own goals as future teachers, the respondents drew directly from their own learning trajectory, stressing the importance of creating an emotional connection between the pupils and the language and encouraging self-expression. This endeavour, I argue, should be supported by the teacher-training departments as well. Teacher trainers should emphasise the *legitimacy* of non-native appropriation of the language, expose students to works by multilingual writers, and promote classroom activities allowing self-expression.

At the same time, as my research has shown, most of the interviewees were initially drawn to English by the allure of its foreign, exciting otherness as expressed by songs and movies, only gradually appropriating it for their own uses. Divorcing the study of English from its cultural aspects, as some proponents of EIL would like to do, would disable the widening of horizons and limit the exposure to potential sources of identification, which are the prerogative of every language learner. A middle road has to be found, both allowing the enriching access to a different culture, and presenting the language itself as a tool ready to be appropriated.

mirimtb@gmail.com

References

Giddens, A. 1991. *Modernity and Self-Identity: Self and Society in the Late Modern Age.* Cambridge: Polity Press.

Kumaravadivelu, B. 2006. 'Dangerous liaison: globalization, empire and TESOL' in J. Edge (ed.). *Re-locating TESOL in an Age of Empire.* London: Palgrave Macmillan.

Phillipson, R. 1992. *Linguistic Imperialism.* Oxford: Oxford University Press.

3.6 Teaching culture: what do teachers have to know?

Maike Grau *University of Education, Freiburg, Germany*

For teachers of English as a foreign language, the cultural element can be daunting for a number of reasons: coursebooks and curricula for ELT in public schools are often still based on traditional concepts of teaching culture, which can be seen in the choice of cultures and in the way these are represented in teaching resources. In academic publications, however, these approaches to teaching culture have been criticised for their tendency to reduce and essentialise cultures, and for presenting diverse and constantly changing cultures which are actively constructed by individuals as static and homogeneous entities which are closely linked to nation states. The concept of transculturality has been introduced to emphasise culture crossings, blendings and borrowings across national borders (Welsch 2009), and the English language with its many cultures has been shown to be both part and product of these globalisation processes (Pennycook 2007). However, classroom applications of critical and transcultural approaches in foreign language education are few so far and have mostly been designed for advanced learners of English, often involving discussions of identity formation in post-colonial literature or film (for example, Kumaravadivelu 2008).

This paper considers the gap between theory and classroom practice in the field of teaching culture from the perspective of pre-service teacher education. My small-scale survey study is based on open-ended responses from 32 students enrolled in a German university-based teacher education programme and was carried out in October 2012. While the answers given in this small sample can in no way be generalised, and, like all questionnaires, do not include in-depth comments, they can provide valuable insights for teacher education and starting points for further research. The findings presented here have been generated by computer-supported qualitative data analysis and will focus on a few salient issues including definitions of culture and reasons for teaching culture in ELT.

Key findings

A majority of respondents define culture using terms such as 'country', 'region', or 'area' (17 out of 32), often combined with 'a group of people' (11). Compared with the features emphasised in the current academic discourse, only two students describe cultures as constantly changing and diverse, as opposed to a relatively monolithic and closed representation of a country or a national group.

All 32 participants in the study consider it important to include culture in ELT. Reasons given for this opinion vary, but 21 respondents mention the connection between language and culture, often combined with the argument that language learners need to know about the native speaker's culture in order to be able to understand and communicate appropriately with them. The status of English as an international language is mentioned by only three participants.

Answers such as these give reason to think about the impact the students' own experiences as English language learners in school may have had on their beliefs about the nature of culture and its role in the ELT classroom. However, some responses also reflect the students' personal experience with cultures when travelling, working and studying abroad. These comments include observations about cultural diversity, cultural mixing and the use of English in postcolonial and global contexts. Despite the fact that, in the context of a questionnaire, these are rather short accounts, they include key elements of the current academic discourse in cultural studies.

Conclusions

How can future teachers of English be supported in developing a critical approach to teaching culture?

1 *Classroom applications:* Ways of putting a critical approach to teaching culture into practice need to be developed and evaluated in teacher education courses, considering English as a language of many cultures, including traditional 'target cultures'. This is especially true for English in primary school and in the first years of secondary education.

2 *Culture-general topics:* While English teachers should be aware that English is, of course, used in communication with native speakers and culture-specific knowledge is, therefore, required, there should also be an element of 'culture-general' topics in teacher education, including a discussion of current issues raised in the research literature.

3 *Reflective approach:* This small-scale survey study has indicated that students' experiences as learners of English may have been based on cultural knowledge transfer and a fairly closed notion of culture. Relating to more recent personal experiences could provide a counter-balance in the process of developing a view on language and culture which reflects more adequately the nature of today's globalised world.

maike.grau@ph-freiburg.de

References

Kumaravadivelu, B. 2008. *Cultural Globalization and Language Education.* New Haven and London: Yale University Press.

Pennycook, A. 2007. *Global Englishes and Transcultural Flows.* London and New York: Routledge.

Welsch, W. 2009. 'On the Acquisition and Possession of Commonalities' in F. Schulze-Engler and S. Helff (eds.). *Transcultural English Studies.* Amsterdam and New York: Rodopi.

3.7 Practical activities to enhance L2 identity

Alexandra Reynolds *Sussex University, Brighton, UK and Université de Nantes, France*

The aim of this workshop was to explore some in-class activities which could be used to motivate learners to think about who they are in relation to a wider English-speaking community. These activities can be used in the English language classroom, on a one-to-one basis or as a stimulus to further discussion in the context of an interview.

The participants of this workshop were asked to carry out these tasks themselves so that they could then transpose them to their own ELT contexts. The focus of this paper will be a mind mapping activity and a word list used to describe the English language. Approximate times are given for how long these activities last.

Mind mapping the self

Approx. 20 minutes for drawing and 20 minutes for sharing
This activity requires learners to describe themselves using an initially non-verbal cue. This means that this activity can be used with many different levels of learners. Mind maps and language maps have been used by researchers such as Busch (2012)

and Wheeldon and Faubert (2009) as a starting point for further discussions about identity. The maps are a good reference point for a conversation between peers.

Instructions

> On a piece of paper, draw a mind map of your brain. You can use words and/or pictures. The picture can be any shape or form. It doesn't have to look like a real brain, but it should act as a container. Refer to who you are, what you are good at and what you like. Someone who knows you well should be able to recognise you from your mind map.

After the learners have finished their mind maps, they can either present them for-mally to the class, swap with a neighbour or wander round looking at other drawings and asking questions. Every mind map is unique, and they are an excellent starting point for further discussion. Figure 3.7.1, drawn by a third-year physics student at a French science faculty, shows the different linguistic, cultural and intellectual centres of her life. The drawing proved a useful reference point for discussion, where her interlocutors could ask her questions about the elements in her drawing.

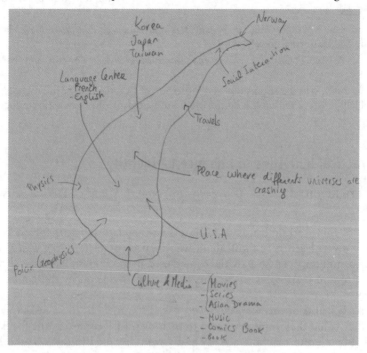

Figure 3.7.1: An example of a mind map

The story of English in 10 words

Approx. 6 minutes for word list and 20 minutes for sharing

This in-class activity is based on a presentation given by David Crystal at the Edinburgh Book Festival in August 2012. Crystal was presenting his own 100 words of the English language, which he revealed to be as much a reflection of who *he* was as a description of the English language itself (see Crystal 2011). It gave me the idea of trying out such a word list with my own students on a smaller scale. I was interested in finding out what words they would choose to describe the English language.

This exercise explores the images or signifiers that we associate with the second language and culture. I asked the participants to list 10 words that they associated with the English language so that I could analyse how my participants related to the objects or concepts they had voiced. I have carried out this test with French students learning English as well as English students learning French. This exercise is useful in exploring the advantages and disadvantages of stereotypes and clichés associated with L2 learning.

Instructions

Make a list of 10 words that you think of when I say 'the English language'. Try not to think too much about it; just note down the first words that come into your head.

The learners then read out their words and the most popular can be tallied. At this point learners can elaborate on why they chose certain words. The learners can be asked to do the same thing with their own country/language. My learners said that the word list associated to their first language and culture (French) was the more difficult because it is 'easier to observe and describe other cultures'. It is also interesting to explore the differences between the language label 'English' and the cultural identities associated with 'British', or 'American', for example. The starting concept offered can be varied depending on what the ELT practitioner wishes to explore.

Learners who are encouraged to think about identity via practical activities of this kind can engage with the L2 on a more personal and intrinsic level.

alexandra.reynolds@univ-nantes.fr

References

Busch, B. 2012. 'The linguistic repertoire revisited'. *Applied Linguistics* 33/5: 503–23.

Crystal, D. 2011. *The Story of English in 100 Words*. London: Profile Books.

Wheeldon, J. and J. Faubert. 2009. 'Framing experience: concept maps, mind maps, and data collection'. *Qualitative Research* 68–83.

4 Classroom dynamics

This chapter takes us into the heart of the classroom and focuses on learning styles and classroom dynamics. The first paper here, by **Marjorie Rosenberg**, encourages readers to develop an awareness of different learning styles. **Elena Onchevska Ager** highlights the discrepancy between teacher beliefs regarding classroom dynamics and what actually happens in class, while **Wioletta Szóstak** presents humanistic activities designed to encourage positive class dynamics. We move on to two papers on the language used by the teacher. **Brian Tomlinson** argues in favour of teacher talking time, showing how it can benefit learners in the classroom. **Julie Humble** then goes on to explore the challenge of explaining language to elementary-level learners; she discusses the meta-language that teachers should use to ensure comprehensibility. The next group of papers all describe the challenges experienced by those involved in teaching ESOL classes: **Anne Crappsley** outlines measures taken to promote cohesion within a class with a rolling intake; **Thomas L. Lloyd** emphasises the necessity of providing support to learners with emotional issues; and **Rosie Quin, Christine Palmer and Jenifer Martin** present projects designed to accelerate asylum seekers' and refugees' integration into the community. The final three papers in this chapter deal with specific aspects of classroom dynamics. **Vera Cabrera Duarte** shows how the use of drama is effective in increasing motivation, while **Tilly Harrison** presents her experiences of using games in language instruction. Finally, **John Rodgers** questions the place of religion in the ELT classroom.

4.1 Spotlight on learning styles

Marjorie Rosenberg *University of Graz, Austria*

Introduction

Have you ever wondered why some learners enjoy parts of lessons while others find those same activities boring? Have students' evaluations surprised you because aspects of your lessons received both praise and criticism? Do some learners love group work while others find it distracting? The answers to these questions may simply lie with the fact that your students span a variety of different learner types. The aim of this workshop was to examine this issue and explore different ways of dealing with it.

Defining learning styles

We began by discussing perceptual filters, learning strategies and individual patterns of behaviour in order to pinpoint what is meant by 'style'. We then went on to consider the role of learning styles in the classroom. Some of the main points were:

- Teachers often teach in the way they learn.
- Mixing methods can help to reach different learners.
- Learners can learn to stretch out of their comfort zones once they know about their preferred styles.
- Consider first harmonising with and then challenging learners.
- Metacognition of styles can provide learners with insight into learning processes and help build tolerance for other types

We also looked at some of the preconceptions of learning styles and what they are not:

- An excuse;
- a reason to pigeon-hole learners;
- right or wrong;
- an indication of competence; or
- limiting.

Three learning style models

The next step was to look more closely at three different models. We began with the sensory-perception model researched in the late 1970s by Walter Barbe and Raymond Swassing (Barbe and Swassing 1979). These 'modalities', as they called them, affect how we take in, process, store and retrieve information. We then moved on to cognitive processing which deals with the thought processes we are most comfortable using. Herman Witkin, who carried out research from the 1940s to the 1970s, coined the phrases 'field-dependent' (global learners who are greatly affected by their surroundings) and 'field-independent' (analytic learners who can distance themselves from influences around them) (Witkin and Goodenough 1981). The last model, mind organisation, based on April Bowie's research in the mid-1990s, looks at the behavioural characteristics of different learner types (Bowie 1997). By filling out a questionnaire, learners determine if they perceive information concretely or abstractly, and if they organise it systematically or non-systematically, resulting in four distinct styles. After briefly discussing the characteristics of the styles, participants tried to categorise themselves and in the ensuing discussions we saw that the individual profiles in the room varied greatly from person to person.

Activities designed for different learner types

In order to show how awareness of style could be 'translated' into classroom implementation, we tried out several activities designed to appeal to different learner types. Starting off with an activity for visual learners, participants looked around the room and then closed their eyes while one person announced that he or she had seen an item of a particular colour. The others tried to guess what it was by asking questions about it. The next activity was for kinesthetic motoric learners and, one-by-one, several participants created a living statue for the others to see. It was pointed out that this activity helps learners who need to physically 'feel' abstract concepts such as use of the past tense since once the learners again take their seats, the 'art work' they created is gone. Analytic learners were then targeted in an activity in which participants had to answer questions without using 'yes' or 'no', demonstrating how thought processes work when learners have to carefully consider different ways to answer simple queries. The activity for global learners appointed several people as programmers who then instructed their robots to carry out different physical tasks. Within the mind organisation model, the 'expert investigators' had to decide which of three statements was most likely to be false and the 'flexible friends' had the chance to ask questions about personal events found in a mind-map.

Where learning styles fit in

The workshop concluded with a summary of how learning styles can be used in the classroom:

- to raise awareness;
- to encourage active participation by learners;
- to increase motivation; and
- to help learners develop successful strategies.

Reflection

In reflecting on the workshop, participants were asked which activities they liked best and how these activities related to their personal styles. They left with the task of thinking about which activities would work well for them and how they could adapt them to their teaching situations. It was stressed that this short introduction was only the beginning of the journey; how they chose to go on was left to them.

mrosenberg@aon.at

References

Barbe, W. B. and R. H. Swassing. 1979. *Teaching through Modality Strengths: Concepts and Practices*. Columbus, OH: Zaner-Bloser Inc.

Bowie, A. 1997. *Mind Organisation*. Seattle, Wash.: The Learning Styles Institute.

Witkin, H. A. and D. R. Goodenough. 1981. *Cognitive Styles: Essence and Origins*. Madison, Wis.: International Universities Press.

4.2 From knowing the way to walking it: teachers' beliefs

Elena Onchevska Ager *Ss Cyril and Methodius University, Skopje, Republic of Macedonia*
Pilgrims Teacher Trainer Journal Scholarship winner

Introduction

The educational group is considered to be a powerful source of motivation for English language learning (ELL) as it possesses greater resources than any individual group member and is a key factor in shaping the atmosphere in the classroom (Dörnyei and Murphy 2003). However, limited research has been carried out into (a) how teachers view the potential of the educational group to improve the quality of their students' ELL; and (b) what they do to tap into it.

This talk reported on aspects of the author's doctoral research into the attitudes of Macedonian university teachers of EFL about the influence of group dynamics on students' ELL, as evidenced by the teachers' expressed beliefs and as inferred from their observed behaviours. It also looked into the relationships between the teachers' attitudes and their related practices.

The study

The study attempted to answer the following research questions:

1 What are teachers' perceptions about the influence of group dynamics on ELL?
2 What is the relationship between teachers' beliefs about group dynamics and their teaching practices?

The data was gathered by means of questionnaires, classroom observations, interviews, teachers' reflections on their observed classes and teachers' syllabi. The data was interpreted using theoretical tools borrowed from the relevant literature and research on teacher education, group dynamics and EFL motivation.

The vast majority of the teachers (95 per cent) shared the belief that group dynamics have the power to affect the quality of the students' ELL, with 88 per cent of the teachers reporting that they use strategies to tap into the group dynamics in their teaching contexts. Among the strategies most frequently elicited from the teachers were group work opportunities in class, teacher availability, relaxed classroom atmosphere, fun activities for getting to know each other, and so on. A few teachers mentioned out-of-class activities, drama techniques, conflict resolution activities, use of language which evokes immediacy ('us', as opposed to 'me' or 'you'), indirect error correction, and others.

On a more careful inspection of the data, however, serious discrepancies surfaced regarding the attitudes of the teachers and their observed practices. It transpired that even though the teachers demonstrated awareness of the importance of developing positive interpersonal relations in the classroom for successful ELL, in the observed classes they predominantly organised opportunities for individual work embedded in autocratic, classical humanist educational settings. Further to this, the seating arrangement was predominantly linear, even though the classrooms offered opportunities for alternative, more group dynamics-friendly seating arrangements. In fact, the teachers' observed practices clashed with their expressed beliefs in as many as 44 per cent of cases.

Implications for teaching and training

The study confirmed the author's intuition that most EFL teachers know the way, but few actually walk it. It identified a lack of consistency between the three types of teacher knowledge outlined by Malderez and Wedell (2007): knowing *about*, knowing *how* and knowing *to*. The potential mismatch between the different types of knowledge teachers possess—to be more precise, between their beliefs and practices—needs to be appropriately addressed in teacher training contexts.

One way to tackle such inconsistencies is via constant focus on teacher beliefs or, as Johnson (1999: 30) likes to refer to them, 'the rock we stand on'. In order to successfully support teachers in managing their own belief systems, trainers can choose from a number of belief-surfacing strategies: teachers' own (observed or not) teaching experiences, observation of others' teaching, reflection on their past and current teaching practices (Malderez and Wedell 2007), as well as critical friendships and reflection on their past experiences as students (Johnson 1999). Malderez and Wedell underline the importance of the relaxed environment that teachers' professional development should be embedded in and recommend the use of fun, fiction, metaphors, etc. during teacher training.

Analysing and understanding one's own and others' professional belief systems is expected to help English language teaching professionals to be better equipped to notice and process any inconsistencies in their own professional belief systems as part of their continuous professional development. In this way, teachers will be better able to steer the interpersonal processes in the classroom in directions that motivate students and create conditions for better quality English language learning.

elena.oncevska@gmail.com

References

Dörnyei, Z. and T. Murphy. 2003. *Group Dynamics in the Language Classroom*. Cambridge: Cambridge University Press.

Johnson, K. 1999. *Understanding Language Teaching: Reasoning in Action*. Boston: Heinle & Heinle.

Malderez, A. and M. Wedell. 2007. *Teaching Teachers: Processes and Practices*. London: Continuum.

4.3 Communication and relationships in the classroom

Wioletta Szóstak *University of Szczecin, Poland*
IATEFL W.R. Lee Scholarship winner

Introduction

The aim of my workshop was to present several humanistic activities which help improve group dynamics and, at the same time, provide communicative language practice. I invited the audience to participate in some of these activities and to discuss their usefulness afterwards.

Hands-on experience

Activity 1: Sweet warm-up

The participants talked about their achievements, their first impressions from the Conference and their plans for the future. The activity was organised as group work, and the choice of the topic was determined by the colour of the sweets each participant had chosen beforehand. Feedback showed that the most interesting topic was 'First impressions from the Conference', as all participants were eager to hear what presentations the others had attended so far and what they had learned from them. I pointed out that the same activity could be organised with toilet paper (Wasilewska 2009) instead of sweets, and it turned out that some participants were already familiar with this idea.

Activity 2: True or false?

I started out by giving two statements about myself, one of which was accompanied by a photo. The audience had to guess if my statements were true or false. This served as a demonstration of the activity, which was then carried out in pairs and turned out to be very enjoyable. Feedback consisted of sharing what the participants learned about each other in this way.

Activity 3: Who wrote it?

I divided the audience into two groups and appointed group leaders. Each group member received a piece of paper and had to write one sentence about himself or herself in the past tense. The group leaders collected the sentences, read them out and groups guessed who had written each sentence. Participants could also ask follow-up questions to the author. For feedback, the group leaders shared some of the most interesting or funniest sentences together with what they had learnt about their authors.

Input and discussion

The audience were not familiar with the concept of humanistic activities, so I introduced them as activities which meet the following criteria (Hadfield 1992):

- They enable learners to get to know each other, promoting friendship and acceptance in the group.
- They enable the teacher to get to know the learners and establish a good relationship with them.
- They create context for personalised and communicative language practice.
- They encourage cooperation and fluid seating arrangements.
- They create a positive, relaxed atmosphere in the classroom.

I invited the audience to discuss possible variations on the activities we had done. The conclusion was that the activities could be easily adapted to suit different levels, needs and contexts, regardless of the resources available; this was considered to be their greatest advantage. I pointed out that the demonstrated activities were only frameworks, and that they could be used as warm-ups, ice breakers, revision games or speaking activities, depending on the aims and structure of the lesson (Woodward and Lindstromberg 1995).

I also invited the audience to share their own ideas for humanistic activities. One of the most interesting ideas suggested was a mingle activity with mobile phones in which learners share and discuss photos from their private galleries.

Afterwards I presented two more activities:

1 **Autograph collections:** a mingle activity based on the bingo framework. Each learner needs a grid with the names of actions (for example, climb a mountain). The winners are the first three students who collect three autographs (horizontally,

diagonally or vertically) from the others. The autographs are given by students who answer 'yes' to the winner's questions (for example, 'Have you ever climbed a mountain?'). The winners tell the class whose autographs they have collected and for which actions. The class ask follow-up questions to find out more about the actions performed by others.

2 **Dice conversations:** a speaking activity organised in groups. The teacher prepares a set of topic cards and a die per group. Students take turns to draw one topic card (for example, my home town) and throw a die, which determines the manner in which they talk about the topic (for example, 1 = tell lies, 2 = compare, etc.).

wszostak@autograf.pl

References

Hadfield, J. 1992. *Classroom Dynamics.* Oxford: Oxford University Press.

Wasilewska, M. 2009. 'Ice-breakers, warm-ups and closers—how to start a new year effectively.' Workshop presented at the 18th IATEFL Poland Conference, Poznań, Poland, 11–13 September 2009.

Woodward, T. and S. Lindstromberg. 1995. *Planning from Lesson to Lesson.* Harlow: Longman.

4.4 Let the teacher speak

Brian Tomlinson *Leeds Metropolitan University, UK and Anaheim University, CA, USA*

Introduction

As my presentation was called *Let the Teacher Speak,* I started by inviting any teacher in the audience to interrupt me at any point to ask a question, raise a point or just tell me that I was talking rubbish. Many teachers did interrupt to ask questions and make points, but nobody expressed disagreement with my main point that teachers should be encouraged to talk more in class and not less.

I then told a story as an example of a teacher starting a class by exposing learners to language in use, and I read a poem as a deliberately provocative example of the danger of restricting teacher talking time in class. Both examples were then shown to illustrate my point that we've made a huge mistake in being dogmatic about teacher talking time.

To reinforce this point I showed on PowerPoint some examples from page 1 of 'teacher talking time' on Google. These included:

- 'It's amazing how almost every new EFL teacher has the same problem—talking too much. It's so standard that the phenomenon has a name: TTT (teacher talk time). The whole idea is to reduce it.'
- 'TTT stands for Teacher Talking Time, and that's something you can't have too little of.'
- 'You should do everything to maximise STT and minimise TTT.'

I also told the audience how I'd recently overheard a moderator of an initial TEFL training course agree with two instructors that 'she's a fail—too much teacher talking time.'

Learners need teachers to talk

I made the point that we've instructed teachers to cut down on teacher talking time; yet teachers need to talk in the classroom in order to

- provide their learners with exposure to the target language in use (especially as in many contexts they are the learners' only source);
- engage their learners both cognitively and affectively;
- develop a positive rapport;
- provide communicative feedback; and
- model functions other than just English for interrogation and instruction.

My recommendations

I recommended that we should reduce teacher teaching time (after all, there's no evidence that explicit teaching of language has any long-term effect on acquisition), but that we should increase *quality* teacher talking time. I then suggested and exemplified the following ways of doing this, by making use of the following:

1 Teacher performance, for example:
- Task-free activities at the beginnings of lessons in which the teacher tells a joke or story or reads extracts from books or magazines. The teacher doesn't ask any questions about the 'text' but makes it available for learners to take away and read at the end of the lesson.
- Acting of scenes from plays (either with solo performances from the teacher or with classes joined together so that more than one teacher can perform).
- Teacher debates, in which teachers from different classes debate an issue of relevance to their learners.
2 Responsive teaching, i.e. providing language, content and advice to learners during an activity when they need it.
3 Teacher intermingling, i.e. walking around unobtrusively but availably when learners are engaged in an activity.
4 Teacher task participation, for example, describing their own experience, offering their own opinions, articulating their own discovery, being a member of a group, playing a role (for example, a manager who could come in and help when a service transaction is going wrong).
5 Teacher chat in which the teacher interacts informally with the learners before, in between and after learning activities' this is described as 'the most authentic and meaningful exchange between student and teacher' (http://bogglesworldesl.com/glossary/teachertalk.htm).

Conclusion

I ended my presentation by doing three things:

1 Firstly, I read the following extract from an 'authentic' conversation between a CLIL teacher and a student, which demonstrates the value of teacher talking time in stimulating learners to do more than just answer questions.

> Teacher (pointing at a maths problem on the board): Miguel, I'd like you to look at this problem.
>
> Miguel: Aren't there enough problems in the world?
>
> Teacher (realising the student's question is hypothetical): I've got five bottles in one hand and six bottles in another. What have I got?
>
> Miguel: A drinking problem?
>
> Teacher: No! I've got 11. The answer is 11 bottles!
>
> Miguel: That's still a lot. Maybe you should look into counselling.

2 Secondly, I gave another example of localised task-free activity.
3 Finally I exhorted everybody to let the teacher speak!

In discussion many members of the audience told stories of the damage done to new teachers (and their learners) by teacher trainers insisting on restricting teacher talking time.

brianjohntomlinson@googlemail.com

4.5 Explaining language to low-level learners: rising to the challenge!

Julie Humble *Lydbury English Centre, UK*

This awareness-raising workshop, aimed at experienced teachers, explored the challenge of explaining language to elementary-level learners and focused on providing answers to the following questions:

- Are we making the lives of low-level learners unnecessarily difficult by using too many 'complex' words to present and explain language?
- Do we assume that these learners will understand certain key words which we (and coursebooks) use to talk about language concepts?
- What are the implications for course design and initial teacher training?

After a brief personal introduction describing my own working environment, i.e. teaching predominantly adult learners, mostly business and professional people, on a one-to-one or very small-group basis, I explained my interest in exchanging ideas and hearing what the audience had to say about the above points.

Next, I proposed three 'types' of language which I felt worthy of discussion. I then wrote these as headings on the whiteboard as in the table below, giving two or three of my own examples before dividing the participants into three groups. Each group was asked to contribute further examples of words for their allocated category which they felt could be misunderstood or not understood at all, or which could cause confusion to low level learners (see Table 4.5.1).

'About language' words	'Instructional' words	General vocabulary
noun	try	decide
perfect	tick	certain
simple	compare	reason

Table 4.5.1: Problematic words

This task generated a lot of discussion, and each group came up with several more examples. We then compared these with my own longer list, and found that the groups had come up with many of the same words (Table 4.5.2):

'About language' words	'Instructional' words	General vocabulary
noun	try	decide
perfect	tick / check	certain
simple / continuous	compare	reason
adjective	explain	always
pronoun	show	usually
preposition	label	important
present	draw	maybe
subject / object	describe	meaning
past	add	arrow
verb	pronounce	
future	spell	
adverb	count	
rule / exception	match	
statement	circle	
passive		
negative		
tense		

Table 4.5.2: Problematic words: longer list

We agreed that various factors relating to learner profile, especially L1 and the student's language learning experience, were instrumental in affecting which words we can expect learners to understand. For example, a learner whose L1 is Latin-based is much more likely to understand words of Latin origin, for example 'decide' or 'pronounce', than those with non-Latin origins.

Finally we looked at some implications for course design (especially on short, intensive programmes) and initial teacher training, and ways in which we can help our lower level students to optimise their learning. These can be summarised as follows:

1　As teachers we all need to monitor our *own* language, possibly by recording our own sessions and analysing the language used to see if it is too 'complex' or if the 'messages' we are giving out could cause confusion. As far as initial teacher training courses are concerned, is enough emphasis placed on the choice of language items used by trainees? Perhaps some kind of language awareness-raising activities would be useful here.

2　Teachers, whether experienced or newly qualified, need to become more aware of aspects of their learners' L1, so that they can try to select a word that the learner is most likely to understand; for example, it is easier for a learner whose L1 is German to understand the expression 'helping verb' rather than 'auxiliary'!

3　It was also suggested that we should try to use as many words as possible that students are likely to be familiar with, for example, those related to PCs, mobile devices, computer games, social networks etc., rather than assuming they will know a more 'common' or seemingly 'easier' synonym.

4　Another idea was to write more of the words we use on the board so that learners are not only relying on their ears, i.e. what they *think* we have said, especially as so many learners these days seem to be more visual than auditory. This will also help to raise their awareness of the sound versus spelling correlation. More use of symbols or shapes, for example, to explain the imperative (circle) or ✔ 'tick' would also be helpful.

5　Finally I proposed that a 'basic lexical core' (BLC) be developed, in consultation with authors and publishers, consisting of language items that need to be at least 'understood' by low-level learners, and which could be used throughout the industry. This could be pre-taught or learnt through translation prior to, or at the beginning of, the course, thus minimising the time needed to explain this during the course itself, and helping our lower level students to optimise their learning.

julie.humble@lydbury.co.uk

4.6　Maintaining class dynamics with a rolling intake

Anne Crappsley *Regent Scotland, Edinburgh, UK*

I love that buzz when a lesson goes well: motivated students, relevant questions, positive and supportive interaction throughout (Hadfield 1992). Doesn't everybody? I truly enjoy teaching, though it often surprises me how a multinational group can lack dynamism at times. As a result, I chose to explore potential barriers and aids to a dynamic class.

I work in a school with a rolling intake, so we accept new students every Monday from one week to about 11 months. I feel that schools with this system are often perceived negatively by a number of teachers—with some justification, perhaps, because they feel it breaks course continuity or class rapport. That said, this system produces countless opportunities for students to exchange experiences concerning culture, language, and achievements or struggles with the English language.

When I began exploring class dynamics, I considered my own education, recalling times and reasons for educationally successful yet dynamic classes; however, the dynamism corresponded more with teacher or student charisma rather than any particular method or activity. Eventually I remembered a university lecture which was dynamic due to structure: one hour divided into three distinct sections with a two-minute break after every 20 minutes in which we were shown a clip from *Absolutely Fabulous,* a comedy television show. Most students engaged for the hour, eager to receive rewards for their attentiveness. I researched this idea and found that, on average, adults can hold their attention to a freely chosen task for approximately 20 minutes. Of course, several variables include age, hunger, fatigue, stress and motivation (Dukette and Cornish 2009).

I began experimenting with this concept by dividing my classes into four 15-minute segments, each with one main objective. This approach helped me maintain pace which, in turn, encouraged students to focus and engage more readily. Obviously, the segments are not fixed and I certainly do not condone using this framework for every lesson as it only becomes routine and consequently, devoid of dynamism. Nevertheless, I find it a useful planning tool, helping me to focus ideas.

Additionally, insight into students' thoughts on a rolling intake and class activities was significant, so I conducted focus groups and asked:

1 What do you prefer to do in class: many short activities or extended activities?
2 Do you prefer to work alone, in small groups or as a class?
3 What types of activities do you like doing in class?
4 Does your preference of class activity change depending on class size?
5 Does your preference of class activity change depending on how well you know your classmates?
6 Are you more motivated to come to class when you know there might be new students in the class?

The responses varied but included several similar to: 'I like many short activities, otherwise it's boring. About 15 to 20 minutes' and 'I like meeting other people from different countries—it's an occasion to get to know other cultures, too'. On reflection, some students show a slump once they are well into their course, and a rolling intake can help counter this to a certain extent.

Regarding activities, I tried to develop frameworks to help me inject enthusiasm on occasion in order to create a more dynamic atmosphere. A variation on *Just a Minute,* a radio game show, sees students choose six topics they *enjoy* speaking about and 10 words to revise. They speak for one minute on a topic and use a minimum number of words. There are three rules: no hesitation, no repetition and no deviation. I have used this activity in various ways, and it affords students the opportunity to practise social skills in a challenging yet positive way and promotes a sense of achievement.

A further activity, *Distraction*, involves the use of a coin or large counter. A pair sit facing each other, each with an outstretched, unmoving hand towards their partner, palm upwards. In this hand they rest the coin. Students converse whilst attempting to steal their partner's coin but protect their own. Again, this is flexible and adaptable, and the benefits are similar to the previous activity, but it is far more challenging.

Finally, a rolling intake provides change and interest, helping considerably to propel students through difficult times in what is often a challenging and demanding course. If a change is as good as a holiday, then I believe we should be providing such opportunities.

References

Dukette, D. and D. Cornish. 2009. *The Essential 20: Twenty Components of an Excellent Health Care Team*. Pittsburgh, Penn.: RoseDog Books.

Hadfield, J. 1992. *Classroom Dynamics*. Oxford: Oxford University Press.

4.7 Providing emotional support to ESOL and EAL students

Thomas L. Lloyd *Waltham Forest College, London, UK*

Background

The prevalence of emotional and mental difficulty in ESOL and EAL teaching is attested to by research (Ward 2007) as much as it is by the personal experience of any individual working with these learners. Indeed, following my talk at IATEFL one of the audience members was kind enough to send me details of a study (Roberts *et al.* 2004) highlighting the severity of this issue, and in turn the necessity of doing all we can to help our students who may be suffering in this way.

This research was a summary of five case studies of differing groups of ESOL students in the UK. What marked out one of these case studies in particular was that one of the subjects, a young man from central Asia who had arrived in the UK as an unaccompanied minor, reported that he had been suffering from sleeplessness and panic attacks. This was in part related to anxiety as to whether the UK Home Office would refuse his application for asylum and deport him to his country of origin. What catches one's attention most, however, is the postscript at the end of this report which states that after the conclusion of this research, the student in question had taken his own life on the last day of term.

It is cases like this which highlight the importance of emotional support in ESOL and EAL, and perhaps even the wider context of ELT as a whole. For this reason, I would like to cover the basic approach to providing emotional support as outlined in my talk and also comment on the value of giving our time to our students who may be dealing with these issues.

Basic approach to providing emotional support

While there are many different methods of counselling and emotional support, my personal approach is based on the tenets and training of the Samaritans. Transposed into the ESOL context it consists of three principal aims: to create appropriate time and space for support, to listen without judgement and to concentrate on the student's feelings and not his or her story.

- **Create time and space.** Although most teachers are time deficient, creating the appropriate time and space for your student to talk is vital. Try to conduct all support away from the rest of the class in a one-to-one situation.
- **Listen without judgement.** Non-judgmental listening is one of the cornerstones of emotional support. It is the space into which we invite the person we are supporting to express how they feel without fear of being belittled, criticised and so on.
- **Concentrate on the feelings and not the story**. The story is the account of who did what to whom: a cavalcade of victims and perpetrators. By its very nature, it assigns blame and concomitant feelings of guilt or resentment. Such sentiments entangle one's thinking with the past to the point where moving on becomes difficult or impossible. By concentrating on the feelings, we allow the student to face the emotional difficulty they are experiencing now without any further burden of guilt or resentment. Creating this acceptance is the only way that we able to begin letting go of the past in any meaningful way.

The value of 'being there' for a student

Finally, it is worth noting that short talks with a teacher can be overvalued and undervalued in equal measure. Returning to the student previously mentioned, if someone is suffering from extreme emotional distress it is undeniable that coming to terms with what they are dealing with will be extremely difficult. Obviously, taking ten minutes after class to talk to the teacher is not going to take away all the emotional pain the person is feeling. At the same time, however, one of the truisms of teaching is that we can only ever be there for our students in that particular moment, and being there for a particular student at a particular moment in time may be all that the student needed at that moment in time. Being there may mean that we are showing our students some care and consideration, giving them a sense that they are not alone, that there is someone out there who will listen and can at least get some sense of how they are feeling. Small though these comforts are, their value should not be underestimated, particularly to those who are in extreme suffering. Such kindnesses, humble though they may be, could have an unimaginable significance to those whose suffering has been acute and enduring.

tlloyd@waltham.ac.uk

References

Roberts, C., M. Baynham, P. Shrubshall, D. Barton, P. Chopra, M. Cooke, R. Hodge, K. Pitt, P. Schellekens, C. Wallace and S. Whitfield. 2004. *English for Speakers of Other Languages (ESOL): Case Studies of Provision, Learners' Needs and Resources.* London: National Research and Development Centre for Adult Literacy and Numeracy.

Ward, J. 2007. *ESOL: The Context for the UK Today.* NIACE Publications.

4.8 Beyond language: challenging the 'limitations' of the classroom

Rosie Quin, Christine Palmer *and* **Jenifer Martin** *City of Glasgow College, UK*

Feedback from student focus groups made it apparent that our learners (predominantly asylum seekers and refugees) were hungry for new opportunities to put into practice the language skills acquired in the classroom in authentic extramural contexts. Staff and students in the ESOL department set up four projects in an attempt to help develop these learners' social and employability skills, and to benefit other learners in the department as a result.

These initiatives are straightforward and rewarding in their replication and accessible to any institution wishing to equip learners with the tools to make the transition from the classroom to the real world with confidence. They also epitomise the rare 'synthesis of academic and social goals', an ideal combination in any motivating task (Dörnyei 2001: 101).

ESOL Language Café

The ESOL Language Café was set up by a group of students eager to create an opportunity for learners and their children to meet up at the weekend in a social context. These volunteers approached a local museum which allowed them to set up a drop-in café where they now hold monthly meetings; during these meetings they share experiences and tips on adapting to life in their new community. The process of organising this scheme was facilitated by two ESOL teachers, who offered volunteers advice on budgeting funds allocated for drinks and guidance on advertising this initiative through social media.

Learners have now taken ownership of the project and around 30 students attend the meet-up; they view it as an opportunity to socialise, practise their English and feel part of a genuine community. Student volunteers have used this experience as concrete evidence, in CVs and personal statements, of their ability to communicate effectively with others in a team. As a result, students have established autonomy in the management of the scheme and gained skills which simply would not have been replicated in the classroom alone.

Student Mentoring Scheme

Teachers had noticed that higher-level students were informally providing a linguistic support network to our lower-level learners. We knew that some learners had previous teaching experience in their native countries and were eager to source opportunities to draw on this experience in the UK. As a result, a Student Mentoring Scheme was established in which higher-level learners assist teachers in the classroom for up to three hours per week.

The main aim of the scheme is to provide a positive learning role model for lower-level learners, who may have no experience of education in their native countries. We have noticed that this can be particularly beneficial to our female learners, who respond well to contact with female mentors of the same native language. The mentor often works on a one-to-one basis or with small groups to facilitate and monitor classroom activities and often helps assist learners in the acquisition of the digital literacy many of them lack. Mentors are encouraged to record their experience in a reflective diary, which then forms the content of workshops we run to allow them to discuss commonalities and differences between international teaching practices.

Glasgow 2 NYC

A visit to New York by one of the college lecturers inspired her to set up an email exchange between students in Glasgow and a community college in New York. Learners write weekly emails in which they relate experiences of integrating into a new community and share photos, songs and stories; these have now been collated to create a blog. It has also provided an opportunity to compare teaching styles and materials across the pond. Following this success, the department plans to set up more exchanges around the world.

Reading the World Waves

Our students have had a chance to show their creative side by taking part in writing and performance workshops in collaboration with students completing a course in Professional Writing. Students have worked on their own short story or poem through a team-teaching approach involving lecturers from both departments. These stories were then performed live by the students at a creative writing and music evening. It has had a very positive impact on the confidence of the students involved, and several have now gone on to join a writers' group.

Conclusion

The ability to contribute to the society in which they live and to give learners a voice within this society underpins The Adult ESOL Strategy for Scotland (2007). We believe that these four initiatives clearly respond to that and have enabled our learners to take ownership of both their own learning and community experience.

Rosie.Quin@cityofglasgowcollege.ac.uk
Christine.Palmer@cityofglasgowcollege.ac.uk
Jenifer.Martin@cityofglasgowcollege.ac.uk

References

Dörnyei, Z. 2001. *Motivational Strategies in the Language Classroom.* Cambridge: Cambridge University Press.

The Adult ESOL Strategy for Scotland. 2007. (Retrieved from http://www.scotland.gov.uk/Publications/2007/05/09155324/2)

4.9 Learning English through drama: step by step

Vera Cabrera Duarte *Catholic University of São Paulo, Brazil*

This paper presents a proposal for TEFL that results from a research project called *Living Drama in the Classroom: An Experience towards Significant Learning.* The proposal has been implemented in an undergraduate course in English language at the

Catholic University of São Paulo, Brazil, and draws on an interdisciplinary approach involving three areas of study: educational psychology, drama and education, and TEFL. The three fields of study have important interfaces aiming at the development of the student as a whole: feelings and intellect.

The theoretical background in educational psychology is based on the humanistic approach, especially on the person-centred approach, as proposed by Carl Rogers (1969). The American psychologist transposed to the learning context the hypotheses formulated in psychotherapy and highlighted the contribution of affect to significant learning.

Rogers' ideas offered relevant contributions to TEFL in promoting motivation, improving interpersonal relationships, and showing the possibilities of establishing a positive learning environment in the classroom. Many language learning theorists have based their premises on some of these ideas, pointing out their impact on the English language learning process as regards the role of affect (see, for example, Arnold 1999).

Concerning drama and TEFL, Maley and Duff (1998) designed and proposed drama activities for English language classes, suggesting that they can bring high motivation to the classroom as such activities tend to help teachers keep students engaged and interested in working collaboratively.

The English language learning context described in this paper is called Drama Workshop. Students taking this subject are freshmen who intend to become either teachers or translators. The 150-minute sessions are held once a week and there are usually around 25 students in each of the two groups taking the subject.

The sessions comprise five steps:

1 **Sensitisation.** This consists of a corporal and/or vocal warm-up exercise, as well as concentration and group interaction activities. I consider these starters for what I call 'group strengthening'.

2 **Improvisation exercise.** This results from thought-provoking texts (a narrative, a poem, or a film, etc.). Such activities prepare learners to work together in harmony and may be seen as elements that will trigger discussions and bring forth conflict, a vital element in their stories.

3 **Choice and preparation.** Students decide which improvisation situation they will concentrate on. They create the story and characters, and they write the sketches, making all the necessary decisions on staging difficulties they may find, in order to dramatise them at the end of term. Divided into acts and scenes, all sketches will contain the following elements: title, super objective, characters, cast, scenes and lines.

4 **Dramatisation.** At this stage, students' work 'goes public', as they perform their sketches to guests at one of the Catholic University theatres. Generally videotaped by the University studio and myself, the sketches are then watched for evaluation by students and their tutor.

5 **Evaluation.** The objectives of each step and the students' performance are discussed at the end of each class.

The writing of sketches is done in groups and I follow up their work, suggesting how they might develop the sketches. We use the Living Drama site (livingdrama.

wikidot.com.br), and students' emails to exchange ideas and to give feedback on students' texts. On the day of the final performance, the students are totally involved in the experience. The general feeling in the class may resemble that of a small acting company.

In the beginning, the students seemed reticent about facing such a new experience, and some were actually resistant. However, they gradually engaged in the process and proved to have learned not only the English language, but also teamwork and how to exercise their 'openness' to new experiences. In one of the students' words: 'We brought English to our lives ... we learned how to work in groups and worried about our colleagues. We developed self-confidence, creativity, and imagination, among other things.'

The vast range of opportunities provided by drama activities for teachers to promote change in the students' ways of learning, the positive impact of the affective component on the learning process are clearly shown in students' reports.

veracabrera@uol.com.br

References

Arnold, J. 1999. (ed.). *Affect in Language Learning*. Cambridge: Cambridge University Press.

Maley, A. and A. Duff. 1998. *Drama Techniques in Language Learning*. Cambridge: Cambridge University Press.

Rogers, C. 1969. *Freedom to Learn*. Columbus, OH: Charles E. Merrill Publishing.

4.10 Bells and whistles: serious play for learning

Tilly Harrison *University of Warwick, Coventry, UK*

Inspiration

The inspiration for this workshop was a day of 'Serious Play' put on for staff at the University of Warwick in July 2012. I learnt for the first time that playing with Lego is now a serious (and franchised) component of many corporate CPD programmes. It struck me that if industry is not too rigid to 'find the fun' as a way of learning, surely higher education and adult teaching can do the same. In the light of this event I wanted to make my existing lectures more fun using games.

Listening game

My first game used (hotel-type) bells in the classroom since they can be heard clearly by the whole class, are somewhat anonymous, surprising and also musical. I hoped it would add laughter to a somewhat dry academic subject. The listening game which I created entailed handing out a bell to groups of four (whistles or any means of making a loud noise would also do). Each group was also given its own secret word based on the lecture I was about to give. The group members needed to choose roles—to listen for the word and ring the bell, to listen for bells by other groups and guess their words, and finally to listen to the lecture and take notes on the content. After the lecture, all the key words were checked. The note taker then explained to their group the significance of those words, summarising the lecture content.

Pre-recorded lecture

In the workshop at IATEFL Liverpool, I wanted the participants to experience this game and then reflect on it to see where it could be improved, what other uses it may have. I also wanted to offer some theoretical content for those who would have felt short-changed without something 'grown-up' in the session. However, I did not want to have to manage the game and give a lecture at the same time. Luckily a newly discovered item of technology came to my rescue: *Present.Me*. I pre-recorded a ten-minute lecture on the theory of games and play with PowerPoint slides one side and my talking head on the other. This allowed me to preview the language of the lecture and choose the key words for the game.

Feedback

After warming up with a general ELT knowledge team game (team scoring was facilitated by another useful online tool, *Triptico*), we played this game listening for words such as 'competition', 'serious' and 'fun'. The feedback on the game was that it went on too long (five minutes would have been better). However, it was felt that it would be good for a class where listening skills vary, as long as the right students got the relevant roles: weaker ones simply listening for one word, stronger ones taking notes. The lecture summary to the group would be helped (hopefully) by the list of salient words, already familiar to them.

Games past and present

The content of my ten-minute lecture covered the increasing recognition of the importance of games, play and fun, not only in education but now in every area including management and marketing. The latter is typically described by the term 'gamification' based on the analysis of the addictive qualities of computer gaming in which four broad types of fun have been mooted (Lazarrro 2004). These are: hard fun (mind-bending puzzles); easy fun (attention-grabbing ambiguity or incompleteness); social fun (cooperation and competition); and serious fun (personally meaningful engagement). Games with their rules, purpose and possibly competitive nature are not, however the same as 'play' which may be simply creative and imaginative.

Games in ELT

In ELT there has long been a tradition of using games for language learning. According to Bill Lee (1986), founder of IATEFL, games offer many useful elements to a teacher: friendly competition (with others but also with oneself), a stimulating goal, cooperative teams, a relaxed but motivated atmosphere, a focus on meaning and communication but perhaps most usefully, plenty of language repetition which is often built in.

The aim of this workshop was 'loop input'—teachers having fun learning about learners having fun learning. I had some enthusiastic thank yous at the end so perhaps for some (hopefully most) of those attending, this purpose was fulfilled.

Tilly.Harrison@warwick.ac.uk

References

Lazarro, N. 2004. 'Why we play games: four keys to more emotion without story'. *Player Experience Research and Design for Mass Market Interactive Entertainment.* (Retrieved on 21 June 2013 from http://www.xeodesign.com/xeodesign_whyweplaygames.pdf)

Lee, W. R. 1986. *Language Teaching Games and Contests* (second edition). Oxford: Oxford University Press.

4.11 TESOL and religious belief: a dangerous mix?

John Rodgers *Cambridge Tutors College, Croydon, UK*

This workshop focused on the role of religious belief in English language teaching. Participants were given a questionnaire and asked to discuss their views in small groups, after which a general discussion followed. It became clear during our discussion that the group represented a wide range of religious beliefs, from Christians and Muslims to atheists. Along with contributions from participants, I shared answers from the 44 written survey responses I had previously collected from EFL teachers. Here are some of the main topics covered, with a summary of the 44 questionnaire replies. Unfortunately I am not able to include comments from workshop participants as these were not recorded.

Respondents were asked: 'Do you think it is OK for a language teacher who has religious beliefs to share those with his/her students?' The most popular response was, 'It depends' (18/44), with 17 agreeing and 8 disagreeing. Eight respondents felt it was acceptable so long as it was at the students' request. Even then, reservations were expressed: 'There might be a danger that, if the teacher expresses a strong preference for a particular world view, then students would feel pressured into agreeing with that' (Respondent 29). Fifteen respondents stated that teachers must not try to impose their views on the students: they must not 'preach' (R2), 'attempt to convert students' (R11), 'try to make/convince others that they should see the world in the same way' (R20), or 'impose some specific political ideology or religion on their students' (R24). The views of many are summarised by R19: 'Fine to talk about almost anything in class as long as you are not ramming beliefs down students' throats.'

Respondents mentioned a large number of factors which would determine whether or not sharing was appropriate. R15 wrote: '… although I feel that teachers (like students) should be able to share their own thoughts and opinions in the classroom, it is only under the condition that they accept that they do not have a monopoly on the truth.'

This view is echoed in some of the literature on this subject: 'notions of truth and certainty … exist uneasily alongside values such as subjectivity, contingency, and moral and cultural relativism that lie at the core of the postmodern occupation of ELT' (Johnston and Varghese 2007: 195). This can be questioned; obviously the supposed danger of certainty is itself presented as a certainty. Furthermore, it is questionable whether certainty about some aspects of one's religious beliefs prevents a person from being open in other aspects, including teaching. Moreover, it is no doubt true that 'all teachers proselytize in the classroom, that is, whether consciously or unconsciously, they try to persuade students by words and actions to accept their beliefs and values' (Baurain 2007: 208). A final comment on the suitability of religion as a subject for discussion from a respondent with no religious beliefs is instructive, both for its openness and pragmatism:

> Our beliefs or non-belief is inevitably an important part of many people's personality. It contributes to our morals, our behaviour, etc. To entirely close this out of the classroom would be to close off one of the most important things in our world. Outside of the classroom, it is inescapable. Not talking about the subject closes off the language related to that subject. Students may want that language.

I would like to conclude this summary with this advice to teachers from Stevick (1982: 201) with which I also concluded the workshop:

> Teaching language is only one kind of teaching, and teaching and learning are only two limited aspects of being human. I therefore hope, first of all, that you will take time to sit down and read again whatever philosophical or religious writings you have found most nourishing to you.

jmhrodgers@hotmail.com

References

Baurain, B. 2007. 'Christian witness and respect for persons'. *Journal of Language, Identity, and Education* 6: 201–19.

Johnston B. and M. M. Varghese. 2007. 'Evangelical Christians and English language teaching'. *TESOL Quarterly* 41/1: 5–31.

Stevick, E. W. 1982. *Teaching and Learning Languages*. Cambridge: Cambridge University Press.

5 Choosing, using and developing ELT materials

As ELT and the publishing industry evolve, questions are raised about the future of published teaching materials. **Simon Greenall**'s opening paper outlines the current state of ELT publishing and suggests that, despite reports to the contrary, traditional coursebooks continue to play a key role in ELT around the world. Next, in their report of the *ELT Journal*/IATEFL Debate, **Scott Thornbury and Catherine Walter** present their views on whether or not coursebooks reflect the lives and needs of learners. The 'coursebook debate' is continued by **Rachael Roberts**, who suggests that coursebooks are not incompatible with a Dogme approach to ELT. **Muhammed Shelby**, writing from the perspective of an Arabic speaker, shows how the adaptation of coursebooks is necessary to meet the needs of learners from specific linguistic backgrounds. We then move on to advice on writing teaching materials. **Felicity O'Dell** provides guidelines on how to write a good task, while **Sue Kay** outlines the services offered by ELT Teacher2Writer in helping potential materials writers to make contact with publishers. The final two papers in this chapter deal with specific types of materials that may be used in class. **Thorsten Merse** explores the use of gay-themed literature and **Chris Lima** shows effective uses of the works of Shakespeare in the ELT classroom.

5.1 The decline and fall of coursebooks?

Simon Greenall OBE *Freelance, Oxford, UK*

Over the 30 years I have spent as a coursebook writer, one feature of ELT coursebooks which has remained constant is the criticism levelled against them by practitioners who resent the limitations which coursebook methodology imposes on the learners. This has led to predictions that the use of coursebooks will gradually decline in favour of other methodologies or means of delivery.

The presentation looked at the extent to which these predictions were valid and considered five questions:

1 What's wrong with coursebooks?

The criticisms include the accusation of pre-packaged ideas and of content which lacks the hard edge of real life. It has also been claimed that coursebooks disempower the non-native speaker teacher, deprive all teachers of choice, and apply excessive control over the learner. Finally, the ELT publishing industry stands accused of commercialism.

2 Where are we today?

It has been estimated that there are at present 1.5 billion learners of English world-wide. There are also 11.5 million teachers of English in the public education sector (PES) and in private language schools (PLS), of which 90 per cent are non-native speakers. The PLS system has about 200,000 teachers, of which approximately 100,000 are CELTA/DELTA trained, and who often have the opportunity to teach without using a coursebook. However, because of curriculum requirements by most ministries of education, we can assume that up to 11.3 million teachers continue to use coursebooks.

Today, the requirements or objectives of those involved in ELT go beyond the relationship between the student and the teacher. On the level of the individual, there is a general awareness of the salary gap between those who speak English and those who don't. On a national level, especially in developing countries, English speakers are needed to develop trade and to attract inward investment: the greater the number of speakers of English there are, the greater the inward investment will be. So English has a beneficial effect on both the wealth of the individual and the state he or she belongs to.

ELT today is no longer a 'backpacker's profession', but one which has extensively trained teachers. Like all industries, the profession has to show accountability, usually in the form of assessment. Coursebooks have to serve the function of interpreting complex curriculum requirements, including the standards expected by systems of assessment.

3 What are the alternatives to coursebooks?

There are three main alternatives. The first is alternative methodologies, such as a Dogme approach or Task-Based Learning, and the second is alternative content, such as Content and Language Integrated Learning (CLIL). While both have undoubted merits, both require training and experience which many teachers may not have.

The third alternative is digital solutions. The opportunities for more varied forms of delivery and content are significant, and they can replicate the functions of the traditional print coursebook, such as offering guidance to teachers and interpreting the curriculum. However, the granularity of digital components can sometimes work against the holistic and integrated benefits of a communicative approach.

4 Who are today's stakeholders in ELT?

As we have already seen, the relationship between the teacher and the student is not the only one with responsibilities and obligations. Other stakeholders include directors of studies, head teachers, parents, employers, third-party funders, exam boards and ministries of education. All of these co-exist in a kind of educational, economic and social eco-system, all dependent on each other. The teacher's choice not to use a coursebook may be in conflict with the requirements or expectations of the other stakeholders. So if there are failings in the system, they are not the sole responsibility of the coursebook; to achieve success would require the reform of the whole eco-system.

5 What's the future for coursebooks and course material?

The ELT publishing industry is at present undergoing a process of fundamental change, which may contribute towards the decline of coursebooks. We can predict greater customisation of materials, and a closer link between content and assessment, all of which will enhance the effectiveness of traditional print or digital resources. But any alternative or replacement for coursebooks needs to supply the same functionality of covering the curriculum, interpreting the complex language requirements of the ELT eco-system, and respecting the professionalism of the industry today.

So while the use of traditional ELT coursebooks may indeed be in decline, reports of their terminal demise have been exaggerated, and they continue to serve their original functions in many learning contexts around the world.

simon.greenall@btconnect.com

5.2 *ELT Journal*/IATEFL Debate: Published course materials don't reflect the lives or needs of learners

Scott Thornbury *The New School, New York, USA and* **Catherine Walter** *University of Oxford, UK*

Scott Thornbury, proposing the motion

Do published course materials reflect the lives and needs of learners? At issue here is a question of representation. It is not an issue of the rights and wrongs of coursebooks *per se*, nor even whether they *should* reflect the lives and needs of learners. The question is whether they *do*. It is self-evidently true that they do not.

How can they? Given the diversity of learners and learning contexts around the world, this would be a tall order. Even coursebook writers themselves admit as much:

No coursebook can cater for all the individual needs of all learners … With international materials it is obvious that the needs of individual students and teachers … can never be fully met by the materials themselves (Bell and Gower 1998: 114, 116).

Of greater concern, however, than their *not* representing the lives and needs of learners, is the fact that coursebooks intentionally *mis*represent their lives and needs. Especially their lives. The cosy, uncomplicated and inconsequential lives of coursebook characters have a long history. Open any textbook from the last or the preceding century, and you'll find it peopled with well-heeled, white middle-class individuals dining out, motoring or being measured for a suit. Despite appearances, I would argue that little has changed. The typical double-page spread in a contemporary general English coursebook, borrowing heavily on the iconography (and ideology) of advertising, shows physically attractive, ethnically mixed, well-dressed and youthful characters, often surrounded by iconic consumer items that reflect their upwardly mobile, middle-class aspirations. They exemplify the observation made in a recent survey of general English courses by Tomlinson and Masuhara (2013: 248) that 'there seems to be an assumption that all learners are aspirational, urban, middle-class, well-educated, westernized computer uses.' Such representations are reinforced by what Gray (2010: 727) describes as 'the new salience of celebrity in textbooks', indexing a neoliberal agenda that associates the use of English with success, individualism, glamour and wealth.

You have to look hard to find any text or image that reflects the economic woes, racism, inequality and injustice that is being experienced in many regions where English is taught. Nor are the linguistic means available to even talk about alternative identity constructions, whether related to religion, social class, sexual orientation or ethnicity, to name but a few.

The 'erasure' of potentially problematic content is enshrined in the guidelines that writers are given. As Ravitch (2004: 46) points out (with regard to textbook production in the US), 'the world may not be depicted as it is and as it was, but only as the guideline writers would like it to be'.

So much for the *lives* of the learners: what about their *needs?* Again, published course materials have a poor record in terms of matching their content to the likely linguistic needs of multicompetent English users in a globalised, multilingual world. The persistent focus on a relatively narrow set of canonical grammar items (primarily verb forms), and the continued allegiance to written grammar over spoken grammar, means that vast areas of linguistic competence, such as lexis, phraseology and discourse features, are often dealt with peripherally, even accidentally, and certainly unsystematically.

And, despite the growing recognition that the majority of learners need English for lingua franca purposes (Jenkins 2012), most course materials still adhere to native speaker models of pronunciation, while nothing has been done to uproot their entrenched monolingualism. As Cook (2010: 111) notes, 'If we think further about what [learners'] needs really are, rather than what course designers assume them to be, we find that they are at least as likely to be cross-lingual as intra-lingual and therefore to involve translation.' And Canagarajah (1999: 86), in critiquing the coursebooks available in his native Sri Lanka, observes, 'Little consideration is given to how the students' own linguistic and cultural backgrounds might affect or enhance their language acquisition.'

On all counts, then, published course materials fail—catastrophically—to reflect the lives and the needs of their end-users.

Catherine Walter, opposing the motion

Scott Thornbury claims that published course materials don't reflect the lives or needs of learners. Surprisingly, he does not fall back on his usual Dogme/Teaching Unplugged viewpoint—that teachers should not bother with course materials. Instead, he begins from the weaker premise that course materials could be improved—not very contentious. Scott began his presentation by showing images of early 20th-century books. This is hardly germane to the discussion; it is as if the nutritional value of deep-fried Mars Bars gave a picture of the contemporary diet. He maintained that there is a prevalence of employed, white, heterosexual, male, middle-class characters in current materials. This doesn't correspond to activities my students regularly do: counting and classifying representations in materials, where some materials do very well indeed. Scott also suggested that vocabulary syllabuses are not based on frequency, and that spoken grammar is not well represented. Both of these points are empirically falsified.

My view is that there are high-quality materials available today from international and national publishers. Most learners globally learn from materials in countries where English is not a dominant language, in large classes that meet two to three times a week, and where access to other materials or the Internet may be poor. Many are young beginners. The book is still a valuable technology here; it can be a doorway to different combinations of supplementary materials, in whatever media teachers and learners can access.

Reflecting learners' lives?

When I was learning a foreign language as an adolescent in a semi-rural working-class industrial town, I did not want language materials to reflect my life—I wanted them to take me out of it, to show me other ways of living. Materials that are too firmly anchored in the here-and-now of the learner will not prepare them for the future. Of course, there are some ways in which course materials should and do reflect learners' lives, for example, by being based on knowledge about learning at different ages, or by comparing learners' lives to those in other places.

Reflecting learners' needs?

- Learners need to learn the language, not just those bits of the language that might happen to emerge in a lesson. Course developers think very carefully about the range of language learners need, and they cover it. Individual teachers don't have the time or the resources for this.
- Learners need classroom time to be used effectively. Typically there isn't much of that time. Course materials offer clear, efficient ways of teaching language; Norris and Ortega (2000) and Spada and Tomita (2010) show that this works and results in lasting acquisition.
- Learners need materials that will help them with the next English language situation they will meet. Course materials provide structures and contexts for out-of-classroom situations.
- Learners need access to extra resources that can be tailored to their needs. Modern courses offer pathways to suit different learners.
- Learners need clear goals and records of progress. Learners value materials because they provide these.
- Learners need teachers who are well supported. Scaffolded by course materials, teachers can replace, reinvent, innovate and fine-tune materials for learners.
- Learners need teachers who have access to professional development activities. Teachers in the majority three-hour-a-week context, and elsewhere, regularly report on how they benefit from the teacher's materials in their coursebooks for their development as professionals.

There is an unprecedented choice of materials available today; teachers don't need to feed their students deep-fried Mars Bars. Materials can give teachers something to depend on, something to kick against and something to improvise from. How teachers nourish their students' learning will always stem from the teachers' creativity and their awareness of learners' needs and lives.

scott.thornbury@gmail.com
catherine.walter@education.ox.ac.uk

References

Bell, J. and R. Gower. 1998. 'Writing course materials for the world: a great compromise' in Tomlinson, B. (ed.). *Materials Development in Language Teaching*. Cambridge: Cambridge University Press.

Cangarajah, S. 1999. *Resisting Linguistic Imperialism in English Teaching*. Oxford: Oxford University Press.

Cook, G. 2010. *Translation in Language Teaching: An Argument for Reassessment*. Oxford: Oxford University Press.

Gray, J. 2010. 'The branding of English and the culture of the New Capitalism: Representations of the world of work in English language textbooks'. *Applied Linguistics* 31/5: 714–33.

Jenkins, J. 2012. 'English as a Lingua Franca: from the classroom to the classroom'. *ELT Journal*, 66/4: 486–94.

Norris, J. M. and L. Ortega. 2000. 'Effectiveness of L2 instruction: a research synthesis and quantitative meta-analysis'. *Language Learning* 50/3: 417–528.

Ravitch, D. 2004. *The Language Police: How pressure groups restrict what students learn*. New York: Vintage Books.

Spada, N. and Y. Tomita. 2010. 'Interactions between type of instruction and type of language feature: a meta-analysis'. *Language Learning* 60/2: 1–46.

Tomlinson, B. and H. Masuhara. 2013. 'Survey Review: Adult Coursebooks'. *ELT Journal* 67/2: 233–49.

5.3 Of course! Using a coursebook *and* engaging with emergent language

Rachael Roberts *Freelance, Leamington Spa, UK*

We hear a great deal about the so-called 'coursebook debate', with the strong implication being that you have to be either 'for' or 'against' coursebooks. Those who believe in dealing with language as it arises will generally be considered to be anti-coursebook. But surely coursebooks are ultimately a collection of topics, texts and tasks. Why shouldn't it be possible to use a coursebook *and* deal with emergent language?

To be fair, Scott Thornbury, the first proponent of Dogme, has often said that coursebooks aren't the fount of all evil, they just shouldn't be 'the tail that wags the dog' (Thornbury and Meddings 2002: 36-40). It's probably true to say that Thornbury's biggest gripe about coursebooks is the way they are generally built around a structural syllabus. Each unit has a handful of language points, which he refers to as 'grammar McNuggets', and the assumption is that these points will be presented, practised and learnt.

It's admittedly something of a false assumption. Language doesn't develop in a linear and predictable fashion and while we may hope to teach a particular point, ultimately all we can do is to expose students to stretches of language, create opportunities for meaningful dialogue and opportunities to notice and, crucially, enable students to *engage* with language. But none of this militates against using a coursebook as a basis.

Engaging students

A key tenet of Dogme is that the learners' experiences, beliefs, knowledge and so on should be the content, rather than what's on the page. As Meddings and Thornbury put it in *Teaching Unplugged* (2009: 7), 'Materials-mediated teaching is the 'scenic route' to learning, but the direct route is located in the interactivity between teachers and learners and between the learners themselves.'

For me, however, the really interesting interactions lie not just between the people in the classroom, but also between what's on the page (or video) and where the learners currently are. By bringing material into the classroom, we can provide learners with content which is *outside* their experience, which stretches them to see things differently. Rather than materials mediating teaching, surely one of the primary roles of the teacher is, in fact, to mediate the material to ensure that the students are engaged and challenged. For example, if they're reading an article, what can you do before they read to help them to see the relevance to their own lives or to have some investment in finding out what the article says?

Noticing and restructuring

As Jack Richards put it in *Moving beyond the Plateau*, 'For learners' linguistic systems to take on new and more complex linguistic items, the restructuring, or reorganization, of mental representations is required, as well as opportunities to practice these new forms' (2008: 8). In order to restructure, students need to actively notice language. Increasingly, coursebooks do provide opportunities for this. That doesn't mean, however, that we can't build in further noticing, repetition and recycling activities. For example, we can follow up work on language in texts with dictogloss activities; or, we can ask students to translate the text into their L1 and then, a few days or a week later, ask them to translate it back. Both of these activities will enable students to notice their individual difficulties and the language which they need to focus on.

Alternatively, we can try some self-recording and transcription tasks. Students can record themselves carrying out a short speaking task and then make a transcription of what they say, making any changes they wish before handing it in. The teacher can then reformulate what each student has written, as appropriate, and the students can compare their versions with the teachers' version. (With a large class, this can be done with one or two anonymous examples, looking at them with the whole class.)

Conclusion

Ultimately, whether or not you use a coursebook, your lessons need to be engaging, motivating and relevant, with plenty of opportunities for noticing, restructuring and recycling.

A coursebook is like a set of recipes. Some people will prefer to stick to the recipe—at least to start with—and just produce what's in the book. Some will start experimenting and producing their own take on the recipe, and some people just love making everything from scratch. No one wants to live on a diet of grammar McNuggets, but pre-prepared food (or lessons) can also be nutritious, delicious and definitely labour saving!

References

Meddings, L and S. Thornbury. 2009. *Teaching Unplugged*. Peaslake: Delta Publishing.

Richards, J. 2008. *Moving beyond the Plateau*. Cambridge: Cambridge University Press.

Thornbury, S and L. Meddings. 2002. 'Dogme and the coursebook'. *Modern English Teacher* 11/1: 36–40.

5.4 Adapting coursebooks to teach yes/no questions to Arab learners

Muhammad Shelby *Taibah University, Medina, Saudi Arabia*

Introduction

There are some similarities between Arabic and English in the formation of yes/no questions that have not been fully exploited to help Arab students learn this structure. The main purposes of this article is to propose a minor adjustment to English beginner coursebooks that can make a huge difference in low-level Arab learners' ability to form positive yes/no questions in English. Here I will discuss the six 'tenses' that most beginner coursebooks start with: present and past tenses with simple and progressive aspects. First, the formation of yes/no questions in Arabic and English will be explained. Then the adaptation will be discussed.

Comparison of the formation of yes/no questions in English and Arabic

These are called yes/no questions because the answer (which may be expressed or just implied) is 'yes' or 'no'. In English, the general rule for forming positive yes/no questions from declarative sentences is to invert the positions of the operator and the subject: 'This is a book' ~ 'Is this a book?' In sentences without an operator, a suitable form of dummy 'do' is positioned at the beginning of the questions: 'He wrote a book.' ~ 'Did he write a book?'

On the other hand, all positive yes/no questions in Modern Standard Arabic (MSA) start with the article *hal*. Unlike in English, inversion in Arabic occurs if there is an operator (*kana*: 'was'), in the past tenses only (see examples 4 and 5).

1. Present simple (copular 'be')	Affirmative sentences	Yes/no questions
Sentence in English →	He is a policeman.	Is he a policeman?
Transliteration →	Hua shurti.	Hal hua shurti?
Literal translation →	He policeman.	He policeman?

2. Present progressive	Affirmative sentence	Yes/no questions
Sentence in English →	He is drinking milk.	Is he drinking milk?
Transliteration →	Hua yashrabu laban.	Hal hua yashrabu laban?
Literal translation →	He drink milk.	He drink milk?

3. Present simple (lexical verb)	Affirmative sentence	Yes/no questions
Sentence in English →	He drinks milk.	Does he drink milk?
Transliteration →	hua yashrabu laban.	Hal hua yashrabu laban?
Literal translation →	He drink milk.	He drink milk?

4. Past simple (copular be)	Affirmative sentence	Yes/no questions
Sentence in English →	He was happy.	Was he happy?
Transliteration →	Hua kana saidan.	Hal kana hua saidan?
Literal translation →	He was happy.	Was he happy?

5. Past progressive	Affirmative sentence	Yes/no questions
Sentence in English →	He was drinking.	Was he drinking?
Transliteration →	Hua kana yashrabu.	Hal kana hua yashrabu?
Literal translation →	He was drink.	Was he drink?

6. Past simple (lexical verb)	Affirmative sentence	Yes/no questions
Sentence in English →	He drank milk.	Did he drink milk?
Transliteration →	Hua shariba laban.	Hal hua shariba laban?
Literal translation →	He drank milk.	He drank milk?

From the examples above we can foresee two major issues:

1 Choosing which word to start the question with; whereas in Arabic it is always *hal*, in English the learner has to choose from: 'am', 'is', 'are', 'was', 'were', 'do', 'does' and 'did'.

2 Inversion occurs in all six tenses in English, whereas it occurs in only two tenses in Arabic.

In Mukattash's (1980) analysis of 585 mistakes made by 600 university students in forming yes/no questions from affirmative sentences, 89.2 per cent were due to mistakes in these two areas. In the writer's small-scale replication of Mukattash's analysis, the percentage of mistakes in those two areas was 68.8 per cent.

Adapting coursebooks

The order coursebooks present those six tenses makes it difficult for learners to learn them. For example, *New Headway Beginner* (Soars and Soars 2009) presents five of them in the following order:

1 present simple copular
2 present simple lexical
3 past simple copular
4 past simple lexical
5 present continuous

This order is particularly confusing for learners as it keeps switching between inversion using the operator in the declarative sentence (in 1, 3 and 5) and no inversion using the dummy 'do' (in 2 and 4). I suggest that, for Arabic speakers, beginner coursebooks teach those six tenses in the following order:

1 Past simple copular
2 Past progressive
3 Present progressive
4 Present simple copular
5 Present simple lexical
6 Past simple lexical

This new order has two benefits. First, it starts with the two tenses that are most similar to the learners' L1, Arabic, thus benefiting from positive L1 transfer (Yule 2010). Second, it presents a rule for learners to follow in the first four tenses: 'inversion using the operator in the declarative sentence', and moves smoothly to the opposite rule of 'no inversion using the dummy 'do".

mshelby@emw-edu.com

References

Mukattash, L. 1980. 'Yes/no questions and the contrastive analysis hypothesis'. *ELT Journal* 34/2: 133–145.

Soars, L. and J. Soars. 2009. *New Headway Beginner*. Oxford: Oxford University Press.

Yule, G. 2010. *The Study of Language*. 4th ed. Cambridge: Cambridge University Press.

5.5 How to write a good task

Felicity O'Dell *Language Testing 123, Cambridge, UK*

This workshop focused on the issues that teachers need to bear in mind when developing tasks for use in the classroom. After discussing what is meant by 'task' in an ELT context, participants analysed an inadequate task and decided how to improve it. Finally, the workshop considered a possible checklist for evaluating any language learning task.

What do you mean by 'task'?

The first part of the workshop, the attempt to define what exactly a 'task' is, drew heavily on an *ELTJ* article (Littlewood 2004) that usefully summarises different types of language learning activities; these range along a continuum from a simple non-communicative learning activity, such as a substitution exercise, through to authentic communication, such as a class discussion. Littlewood points out that 'task' has variously been used both as an umbrella term covering all these activities, and also as a term only applying to activities closer to the authentic end of the continuum. Although the main example of a task discussed in the workshop would come towards the authentic end of the continuum, the characteristics of a good task highlighted in the workshop could be held to apply to any type of language learning task.

Setting the context

The first consideration when designing a task has to be the context in which it is used. The context for the task considered by the participants in the workshop was a group of 20 B2-level students with a range of L1s on a pre-sessional course for engineering students at a UK university. The language learning task that workshop participants considered asked students to read an article at home, present it to their classmates in a lesson and do a piece of writing as a follow-up homework exercise.

(Plenty of) room for improvement

While the basic task was essentially not an unreasonable one, looking at it in detail showed it to be flawed in terms of its appropriacy for its specific context. Its other inadequacies were as follows:

- Its objectives did not relate closely enough to the actual task.
- The task would be unlikely to engage the learners.
- The instructions were not in the most helpful order.
- The learners were not given precise enough guidance.
- One part of the task was inappropriate in terms of level.
- The task included an activity that might encourage poor learner training habits.
- The follow-up task did not consolidate the work of the activity.
- The task did not facilitate the provision of constructive feedback for the learners.

Having identified the inadequacies of the task, participants then shared ideas about how to improve it, while keeping the same basic format of preparing a reading text with a view to sharing information with classmates and then doing a follow-up homework activity. Several much-improved tasks were produced by participants and compared with a revised form of the task prepared by the presenter.

What makes for a good task?

Having considered a specific task for a specific context, the workshop went on to discuss the following list of characteristics of a 'good' task:

- It is rooted in clear and appropriate linguistic objectives.
- It is fit for purpose (in terms of suiting its linguistic objectives and teaching context).

- It is at the right level (allowing for some degree of differentiation).
- It is engaging for learners.
- It has clear and unambiguous instructions.
- It is effectively presented in the best possible way (e.g. using different media appropriately).
- It will allow the learner to receive useful feedback (either from the teacher or in some other way).

It was felt that these characteristics could apply to any task, whether it is written for publication or with one specific class in mind. While some of the characteristics might assume a greater or lesser importance in specific contexts, it was also felt that they would apply to any task, wherever it might be placed on the continuum of language learning activity types.

felicity@languagetesting123.co

Reference

Littlewood, W. 2004. 'The task-based approach: some questions and suggestions'. *ELT Journal* 58/4: 319–26.

5.6 Learn to write ELT materials ... and get published!

Sue Kay *ELT Teacher 2 Writer Limited, Oxford, UK*

Overview

ELT Teacher 2 Writer was set up and is run by Karen Spiller, Karen White and Sue Kay. ELT T2W was set up in response to three perceived problems in the ELT publishing industry.

Where are the new writers?

Firstly, publishers often have difficulty finding new writers. Publishers need more writers than ever before because modern courses typically consist of a large number of components, and it would be impossible for the writer or writers of the main student's book to write them all themselves. ELT editorial departments, who are responsible for commissioning new product, are still largely based in the UK or the USA, and therefore contacts 'in the market' are often seen as the preserve of marketing departments and sales teams. Publishers need to find new writers because they are the pipeline of the future. But they also need to find new teacher-practitioner writers because they bring layers of knowledge with them that full-time generalist writers don't have, such as practical knowledge of what works with their students in their classrooms, understanding of their students' expectations, and so on.

Solution

So, our first challenge was to help publishers find new writers. To facilitate this, we set up a writers' database. The writers register online and provide detailed information about their teaching experience, where they've taught, the kind of students they teach, and more. Publishers are given their own login codes and can carry out confidential and independent, highly targeted searches, and then make direct contact with the writer or writers who match the profile they're looking for. It's free for writers to be in the database and free for publishers to use it. The logos of the publishers using the database are displayed on the website.

How can teachers develop a relationship with publishers?

Secondly, most teachers don't know how to get into writing, or how to make contact with and get known by publishers. There is often a lot of luck involved in making initial contact—a random conversation at the publisher's stand, or someone from a publisher happens to attend a teacher's talk and likes what they hear.

Solution

Our second challenge was to provide teachers with the wherewithal to make themselves known to publishers. As part of the registration process, writers are invited to accept a list of other forms of collaboration with publishers, such as writing readers' reports, attending focus groups. Activities such as these allow publisher and writers to get to know each other and start developing a professional relationship.

How can teachers learn to write?

Thirdly, writers need to be able to 'hit the ground running' rather than learning on the job, so they need training. Publishing schedules get faster—never slower!—and publishers simply don't have time to train new writers. Furthermore training writers isn't often planned in a systematic way. In practice writers learn to write by 'having a go' and then getting feedback from the publisher. Giving feedback, of course, is a skilled art, and itself the subject of training courses, but why isn't there any structured material that teaches the craft of writing? It seems surprising that there are training courses in journalism, writing fiction, biographies, and so forth, but nothing for ELT materials writers. Training isn't just relevant for getting writers up to speed quickly for the purposes of writing for publishers; many teachers produce their own materials to use with their students, and see honing these skills as part of their professional development.

Solution

We needed to provide training for new writers. We believe that you can unpack the craft of writing ELT materials and teach someone—with aptitude—to write. We've devised a series of training modules which cover core writing skills (e.g. how to write vocabulary presentations and practice), component-specific writing skills (e.g. how to write teacher's books), and market-specific skills (e.g. how to write ESP). We then commissioned experienced and successful ELT writers to write modules in their particular field of expertise. As word spread, these writers started approaching us and suggesting new titles for the series, and offering to write them!

Reference

sue@eltteacher2writer.co.uk

ELT Teacher 2 Writer. (Retrieved from http://www.eltteacher2writer.co.uk)

5.7 Gay-themed literature in the EFL classroom

Thorsten Merse *Westfälische Wilhelms-Universität, Münster, Germany*

In the field of ELT, it appears that lesbian, gay, bisexual, transgender and queer (in short, LGBTQ) topics have been conspicuous in their absence. Therefore, it comes as no surprise that the emerging body of LGBTQ-themed literature has largely been overlooked for classroom usage, even though literary texts have long held an established position in ELT.

From silencing to welcoming LGBTQ voices

I put forward the thesis that literature selection for EFL classrooms follows heteronormative standards. This means that texts are chosen only in which heterosexuality is the natural norm of forming relationships or expressing love and sexual desire. As a result, literary texts which foreground LGBTQ voices are excluded and have not yet found their way into curricula and literary canons. With a view to overcoming this silencing discourse, it is important that teachers begin to welcome LGBTQ literature into their classrooms. This action call is supported by Nelson (2009), who argues that language classrooms are still constructed as heterosexualised zones, but that they should increasingly mirror the worldwide visibility of LGBTQ diversity in order to keep language learning socially relevant and culturally pluralistic. In addition, Norton and Toohey (2011) emphasise that learners from various identity positions must be able to claim their voice in the classroom; this also includes LGBTQ identities. In linking these positions with teaching literature, I suggest that LGBTQ texts provide a springboard for actively discussing LGBTQ diversity and exploring norms of sexuality.

The classroom perspective

But how can teachers select LGBTQ-themed literature for their classrooms? Depending on their specific teaching aims and plans, teachers could choose among the following:

- problem novels in which LGBTQ characters encounter a rather hostile environment, e.g. John Donovan's *I'll Get There. It Better Be Worth the Trip* (1969);
- stories with more positive LGBTQ representations and coming-out narratives, as can be found in the 1994 short story collection *Am I Blue? Coming Out from the Silence*;
- texts that explore the whole range of gender and sexual diversity or depict queer utopian settings, e.g. David Levithan's *Boy Meets Boy* (2002) and *The Lover's Dictionary* (2012), Alex Sanchez's *Boyfriends with Girlfriends* (2011), Julie Anne Peter's *Luna* (2004) and Madeleine George's *The Difference Between You and Me* (2012);
- visual literature, e.g. Alison Bechdel's graphic novel *Fun Home* (2006) or picture books such as *And Tango Makes Three* (2005) and *Heather Has Two Mummies* (1989).

Another option for finding suitable literature is to turn to literary organisations such as the Lambda Literary Foundation or the American Library Association with its Rainbow Project. They offer immensely helpful websites containing diverse lists and reviews of LGBTQ literature. Still another possibility is to check typical distribution channels such as local or online bookstores and publishing houses for LGBTQ literature.

Along with finding suitable texts, a further challenge is to actually use LGBTQ literature in ELT classrooms because non-normative sexuality is still a controversial issue in many contexts. It is, therefore, advisable that teachers first of all find out if their institution would allow for an LGBTQ-sensitive approach and how potential skepticism can be argued against. Teachers should anticipate their students' reactions and implement an LGBTQ text carefully to avoid homo- or transphobic backlash, e.g. by giving students a say in what text they want to read or by introducing LGBTQ texts as natural rather than pointing out their 'exotic peculiarity'. On a methodological level, teachers could evoke students' heteronormative reading expectations and have them compare these with the actual plot developments. Furthermore, a close reading of text passages and follow-up activities that create a change of perspective would allow students to see the world through an LGBTQ character's eyes. Students could also visually represent an LGBTQ text through producing comic adaptations or freeze frames, which would push their imaginations further and invite them to explore critically the way they see and depict LGBTQ people.

Concluding remarks

In conclusion, as Renzi *et al.* state: 'Bringing LGBTQ texts into the classroom is not easy. It takes preparation and careful planning. It takes asking some hard questions. But isn't it worth it?' (2012: 132). Participants in this presentation answered this question with 'It is worth it.' After all, it is our responsibility as teachers to prepare students for valuing diversity and social justice and to develop a respectful understanding of LGBTQ phenomena. Thus, teachers can become part of a process in which the diversity of topics that are represented in ELT is continuously increased and re-negotiated.

t.merse@uni-muenster.de

References

Nelson, C. D. 2009. *Sexual Identities in English Language Education: Classroom Conversation.* New York: Routledge.

Norton, B. and K. Toohey. 2011. 'Identity, language learning, and social change'. *Language Teaching* 44/4: 412–46.

Renzi, L., M. Letcher and K. Miraglia. 2012. 'Out of the closet and into the open: LGBTQ young adult literature in the language arts classroom' in J. A. Hayn and J. S. Kaplan (eds.). *Teaching Young Adult Literature Today: Insights, Considerations, and Perspectives for the Classroom Teacher.* Lanham: Rowman & Littlefield.

5.8 Will and the Web: Shakespeare and the Internet

Chris Lima *The Open University, Milton Keynes, UK*

Background information

In this workshop, I shared some of the activities I have developed for course modules on *Shakespeare and Language* taken by undergraduate international students as part of their Erasmus/Study Abroad programmes. The sample activities used in the workshop are part of a two-term course on Shakespeare's plays and are in two handbooks which contain the lesson materials. The design of these materials incorporated accessible and diversified online sources in order to help students engage with themes and topics in the plays as well as work with the language in and outside the classroom.

The materials were developed with a hybrid approach to Shakespeare in mind, which would reflect the needs and interests of both literature and English language students. When compiling and designing them, I had to make a number of decisions regarding students' previous knowledge of the plays and the contexts in which they were created and have been received, as well as learners' level of language proficiency. My main objectives, and challenges, were to find a balance between:

- critical literary analysis of the texts and language work;
- the four skills, while putting a clear emphasis on reading and academic writing;
- the four Shakespearean genres (tragedies, comedies, history plays and problem plays); and
- the analysis of the plays as text and as performance.

Shakespeare and ELT

Shakespeare has always been a man of controversies. To the controversial position of the theatre in Elizabethan England, to the history of his plays' reception in time, and to the authorship controversy (Wells 1986), we can add the controversy of teaching Shakespeare to English language learners. Positions vary from the extremes of his banishment from the ELT classroom to his sacred and untouchable position in the syllabus. There is a wealth of literature on Shakespeare in education, with many titles coming from the USA and Commonwealth countries. Similarly, there is a wealth of myths surrounding Shakespeare's language and its supposed incomprehensibility to modern audiences and readers (Crystal 2008), especially if those are non-native speakers of English.

My own position in relation to the teaching of Shakespeare to language learners is as follows:

1 Shakespeare's imaginative and poetic use of language can help learners to similarly explore grammar and vocabulary in creative and original ways.

2 Themes in Shakespeare still resonate cognitively and emotionally with most of us in different cultures and countries and can help learners to think critically about issues that matter to them.

3 Exploring Shakespeare through performance (Crystal 2009) in the classroom can be a powerful tool to help learners to develop fluency, pronunciation and self-confidence as English language speakers.

4 Using Shakespearean online resources can help students to engage with literature and language outside the classroom and thus become more independent learners.

Above all, I believe to provide language learners the opportunity to engage with Shakespeare is to open a door that gives them access to an extremely rich language resource and to one of the most fascinating body of texts ever written in the English language.

The workshop

The first activity was based on *Henry V.* Participants watched the scene of the St Crispin's Day speech in Branagh's 2005 film version of the play as well as the scene of the Speech to the Troops at Tilbury in Shekar Kapur's film *Elizabeth, The Golden Age.* Using a worksheet as a prompt, participants were invited to discuss the similarities and differences between the two scenes from linguistic and cinematic points of view.

The second activity was based on *Othello.* Participants watched a scene from Branagh's film version of the play and were asked to compare the screen script to the text in the play. Groups then discussed the effects of the film adaptation on their understanding of the play. Discussions in the groups were lively and enthusiastic, and participants were also able to ask questions and comment on the activities they were doing.

To conclude the session, I shared a series of links to YouTube videos, podcasts, websites and blogs devoted to Shakespeare, e-texts of the plays, an online glossary, a Shakespeare concordance, scholarly databases, and mobile and tablet apps. Participants were also invited to join the ELT Online Reading Group where there is a discussion thread devoted to Shakespeare. Participants left with a couple of 'adaptable and adoptable' ideas for activities to bring English literature and creative online material into their lessons.

References

chrislima90@yahoo.co.uk

Crystal, B. 2009. *Shakespeare on Toast: Getting a Taste for the Bard.* London: Icon.

Crystal, D. 2008. *Think of my Words: Exploring Shakespeare's Language.* Cambridge: Cambridge University Press.

Wells, S. (ed.). 1986. *The Cambridge Companion to Shakespeare Studies.* Cambridge: Cambridge University Press.

6 Focus on pronunciation

The five papers in this short chapter all address the teaching of pronunciation from various perspectives. **Jonathan Marks** starts the chapter with an overview of some of the key questions teachers ask about teaching pronunciation; this is followed by **Sasha S. Euler**'s description of a connected speech-based approach to pronunciation instruction. The remaining papers in this chapter address research into pronunciation instruction and the development of pronunciation instruction in three different contexts. **Yolanda Joy Calvo Benzies** presents students' and teachers' views on pronunciation instruction in Spain; **Tatiana Skopintseva** describes the integration of pronunciation into a Russian ESAP programme; and **Sophie Farag** outlines the development of a pronunciation class for university students in Egypt.

6.1 Things to do with a mouthful of air

Jonathan Marks *Freelance, Łeba, Poland*

The title

I began this workshop by explaining its title. W.B. Yeats wrote, in and of one of his poems, that he 'made it out of a mouthful of air'; every instance of spoken language—every word we utter, every conversation we have—results from modifying and shaping a mouthful of air, blocking, channelling and expelling it in various ways. Every piece of writing, too—every email, every poem, every novel—is a representation of these processes and can be converted back into air if we breathe life into it by reading it aloud.

Doubts and questions

I then briefly suggested answers to some of the doubts and questions commonly raised by teachers in discussions of pronunciation teaching:

'Learners find pronunciation work boring.'

They won't if the level of challenge is not too high and not too low, if they can see the point of what they're practising and if they are given the help they need to improve.

'There's no time for pronunciation.'

Attention to pronunciation benefits other skills and can often be integrated into other activities. Specific pronunciation activities often only need a few minutes. If learners pay attention to pronunciation, they get better at noticing how words are pronounced and how phrases and sentences are spoken, so they need less teacher guidance; this saves time in the long run.

'When should I focus on pronunciation?'

Pronunciation work can usefully appear on three occasions:

1 When it is useful to highlight particular pronunciation points that cause difficulty.
2 When introducing new grammar, vocabulary or functional language—is there anything about the pronunciation that learners will need help with?
3 Whenever the need arises, for example, to sort out misunderstandings in discussion or listening activities.

'What type of pronunciation should my learners aim for?'

Current discussion of pronunciation models focuses usefully on what features are important for international intelligibility. However, in some parts of the world there are well-established regional pronunciations of English, while elsewhere prestige is attached to British or American pronunciation, and learners may wish to aim for one of these—indeed, state education systems and exams may expect them to. For many people, accent is an important part of identity. Some relish the opportunity to adopt a different identity when they speak another language, while others resist the prospect. Whatever pronunciation learners aim for, they will benefit from practising *listening* to a wide variety of accents and tuning in to their distinctive features.

'Can I teach pronunciation even if I'm not a native speaker?'

If you share your learners' L1, you can be the best model for them, and you will have an excellent understanding of the problems they face. If your learners speak a different L1 from you, or mixed L1s, you will still be a good model and you will recognise many of their problems. If you are really concerned that your own pronunciation isn't good enough, remember that you can use recorded material for pronunciation work, that learners pick up pronunciation not only from you but from films, songs, etc. and that, with your coaching, they can achieve a level of pronunciation higher than yours.

'Is it easier to teach pronunciation in monolingual or multilingual classes?'

In monolingual classes everyone tends to have similar problems and successes. The disadvantage is that learners can understand each other well even if their pronunciation has substantial elements of L1 interference, but the advantage is that you can do directed pronunciation work which clearly benefits the whole class. The disadvantage of multilingual classes is the greater variety of pronunciation needs. However, learners have more opportunity to discover which features of their pronunciation inhibit intelligibility.

'Is there such a thing as a pronunciation syllabus?'

All elements of pronunciation are needed from the very first lesson. Instead of a separate pronunciation syllabus in the form of a graded progression, it makes more sense to integrate a pronunciation focus into whatever language points you are dealing with, and to supplement this, at any level of teaching, with intensive work on particular aspects of pronunciation which are causing difficulty or confusion.

Activities

In the remainder of the workshop, participants had the opportunity to briefly try out fifteen of the activities in *The Book of Pronunciation* (Marks and Bowen 2012), working on individual sounds, sounds and spelling, clusters, rhyme and alliteration, word stress, strong and weak forms, tonic prominence and intonation patterns, and noticing links with work on lexis, grammar and functions.

jonathanmarks@wp.pl

Reference

Marks, J. and T. Bowen. 2012. *The Book of Pronunciation*. Peaslake: DELTA Publishing.

6.2 Implementing a connected speech-based approach to pronunciation teaching

Sasha S. Euler *City College Trier, Germany*
International House Brita Haycraft Better Spoken English Scholarship winner

Why does connected speech matter?

The way pronunciation is typically taught often does not enable EFL students to understand authentically spoken native speaker English. This is to a large extent because students are not confronted with and systematically taught authentic language rich in connected speech reduction. This situation is further exacerbated because there is no systematic approach and very little and scattered commercially available material. (See Brown and Kondo-Brown 2006.)

Approaches in pronunciation teaching

We can say that there are three components to an approach in language teaching:

- views of language;
- views of learning; and
- views of how language constituents interlock.

These classical components are also valid in approaches to specific areas of the language (such as Lewis' lexical approach). As regards 'views of language', up into the 1970s pronunciation was taught with a primary focus on sounds, informed by articulatory phonetics. In the late 70s and early 80s this started to change, and the state of the art now is to teach top-down, i.e. starting with larger units (intonation contours, rhythm). This kind of instruction, however, is often very unsystematic and impressionistic, so that some (also prosody-centred) alternatives have been proposed, the present approach being one of them.

A connected speech-based approach

In my approach I see connected speech in the centre, as the final language product, conditioned by rhythm and strongly influenced by positional variation (for example, vowel length [*bat* vs. *bad*]), word stress and prominence (thought grouping, nuclear/primary sentence stress). Intonation (in the narrow definition as utterance–final pitch movement) and sound quality are not very significant in comparison. (See Derwing *et al.* 1998 for an empirical study.)

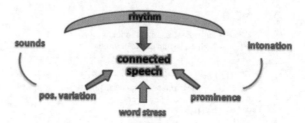

Figure 6.2.1: The connected speech-based approach

An example of how rhythm conditions connected speech can be seen in a sentence like *The KIDS might have been PATting the DOGS*. Because each rhythmical interval has to take about the same amount of time (each interval contains a content word, to simplify), function words need to be reduced somehow. These are the rules of connected speech. In the underlined words initial /h/ is deleted, the vowel in *have* is reduced to schwa, and (in NAmE) /t/ is flapped (produced like a very short 'd') between two vowels across word boundaries, leading to [maɪDəvbɪn]. These processes make it possible to keep the rhythmic timing—and are what makes native speaker speech so very difficult for learners to comprehend.

Teaching principles

As regards 'views of learning', a basic model for pronunciation lessons was proposed by Celce-Murcia *et al.* (2011), going from description and analysis to listening discrimination to controlled practice to guided practice to communicative/free practice (which can, of course, also be done in a patchwork mode). With some re-defining we can, further, utilise principles from vocabulary and grammar teaching, most notably so the notion of collocation and chunking. Conceiving language as chunks lies at the core of contemporary language instruction, and also very much works for pronunciation teaching (as in the 'might have been' before, which, in phonology, is referred to as a phonological/prosodic word). Seeing a sequence of fused ('connected') function words as a single chunk makes English pronunciation significantly more tangible, as learners have informed me from their perspective very many times.

Syllabus of a connected speech-based approach

On a general note it should be said that while instruction in forms must, in principal, be secondary to developing fluency, pronunciation is an integral part of oral competence and respective instruction seems justified on all levels.

In actual implementation (where we have to consider 'how language constituents interlock'), two major questions arise: how is pronunciation best acquired in classroom situations, and how can all the very many individual rules of connected speech be taught?

The first issue is addressed by structuring the syllabus in the four steps shown in Figure 6.2.2, where sounds can also be interspersed when it seems sensible in the specific classroom situation. Connected speech becomes teachable and processable by helping students develop a solid understanding of prosodic areas like rhythm, thought grouping and primary stress allocation. In doing so the issue of individual

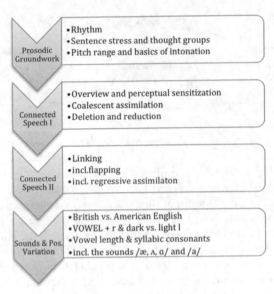

Figure 6.2.2: Syllabus structure

rules, in turn, also becomes less of a problem because they will now appear as somewhat of a logical consequence. In practice, the issue can be tackled by creating larger categories—coalescent assimilation, deletion and linking—and treating individual rules as possible instances that students can discover under the same framework (such as deletion). I have tried this in intensive courses on pronunciation in advanced contexts and as a sub-syllabus in lower-level EFL programs (A1/A2), and it has worked very successfully in both contexts.

eulers@hotmail.co.uk

References

Brown, J. D. and K. Kondo-Brown (eds.). 2006. *Perspectives on Teaching Connected Speech to Second Language Speakers.* Honolulu: University of Hawaii Press.

Celce-Murcia, M, D. M. Brinton and J. M. Goodwin. 2011. *Teaching Pronunciation: A Course Book and Reference Guide.* Cambridge: Cambridge University Press.

Derwing, T. M., M. J. Munro and G. E. Wiebe. 1998. 'Evidence in favor of a broad framework for pronunciation instruction'. *Language Learning* 48/3: 393–410.

6.3 The teaching of pronunciation in Spain: students' and teachers' views

Yolanda Joy Calvo Benzies *University of Santiago de Compostela, Spain*

Introduction

Spanish learners often have serious problems with English pronunciation (Palacios 2000; Estebas 2009); these can be caused by the following:

- the lack of many similarities between the phonological systems of the two languages;
- the irregular correspondence between English spelling and pronunciation; and
- the lack of exposure to spoken English outside the classroom.

Therefore, it would seem logical to state that speaking and pronunciation skills should be emphasised in EFL classes in this country. However, as this study shows, both EFL teachers and students feel that pronunciation continues to be neglected in EFL classes.

Methodology

A total of 135 post-obligatory secondary education (*Bachillerato)* students, together with five EFL teachers, participated in the study. Two questionnaires were used to collect the data; one version was designed for the students and the other for the teachers. Both followed a similar format:

- personal data;
- English outside the classroom;
- general importance and attitudes towards the learning of pronunciation;
- the current role of pronunciation in EFL classes at high school;
- preferences and specific problems regarding English pronunciation; and
- views on the role of pronunciation in their textbooks.

The majority of the items were of a multiple choice nature or used a Likert scale of 1–5. There were also a few open questions in which the subjects were asked to write complete answers.

Results

The results obtained in this study indicate that pronunciation continues to be disregarded in EFL classes in Spain. The first group of participants, i.e. the students, made the following claims:

1 Not enough time is devoted to the teaching of pronunciation in their EFL classes.
2 Oral skills continue to receive less attention than writing, grammar, vocabulary and reading; the first two are particularly emphasised.
3 They themselves as well as their colleagues only speak in English on some occasions.
4 Activities focused on pronunciation are hardly ever carried out; those that *are* suggested are monotonous and boring, namely listening and repeating words and small sentences, with a complete absence of songs, games or computer programs and the Internet.
5 Likewise, the correction system used by their teacher is also very traditional, once again using the 'listen and repeat' technique.
6 They are very rarely tested on pronunciation
7 Tasks that focus on their specific pronunciation problems are rarely carried out.
8 Their textbook includes insufficient pronunciation activities; this does not help them improve.

The EFL teachers surveyed share many views with their students and admit the following:

1 Less attention is paid to listening and speaking in their EFL classes (and, thus, to pronunciation).
2 Not enough time is devoted to the teaching of aspects of this language field.
3 Few pronunciation activities are put into practice in the classroom.
4 They very rarely test and assess their students' pronunciation abilities.
5 Their students only use the L2 on some occasions.
6 They have negative opinions about the EFL textbooks. Not enough pronunciation exercises are included, and those that *are* present follow a very repetitive pattern and rarely help their students to improve their pronunciation.

Conclusions

This study confirms that, according to the views and perspectives of post-obligatory education students and teachers, pronunciation continues to have an inferior role in EFL classes. This is surprising, given the difficulties that native speakers of Spanish have with this aspect of English. It can be concluded that many changes are still necessary in the educational system of Spain. There is a need for a higher degree of exposure and oral production of the target language, as well as a need to test the students' pronunciation. More generally, the frequency and format of the activities used in the classroom should be modified and adapted so that they are really motivating and challenging.

This study is part of a larger project, namely a doctoral dissertation that aims at identifying and analysing the role of pronunciation at different levels of education. Our hypothesis is that these findings and results could be extrapolated to other levels of education, such as obligatory-secondary education and university and even to many other Spanish regions and European countries. If this were the case, a remedial programme for improving the inferior role of pronunciation in EFL classes in Spain will also be proposed.

yolandajoy.calvo@rai.usc.es

References

Estebas Vilaplana, E. 2009. *Teach Yourself English Pronunciation: An Interactive Course for Spanish Speakers*. Oleiros: Netbiblo.

Palacios Martínez, I. 2000. 'Improving learners' pronunciation of English: some reflections and some practical tips' in J. M. Ruiz, P. Sheerin and C. Estebánez (eds.). *Estudios de Metodología de la Lengua Inglesa*. Valladolid: Universidad de Valladolid.

6.4 Teaching pronunciation to Russian learners

Tatiana Skopintseva *New Economic School, Moscow, Russia*

This talk reported on a classroom initiative to integrate pronunciation instruction into an ESAP curriculum; the result was a 40-hour English pronunciation course designed for Russian MA students majoring in economics and finance. The course, called 'Well Pronounced', focuses on teaching the lingua franca core and non-core segmental and suprasegmental pronunciation features that enhance Russian learners' rhetorical competence and ensure intelligibility between Russians and other English-speaking people.

Rationale

With globalisation of the English language and multicultural interactions in the modern workplace, rhetorical competence and performance skills have been brought to the fore in the ESAP curriculum. Making presentations, taking part in debates, participating in meetings and negotiations, and self-presenting at job interviews—all require the learner to speak accurately and intelligibly in cross-/multicultural settings. Meanwhile, most intelligibility problems in oral communication are caused by L1 interference; this can lead to an underestimation of the rhetorical competence of non-native speakers. With this in mind, teaching pronunciation has become an essential item on the ESAP agenda.

The assumption that positive attitude towards the L1 accent and the acquisition of some degree of native speaker accent are necessary to ensure intelligibility (Jenkins 2000) has proved to be reliable in our course and made the learning goals of the course teachable and achievable.

The 'Well Pronounced' course is a practical application of works by international and Russian phoneticians. It is based on pronunciation features which typically cause communication breakdowns in Russian English speech, affect orthoepic accuracy (i.e. the relationship between pronunciation and spelling) and impede comprehension of discourse in public speaking. Students are taught to elicit Russian-specific pronunciation errors through building their phonological awareness of the items in focus; they are also trained to correct them. By the end of the course the students are provided with a step-by-step algorithm for preparing an oral text independently.

Core features

The following lingua franca core and non-core pronunciation features are taught to Russian speakers to achieve rhetorical competence:

- Aspiration after /p/, /t/, /k/ as in 'company', 'policy', 'public', 'market'.
- The quality of cardinal vowels, particularly the difference between /æ/, /ʌ/ and /ɑ:/ as in 'bag'/'bug', 'stuff'/'staff', and 'much'/'March'; also the difference between /ɔ:/ and /ə:/ as in 'walk'/'work', 'born'/'burn' and 'course'/'curse'.
- Articulation of diphthongs as in 'want'/'won't', 'sells'/'sales' and 'lawn'/'loan'.
- The voicing of consonants in word endings, including '-s' and '-ed' endings as in 'place'/'plays', 'life'/'live', 'price'/'prize', 'wanted'/'want it'.
- Word stress, including word stress in derivatives as in 'contrast' (noun)/'contrast' (verb), 'import' (noun)/'import' (verb).
- Palatalisation of consonants before front vowels.
- Nuclear stress production and placement within tone units with pitch movement on the nuclear syllable to make the word prominent because 'The main prosodic feature for Russian speakers would be intensity (loudness), while English speakers would rather vary the pitch under the same circumstances' (Savina and Skopintseva 2005: 74).
- Flexibility in adopting the rhotic variant /r/, for example, 'card' pronounced as /ka:rd/ or /ka:d/.

- Rhythm, since Russian learners generally produce an impression of speaking too fast, too loudly, or emphasising to many sounds, which creates a 'pushy' effect.
- Register, the so-called 'step-ups' and 'step-downs' to emphasise the discourse structure and to break the monotony of Russian-specific intonation patterns in public speaking.

Implications for course design, material and classroom pedagogy

- The course is organised by gradually building on complexity of pronunciation features. Articulatory setting and syllabic values are considered the starting points to teach English pronunciation, while tones (falling and rising) and register top the pronunciation for public speaking 'teaching ladder'.
- To make the complex learning goals teachable and achievable under ESAP curriculum constraints, it is recommended that teachers rely on pronunciation features with dual advantages. For example, changing register helps to avoid the L1 monotony and broadens the pitch range for rhetorical purposes, which in turn is found to be a sociolinguistic factor indicative of regional, social and stylistic variation of English standard speech (Shevchenko and Skopintseva 2004). Some breathing and relaxation exercises prepare the speech organs for smooth speech production and help to combat stage fright. Carefully chosen articulation warm-ups can be used to articulate specific English consonants.
- It is important to compose pronunciation materials of specific key terms, proper names and foreign words, Latin and Greek vocabulary.
- To make any pronunciation course goals teachable and achievable for ESAP students, teachers should develop a systematic approach to improving students' pronunciation; they need to be persistent in focusing on the pronunciation 'hot spots' in every class, in the same way, for example, as they correct grammar errors.

tatiana.skopintseva@gmail.com

References

Jenkins, J. 2000. *The Phonology of English as an International Language*. Oxford: Oxford University Press.

Savina, I. and T. Skopintseva. 2005. 'Symposium on pronunciation' in B. Beaven (ed.). *IATEFL 2005 Cardiff Conference Selections*. Cardiff: IATEFL.

Shevchenko, T. I. and T. S. Skopintseva. 2004. 'Prosody variation in English: geographical, social, situational' in *The Proceedings of the 2nd International Conference: Speech Prosody 2004*. Nara: SP 2004.

6.5 Teaching an IEP pronunciation course: procedures, activities and findings

Sophie Farag *The American University in Cairo, Egypt*

Background

In the Intensive English Program (IEP) of The American University in Cairo, students attend five hours of EAP a day, but little time is spent on teaching pronunciation.

These students often lack confidence in speaking, and so the IEP Pronunciation Centre was started in September 2011. Classes meet once a week, after the EAP classes, for 40-minute sessions, and students sign up on a voluntary basis.

The course

In surveys administered to students asking them to evaluate the pronunciation classes, students indicated that they wanted more conversation, as opposed to pronouncing separate words. In response to this feedback, each class session is divided into two stages. Stage 1 focuses on pronunciation and on introducing a specific sound or pair of sounds that Egyptian learners have difficulty with. Stage 2 focuses on developing fluency and includes interactive activities. Examples of activities used in each stage are presented below.

Pronunciation activities

Sounds

- At the beginning of the course, the phonemic chart from *Sound Foundations* (Underhill 2005) is introduced to raise students' awareness of how the different sounds are produced. Sounds that are focused on include /p/ vs /b/ and /θ/ vs /ð/.
- Minimal pairs (for example,, /θ/ vs /s/: 'thick' vs 'sick'; /p/ vs /b/: 'peas' vs 'bees'), and tongue twisters (for example, 'Some people pay to park, but I bought a bus pass') act as good warmers and are fun to say.
- Comparing vowel sounds: the website *RoadToGrammar* presents an online interactive rhyming activity that allows students to compare confusing vowel sounds, for example, 'right' rhymes with 'bite' and 'height', but not with 'eight' and 'weight'.

Consonant clusters

- Words ending in consonant clusters, for example, 'desks', 'girls', and past tense verb endings, for example, 'asked', 'watched', tend to be pronounced by Egyptian students as an extra syllable, so practice includes counting syllables to ensure that none are added.

Word stress

- Words that can be both a noun and a verb, for example,, 'protest', 'contrast' are introduced and students practice stressing the first syllable for nouns and the second syllable for verbs.
- The website *RoadToGrammar* presents an online interactive activity that allows students to listen to a variety of multi-syllable words and decide on the stress pattern of each word.

Sentence stress

- Our students tend to speak in a monotone when conversing in English, and sentence stress is difficult for some. Activities include reading poems aloud while stressing the rhythm. Students practice asking questions or saying statements, while stressing different words, to give different meanings. The following sentence gives different meanings when a different underlined word is stressed: '*I* didn't say *you* should *catch* *him*.'

Fluency activities

The second part of each lesson includes interactive activities to practice the newly introduced sounds, to engage the students, and to help them gain confidence and fluency in speaking. These activities depend on using images to elicit conversation among students and can help them develop their vocabulary.

Spot the difference

- By taking turns to describe their picture to their partner, students work in pairs to identify the differences between two pictures that appear quite similar but have several differences.

Describe and draw or guess

- One student in each pair is given a picture of an object or a scene to describe to their partner, who guesses or draws the picture.

Picture sequence

- Stories that are represented through a series of images are cut up and given to pairs or groups of students to put in order. This activity requires students to discuss the story and agree on the sequence. A volunteer from each pair/group tells the story to the rest of the class.

Tell the story

- Images of a scene or people doing an activity are used as a starting point for students to create their own stories. In pairs or groups, students are given a picture and they create a story around it. The story can be simple or complex depending on the language level of the students.

Reflection

The results of a self-evaluation survey conducted at the end of the pronunciation course to measure the impact of the classes on the students showed that those who attended regularly felt more confident and fluent in speaking English, and they enjoyed the classes. These results are a motivation to continue to improve the course. Low attendance is a challenge as students are tired after five hours of English, and actions for improvement include promoting the course more during the first week of classes to stress the benefits.

sophiemf@aucegypt.edu

References

RoadToGrammar for rhyming vowels. (Retrieved from http://www.roadtogrammar.com/rhymer/)

RoadToGrammar for word stress. (Retrieved from http://www.roadtogrammar.com/wordstress/)

Underhill, A. 2005. *Sound Foundations: Learning and Teaching Pronunciation* (2nd ed.). Oxford: Macmillan Education.

7 The early years: from literacy to laptops

The focus of this chapter is language instruction for children and teenagers. The scope and diversity of these papers reflect the breadth of research carried out with young learners around the world. The chapter opens with **Sandie Mourão**'s paper on the importance of play for children of preschool age. The next three papers explore issues related to children in different contexts: **Zarina Markova** explores the relevance of Gardner's Multiple Intelligences theory to Bulgarian children learning English; **Emma Mojoko Evele** presents strategies to improve the reading skills of her learners in Cameroon; and **Senem Ozkul** addresses CLIL in German high schools, with particular reference to the teaching of geography. Next, **Patricia E. Reynolds** discusses the experiences migrant children face in their new schools, while **Gail Ellis** looks at the reasons parents have for enrolling their children in out-of-school English classes. The final three papers in this chapter all address the topic of technology in ELT for young learners. **Michael Carrier** outlines the opportunities available to learners in state schools through the use of one-to-one learning, while **Paul Woods** discusses research into the effectiveness of such programmes. Finally, **Chryssanthe Sotiriou and Dimitris Primalis** show how the teaching of literature to young learners can be enhanced through the use of technology..

7.1 Principles of early childhood education and very young learners: the role of play

Sandie Mourão *Freelance, Portugal*

This presentation was prompted by Tina Bruce's (2011) ten principles of early childhood education, which highlight the importance of creating a rich learning environment with and through language. These principles incorporate the educational theories of Froebel, Montessori and Steiner alongside the socio-constructivist ideas of Piaget, Vygotsky and Bruner.

Play and language learning

Principle 4 of Bruce's principles states: 'Children learn best when they are given appropriate responsibility, allowed to experiment, make errors, decisions and choices, and are respected as autonomous learners' (2011: 47). In early-years language learning contexts this becomes possible if we consider the role of play 'a child's work and the means whereby he grows and develops' (Issac 1929: 9). Through play, children actively manipulate, rearrange and try out as well as act on and reflect upon learning. Language is almost always part of this play.

Play can be seen from two perspectives: adult-led play and child-initiated play. Both afford learning opportunities, but child-initiated play is considered most beneficial for children. In our English classes the moments we spend with our students are structured by the activities and games we prepare to provide opportunities for hearing English and acquiring it; this is adult-led play. The challenge is provide a balance between child-initiated learning and adult-led learning through play.

Formal and informal instruction

To enable play to be productive for language learning purposes we need to consider instruction in two forms: formal instruction and informal instruction. The teacher leads formal instruction—she demonstrates and provides access to the target language through play-like routine activities. These activities contain what Bruner (1983) has referred to as 'formats'. If we dissect a game or activity we will find that it does the following:

1 provides a sequential structure;
2 contains clearly marked roles; and
3 consists of scripts to support communication.

During English classes teacher and children naturally interact, with children gradually understanding the structure and roles and picking up the scripts of these activities.

Informal instruction occurs between peers during child-initiated play, usually outside the English lessons and during free play. It is recognised that children learn just as much from more knowledgeable peers as they do from adults. But what exactly is free play? Free play is the opportunity to explore and investigate materials and situations for oneself. It is through child-initiated free play that our learners take responsibility, make decisions and choices, and become autonomous learners. They can try out the structures and roles they saw in action during adult-led play, and they can imitate and use the scripts they heard and memorised. They can experiment, make mistakes, and not feel threatened.

How can we create opportunities for child-initiated play in English?

Many preschools are set out into learning or activity areas, which are equipped with developmentally appropriate materials for young children to play with and manipulate. Examples are a house area; a writing area, a reading area, a construction area, a water area. My suggestion is that a learning area be set up for English. In fact, such areas have existed for over a decade in schools in Portugal, Italy and Spain. In these English learning areas children interact with English materials (flashcards, puppets, stories, games and picture books) and engage in child-initiated play.

The relationship between adult-led and child-initiated play

The relationship between adult-led play and child-initiated play is shown in the adaptation of Moyles' 'play spiral' (1989: 16) (see Figure 7.1.1). It demonstrates how play supports learning and language acquisition. Children need language to play in English, so this spiral begins with directed, adult-led play. Children engage in directed play with the English teacher; they are exposed to formats during play-like activities. Once English is over, children move into child-initiated, free-play mode, interacting with the English materials in the English learning area. Regular sessions of English provide opportunities for mastering those structures, roles and scripts that make up the routine activities and games, and children go on to restructure their learning during subsequent free play. This leads to a growth in language use and knowledge.

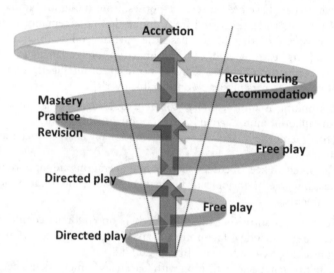

Figure 7.1.1: The play spiral (adapted from Moyles 1989: 16)

Conclusions

Play can support development in the target language by providing children with opportunities to experiment and choose, make mistakes, take decisions and become autonomous learners. Planning for child-initiated, free play to be part of our early-years English classes is essential in the creation of a rich learning environment that involves learning with and through language.

References

sjmourao@gmail.com

Bruce, T. 2011. *Early Childhood Education* (fourth edition). Abingdon: Hodder Education.

Isaacs, S. 1929. *The Nursery Years: the Mind of the Child from Birth to Six Years*. London: Routledge & Kegan Paul.

Moyles, J. 1989. *Just Playing?: The Role and Status of Play in Early Childhood Education*. Milton Keynes: Open University Press.

7.2 Multiple Intelligences reconsidered

Zarina Markova *South-West University, Blagoevgrad, Bulgaria*

Background

The theory of Multiple Intelligences (MI) has received a good deal of attention not only in the English language teaching community, but in educational circles in general. Worldwide, there have been diverse responses, from thoughtful implementation to far-fetched misinterpretations, and from unquestioning acceptance to total rejection. Critics have argued that MI (a) has little scientific value; (b) has little power to enhance students' learning; and (c) is not linked to foreign language acquisition.

However, a comparison between Gardner's concept of intelligences and the characteristics of young learners reveals a considerable overlap:

- Children's thinking is multi-sensory, concrete and lateral; it is boosted through object manipulation, motor activity and emotional involvement.
- Children best memorise images—concrete, emotionally charged material on topics close to their interests.
- Children are likely to keep focused when mental operations are supported by physical motions, by large bright objects, by change and diversity of activities, rhythm and environments.

Therefore, it is not surprising to see researchers on children's cognitive development and learning conclude: 'The notion of multiple intelligences is important for flexibility in teaching' (Goswami and Bryant 2007:20).

Evidence linking language acquisition with Gardner's framework has been accumulating. Although research has predominantly focused on L1 development, evidence suggests that using strategies based on Gardner's model leads to enhanced vocabulary acquisition and better language skills development (Markova 2013). While the growing body of evidence in this area cannot serve as validation of Gardner's theory, there are indications that it may be too early to discard his framework as ineffective for teaching foreign languages, especially to young learners.

The study

In an attempt to throw further light on this topic, a team of teachers conducted a one-year study with four classes of Bulgarian seven and eight year olds. The aim of the study was to explore whether and how the use of Gardner's framework to enrich foreign language instruction can affect young learners' language skills, and their involvement in and attitude towards English lessons. The design was quasi-experimental, with a control group consisting of two classes of 42 students in total, and an experimental group comprising two classes of 48 students in total. The instruction in the control group was based on *Blue Skies for Bulgaria*, including textbook, workbook and handwriting book (Holt 2003). The experimental group used the same textbook complemented by a set of teaching activities aiming to ensure a more balanced approach reflecting Gardner's framework. Data were collected three times throughout the school year: at the beginning, when the control and experimental groups were formed; in the middle; and at the end. The data collection tools included oral and written tests, attitude questionnaires and classroom observation checklists.

The findings

The midpoint and endpoint assessment of the language skills suggests that the instruction in the experimental group was more effective. The results are as follows:

1 In both language tests, the two groups showed no statistical difference in the performance on the reading comprehension tasks.
2 In the mid-test, the experimental group achieved statistically better results on one of the sub-tasks (recognition of sound–letter correspondence.
3 In the final test, the experimental group performed statistically better on the listening comprehension task.
4 In both language tests, there were statistically significant differences between the two groups with regard to students' performance on the spelling tasks and on the composition of short written and spoken messages. It is interesting to observe these differences in skills traditionally considered difficult by Bulgarians.

The different forms of instruction did not statistically affect the degree of students' involvement in the English lessons. However, there was a major difference between the degrees of positive attitudes towards English in the two groups.

Conclusion

The study was conducted with Bulgarian seven and eight year olds using *Blue Skies for Bulgaria*. Done with another coursebook, a different age group and in a different country, it may have yielded different results. Yet, the findings presented in this talk suggest that the question of the application of Gardner's model in foreign language teaching still needs exploration.

zarinamarkova@abv.bg
References

Goswami, U. and P. Bryant. 2007. *Children's Cognitive Development and Learning (Primary Review Research Survey 2/1a)*. Cambridge: University of Cambridge Faculty of Education.

Holt, R. 2003. *Blue Skies for Bulgaria*. Harlow: Pearson.

Markova, Z. 2013. 'The Theory of Multiple Intelligences and Effectiveness of English Language Teaching in the Primary Bulgarian Classroom'. Unpublished PhD thesis. Sofia University, Bulgaria.

7.3 Early literacy in English-medium schools in Cameroon

Emma Mojoko Evele *Cameroon English Language and Literature Teachers' Association, Maroua, Cameroon*

Introduction

This presentation focused on early literacy issues in relation to one of the two English-speaking regions of Cameroon. Although these regions are referred to as

English speaking (Anglophone), English is not a second language here but is taught as such. Early literacy is a complex issue in Cameroon, a country with over 270 indigenous languages. In the Anglophone regions, the lingua franca is Pidgin, which bears a resemblance to English and is used everywhere except in the classroom. English is encountered in school—strictly speaking, in the classroom. Learners leave it in the classroom, switching to the more comfortable Pidgin when outside. Young learners begin their literacy journey in nursery school, which lasts for two years; this is followed by six years of primary education. English is taught daily as a subject. In Form One (the first year of secondary school) some students are still unable to communicate meaningfully enough in English to make it possible for them to have an average of 10/20, the pass mark in the course.

Case study: Bilingual Grammar School, Molyko

A three-month remedial literacy programme helped 48 students to overcome their reading difficulty. I realised that their inability to write correctly was closely related to their inability to read, so they were taught reading using two methods. Based on suggestions that children should be taught to read 'bit-by-bit' and that they need to learn to 'read through reading' (Ellis 1998), I alternated between these methods. There was a focus on the phonic system of teaching reading since some learners could not see a relationship between the letters of the alphabet and the sounds of English. Following suggestions from Slattery and Willis (2001) that the phonic system be used to help improve on spelling and word recognition skills, instruction included work on silent consonants, consonant clusters, diagraphs and phonograms.

Teaching reading 'bit-by-bit'

Learners were divided into groups according to their reading levels. Those students unable to make sense of the letters of the alphabet and their sounds were drilled on sound and word building. Five-minute activities were used, such as aural cloze exercises in which rhyming words were omitted as I read a story aloud to them; wherever I paused, students supplied the missing word. At the end they used the words to retell the story, and they tried to write it in groups. Participants thought these activities could be used in regular classes as well.

Learners built other phonograms using the onset-and-rhyme style, and came up with words in English. Other methods included five stages in teaching spelling: look at the word; repeat its pronunciation after the teacher; look at it and spell it orally; the teacher puts the card away for the learner to write it; then it is brought back for the learner to check. The learner is then encouraged to make a sentence with the word. Short sentences were cut up and put in an envelope; learners tried to reconstruct them. Later, ten sentences were written on ten sheets of paper and put in an envelope for learners to construct the story.

Teaching 'reading through reading'

In a low-resourced multi-cultural context like mine, the use of graded readers proposed by Ellis (1998) was not possible; the absence of such materials necessitated a different approach. Instead, different story books were gathered and reading tasks assigned. Children listened to me read aloud, they repeated, and chunks were written on cards for them to read at a glance. They were asked to complete book report forms after reading little story books. They chose two people to tell the story they had read, and they also listened to two others. After reading stories in groups, some dramatised it, others presented a TV report on it, others tried to draw while others transformed it into a song.

Results

At the end of the project, even though some learners were still considered below average, their literacy skills had improved considerably. Their word recognition skills were stronger, they had become 'book friendly', and they could see what had been wrong in their writing previously.

evelema@yahoo.com

References

Ellis, R. 1998. *First Steps in Reading*. Oxford: Heinemann Educational Publishers.

Slattery, M. and J.Willis. 2001. *English for Primary Teachers*. Oxford: Oxford University Press.

7.4 Learning geography in English: cool or fool?

Senem Ozkul *Augsburg University, Germany*

Introduction

As a result of globalisation and mobility throughout Europe, the student profile in German schools has rapidly changed. The number of classes that include speakers of other languages has increased tremendously. Since non-linguistic subjects are taught through a foreign language in Content and Language Integrated Learning (CLIL) classes, these classes are regarded as meeting points for subject and language. They provide learners with an opportunity to improve their linguistic spontaneity and subject knowledge as well as their communication skills. In this sense, CLIL classes are a valuable approach to language learning in linguistically diversified contexts since the operating language is a foreign language for both L1 and L2 speakers (Piske 2007).

According to the literature, many studies in CLIL focus on the subject and linguistic achievements of learners in CLIL and non-CLIL classes; few have focused on the learners' reasons for taking CLIL classes. In particular, there is a research gap concerning the potential of CLIL for fostering harmony in language learning in linguistically heterogeneous classrooms:

> Within the theoretical discourse in German on CLIL, the fact has usually been neglected that CLIL does not only involve the foreign language and the official school language, but also needs to be related to the linguistic diversity of the learners and the numerous heritage languages that might be represented in contemporary classrooms. For many learners CLIL is not a second language learning activity, but it rather involves three or four languages of various competence levels. (Breidbach and Viebrock 2012: 13)

The project outlined here is an attempt to close the research gap. It focuses on the motivational differences among German L1 and German L2 speakers in relation to CLIL classes. Research questions were as follows:

- Why do pupils prefer learning a school subject in a foreign language (English)?
- Are German L1 and L2 speakers motivated to take CLIL classes for similar reasons?

Method

The research instrument was a semi-structured questionnaire about learning geography through CLIL. Of ten secondary schools (*Realschulen*) in Swabia that offer CLIL classes for the subject of geography, six agreed to participate in this study. Five different forms of bilingual methodology are prevalent in Germany. The subjects of this study were taking the classical form of CLIL, which starts in the seventh grade and continues until the tenth grade. Participating secondary schools administered the questionnaire and returned the completed questionnaires in November and December of 2012. A total of 146 seventh-grade pupils with an average age of 13 (56.2 per cent males; 40.4 per cent females; 3.4 per cent unspecified) responded to seven questions. Besides personal questions about age, gender, parents' linguistic background, mother tongue, and other languages learned, the questionnaire included the following:

- Q.6: Why do you want to learn geography in English?
- Q.7: If geography were offered in other foreign languages, for example, French, would you still decide to participate in CLIL classes? Why?

This article presents results from the last two questions. In Q.6, subjects were asked to choose up to three out of twelve reasons for learning geography in English, and they were allowed to write additional personal reasons into an empty box. Q.7 was an open question; they were asked to state their reasons for learning or not learning geography in another language.

Results and discussion

The responses were analysed by means of SPSS 20. The results showed that there was no motivational difference for learning geography in English between pupils of different genders and linguistic backgrounds. For both genders and for both German L1 and L2 speakers, the most frequent motives for taking CLIL were 'Because it (English) is useful for my future career' and 'Because I want to improve my English'.

A majority of the subjects would not have wanted to take CLIL classes in a different foreign language because of 'insufficient command of another foreign language', and 'extra workload'. Those subjects who were interested in taking CLIL classes in another foreign language would have done so because they had 'motivation for learning other languages'.

Conclusion

The participants in this study were motivated to learn geography in English mostly for linguistic reasons, to improve their English and thus to have a better future career. It was also learned that the number of German L2 pupils in CLIL classes was lower than the number of German L1 pupils. The next phase of this study will examine the motivation of non-CLIL learners of geography with a migration background to find out why they do not prefer to learn geography in English. Moreover, the parents of the non-CLIL learners of geography will be interviewed to learn if they have been informed about this opportunity in schools and if they would find it beneficial for their children.

References

senem.oezkul@phil.uni-augsburg.de

Breidbach, S. and B. Viebrock. 2012. 'CLIL in Germany—results from recent research in a contested field of education'. *International CLIL Research Journal* 1/4: 5–16.

Piske, T. 2007. 'Bilingualer Unterricht an Grundschulen: Voraussetzungen, Erfahrungen und Ergebnisse'. *Grundschule* 4: 28–30.

7.5 Learning the ropes: children crossing cultures in classrooms

Patricia E. Reynolds *University of Mary Washington, Fredericksburg, Va., USA*

Overview

Education for the 21st century means education for an increasingly diverse student population throughout the world. Understanding characteristics of non-native speakers of English, as well as ethnic minorities who speak a language other than English, is becoming a necessity for all educators. Additionally, because of an unprecedented immigration pattern throughout the world over the past 20 years, children must reconcile crossing cultures between the expectations of their first-generation immigrant parents and the expectations of local community schools (Abed and Sheldon 2008; Batalova 2008). Children involved in the process of crossing cultures are labelled 'international students', 'migrants', 'transcultural children', or 'cross-cultural children' in school settings. While most educators agree with the assumption that all children experience changes and difficult transitions throughout their development, for the population of children engaged in this dynamic, the experience of crossing cultures is tantamount to *life altering* (Taylor 2004). Crossing cultural boundaries may also affect children's abilities to garner opportunities in their current academic settings, leading them to lower achievement throughout the overall process.

Where do these children come from?

This session discussed the realities of the 21st-century classroom and the numbers of populations on the move globally. Current statistics worldwide are no surprise to educators who walk into classrooms and look out at the faces of children who present identities from various international cultures. Nations that have relied on homogenous populations of children in their schools have been challenged by this new mix of cultures—a phenomenon that has led to new approaches to teaching children who are *not like us*. But what about the children who have to make this journey across cultures? The question is: How are they doing this? But more importantly, what strategies do they use to do it? Are they successful, or are they simply able to function in heritage communities within the new culture?

Managing the models

In this presentation the current model was discussed; this model was based on research conducted back in the 1950s with college-age students voluntarily entering into a study abroad program. All the session participants agreed this is not a match for school-age children who, for the most part, have had no input into the migration event. These children are then termed 'involuntary immigrants' and find themselves at the forefront of having to make the cross-cultural journey on their own in school settings. The current research conducted indicates that the pattern for an involuntary migrant with developing social, psychological and emotional systems has a very different pattern than the ones previously thought; it is termed *Learning the Ropes*.

Learning the Ropes

The *Learning the Ropes* basic social process looks very different from the models that are currently used in TEFL teacher preparation and is more accountable to the needs of the child in a classroom setting. It takes into consideration that a child is an individual in the process of developing socially, psychologically and emotionally.

Figure 7.5.1: Stages in Learning the Ropes

The presentation discussed the stages presented in Figure 7.5.1, their impact on students crossing cultures in school settings, and how educators in various settings can work with students as they accomplish this daunting task.

The questions raised by looking at this basic social process were indicative of an understanding that educators worldwide are having the same difficulty helping students acculturate to new environments. Many of those in TEFL find that they are faced with a double-edged sword when it comes to accomplishing this task as they are adding a new language which may not be the dominant language in the country where they are teaching English. This complication leads to TEFL professionals feeling this task may be a greater burden on the child and their efforts to teach, now the third language, may be ill advised.

Suggestions for improvement

All educators, but most importantly language educators, need to understand the process children are going through as they not only learn the languages but acculturate to their new environments. Additionally they require professional development in discovering ways to work with students who are acquiring not only language but culture simultaneously. Furthermore, there needs to be recognition that learners are using school settings to accomplish acculturation tasks, and that schools are left with students who may not be achieving and functioning academically to their highest potential. This, in turn, leaves children with unfulfilled promise for the future as well as trajectories for the future that do not match with the dominant culture, which, renders them to low-paying and less-than-adequate employment and opportunities in the new culture.

preynold@umw.edu

References

Abed, N. S. and K. M. Sheldon. 2008. 'Parental autonomy support and ethnic culture identification among second-generation immigrants'. *Journal of Family Psychology* 22/3: 652–7.

Batalova, J. 2008. *Immigrant and ELL education: A demographic overview.* Paper presented at the ETS-NCLR Symposium: The Language Acquisition and Educational Achievement of English Language Learners, Princeton, N.J., 8–10 January 2008.

Taylor, J. T. 2004. 'Teaching children who have immigrated: the new legislation research, and trends in immigration which affect teachers of diverse student populations'. *Multicultural Education* 11/3: 43–54.

7.6 Investigating why parents send their children to out-of-school English classes

Gail Ellis *British Council, Paris, France*

The rapid growth in primary English language teaching is, in part, a result of parental pressure; variation in policy, quantity and quality in the language learning experiences children receive at mainstream school means that many parents are willing to pay for supplementary English classes. As a result, private providers are now contributing to the linguistic future of the next generations and their life in a globalised world.

This session reported on a global study conducted among parents who send their children to British Council English classes. It investigated their aspirations for wanting their children to attend out-of-school classes, the type of teaching approach they expect, and how closely they expect classes to complement the national curriculum in their country. It also investigated how their decisions may be influenced by their own past language learning experiences.

Research background

Parents are key partners and a key customer and influencer group for the broad young learner audience (2–17 years), so a greater understanding of parents' aspirations will help providers, both state and private, to meet and manage parents' expectations regarding their children's English language learning needs. It will also help them to select the most appropriate teaching approach, design age and context-appropriate materials and courses, and to find ways of adding value by becoming more 'customer-friendly' in an increasingly competitive market.

Main research findings

Over 5,000 parents/carers responded to an online survey which revealed very different levels of response by country. Respondents were mainly female although, in the Middle East, they were mainly male. Parents were generally educated to tertiary level and had knowledge of other languages including a high level of English which many used professionally. The ELLiE research (Enever 2011) reports that parents' knowledge and use of foreign languages professionally has a significant impact on children's foreign language achievement. Parents have positive attitudes towards their children's foreign language learning and can be classified as 'enforcers' or 'proactive encouragers' (Solutions Research 2009).

On balance, the majority of parents/carers were quite positive about the quality of their child's mainstream English provision. The single most important reason for sending their child to additional classes is that English is now seen as a basic life skill and career enhancer for a child's future in a globalised world. Typically they believe that the ideal age for a child to start learning a foreign language is 3–4 years old, and that speaking and listening are the key English skills to focus on.

Views on whether classes should follow the national curriculum differed markedly by country. Overwhelmingly, parents advocated a balance between an academic/studious approach and a more recreational/activity-based approach, with interest in a more academic approach as their children get older. They advocated a range of classroom teaching activities from the traditional to the less traditional, more naturalistic activities, and there was preference for activities experienced by parents themselves as language learners. Finally, there was widespread demand from parents for further support, especially among those with younger children, around speaking English at home and Internet use.

Techniques for adding value

It can be seen that parents assign high value to out-of-school English classes as they have high ambitions for their children and recognise that an early start to English language learning will make all the difference to their economic futures. They are

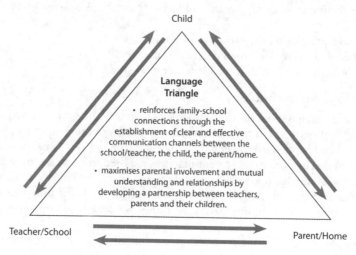

prepared to invest personal time, effort and money in their children's education and want to be involved. Providers, therefore, need to add value by creating child and parent-friendly schools so that parents feel trust and confidence in a school. This can be achieved through:

- the school's ethos and welcoming and inclusive environment that respects diversity;
- ensuring that parents know their child is in a safe, structured and high-quality learning environment;
- providing learning experiences that are age and context-appropriate, relevant and which build confidence and self-esteem;
- establishing effective communication channels, facilitating parental involvement (Brewster *et al.* 2002) and providing support and training for parents via the Language Triangle which highlights the three-way relationship between the child, teacher and parent—see Figure 7.6.1; and
- providing training for teachers to develop the interpersonal and communication skills needed to liaise with parents, to teach children to account for their learning so they can become aware of what and how they learn and report to their parents effectively, and to enhance pupils' and parents' awareness of the possibilities of the out-of-school environment for English language learning by designing tasks that bring the out-of-school context into the classroom and take the in-the-school experience into the home.

Figure 7.6.1: The Language Triangle

References

Gail.Ellis@britishcouncil.fr

Brewster, J., G. Ellis and D. Girard. 2002. *The Primary English Teacher's Guide*. Harlow: Pearson Education.

Enever, J. (ed.). 2011. *ELLiE. Early Language Learning in Europe*. London: British Council.

Solutions Research. 2009. *Positive Activities. Qualitative Research with Parents*. Research Report DCSF-RR142. Department for Children, Schools and Families.

7.7 One-to-one learning

Michael Carrier *Cambridge English Language Assessment*

Across the world there is an exciting new development in the way technology can be used to foster autonomous learning. 'One-to-one learning', sometimes written as '1:1 learning', refers not to one teacher per student but to a new approach where each learner has his or her own handheld device (laptop, tablet, phone); this is used in class or at home to access course and supplementary materials for language learning and practice.

As learners in state education become accustomed to having more autonomy and access to a wider set of educational resources delivered online or by handheld device—whenever and wherever they need them—then they expect to have similar opportunities in their English language courses. 'One-to-one learning' develops autonomous learning and provides anytime, anyplace access to learning materials.

New pedagogical needs mean that we need new types of classrooms with connectivity built in, with interactive whiteboards, and with sets of one-to-one learning devices, or opportunities for students to bring their own devices and connect to the schools' learning materials.

In the ELT context this means that we can use the devices to

- bring more authentic English content into the classroom;
- set up authentic tasks using camera and recorder functions to tell a group-developed story;
- do language practice on the bus or train home;
- develop new forms of pair work activity in class; and
- extend the number of hours available for English study.

Methodology not technology

One-to-one learning is more about methodology than technology. It does require individual handheld devices, but these are becoming more common and in many schools they are provided by the government. What is more complex is the change in curriculum design and classroom management practices required to make the most of this.

We need new and innovative pedagogical models which entwine technology-based study modes with teacher- and classroom-based study modes—ensuring that students are still working in a communicative way, using the devices to stimulate pair and group work.

An example is the 'flipped classroom', where much of the preparation and cognitive learning takes place *outside* the classroom using technology support, and the face-to-face teaching in the classroom is reserved for facilitating learning and building communicative skills.

Where students do not have access to traditional classes it is also possible to use video-conference technology to develop remote learning model. This is happening in Uruguay with Plan Ceibal; the teacher is in a different city from the students and connected by videoconference, and the students have individual handheld devices with software-based activities selected by the teacher to integrate with the curriculum and the video live lessons.

In addition, the provision of individual devices is a way of democratising learning, of giving learners unfettered access and more control over the pace and content of their learning, and extending time on task by using out-of-class time using the same devices as in the classroom. One-to-one learning is about the balance between in-class and out-of-class and self-access learning.

Better outcomes

It is now clear that the global experiments in one-to-one learning can lead to measurable changes in student achievement and student engagement. Bebell and O'Dwyer say, '... access to 1:1 computing led to measurable changes in teacher practices, student achievement, student engagement, and students' research skills compared to the control condition' (2010: 11).

Practitioners have shared their views; Solomon states: 'It is about the *paradigm shift* in how instruction is delivered, and the spark that is created in students that provides a new sense of enthusiasm and ownership in their learning' (2005: 3). The teacher in a British Council pilot in Cairo, Ghada Mohie Ahmed, said:

> The classmate PCs were undoubtedly helpful and enabled me to achieve my aims better. Students looked forward to the lessons and the parents were happy and excited to see their children using the technology. Everyone could see that the kids were more focused and better behaved' (cited in Peachey and Sweeney 2011: 2).

Teacher development

A crucial factor is the need for new types of teacher training to develop the skills and confidence that teachers need to help students make the most of this technology. Teachers need to take action to 'own' the technology, build their confidence in using it, integrate it into their classes and take responsibility for out-of-class learning.

We need to support teachers to develop a set of digital competencies including technology awareness, integrating digital content into the curriculum, developing new forms of classroom management, and using digital tools to create new materials.

mcarrier@btconnect.com

References

Bebell, D. and L.M. O'Dwyer. 2010. 'Educational outcomes and research from 1:1 settings'. *Journal of Technology, Learning and Assessment* 9/1: 1–16. (Retrieved from http://ejournals. bc.edu/ojs/index.php/jtla/article/view/1606/1463)

Peachey, N. and P. Sweeney. 2011. *Enhancing Education with IT Innovation.* London: British Council and Intel Corp. (Retrieved from http://www.intel.de/content/dam/www/public/us/ en/documents/case-studies/education-world-ahead-classmate-pc-british-council-study.pdf)

Solomon, G. (ed.). 2005. '1:1 computing: a guidebook to help you make the right decisions' in *A Special Section of Technology & Learning Journal*: 1–44. San Francisco: CMP Media LLC. (Retrieved from http://www.guide2digitallearning.com/downloads/HP1to1Guide_final2. pdf)

7.8 Do laptops in schools promote learner autonomy and achievement in English language learning?

Paul Woods *British Council, Montevideo, Uruguay*

The jury is still out. Research in Canada suggests they do, but in Peru researchers found that, although using laptops improved students' IT skills, they had little or no effect on test results in English and maths. An innovative project with Plan Ceibal in Uruguay to deliver English lessons in primary schools using remote teachers, however, is using One Laptop per Child (OLPC) laptops to excellent effect.

Benefits of one-to-one initiatives

North Carolina State University studied six statewide one-to-one initiatives in the USA and found positive effects on both student outcomes and instructional practices. The use of laptops was generally found to have a positive impact on student achievement. There were improvements across the board in the 21st-century skills of using technology, innovation, communication and collaboration. In general, the researchers concluded that introduction of one-to-one initiatives led to positive responses, ranging from improved student achievement to shifts in the way in which classrooms are run.

Having a laptop is highly motivating for students for three reasons: learning can take place anywhere; both the teachers and the students are frequently learning together; and even at a very early age pupils can access the vast range of resources on the Internet.

One Laptop per Child

The OLPC initiative driven by Nicholas Negroponte of MIT set out with the mission of producing the '$100 Laptop', which would revolutionise how we educate the world's children. The goal was to provide children around the world with new opportunities to explore, experiment and express themselves. The OLPC XO laptop was rolled out to developing countries in November 2007, and by 2011 worldwide over 2.5 million children and teachers had XO laptops.

However, not all the results have been positive. The Peruvian government spent $225 million to supply and support 850,000 One Laptop per Child (OLPC) laptops in schools throughout the country. An article in the *Economist* in April 2012 with the title 'Error Message: A Disappointing Return from an Investment in Computing' was highly critical: 'Giving a child a computer does not seem to turn him or her into a future Bill Gates—indeed it does not accomplish anything in particular.' The article quoted extensively from an Inter-American Development Bank (IDB) Report whose main findings were that children who received computers did not show any improvement on standardised tests in maths or reading. There was no evidence that access to a laptop increased motivation, or time devoted to homework or reading. Test scores remained with only 30 per cent reaching the required level in reading. The report's conclusion was that the effective implementation of the One Laptop per Child programme was not enough to overcome the difficulties of a project design that placed its trust in the role of technologies themselves. The use of technologies in education was not a magic and rapid solution through which educational problems and challenges could be solved with the simple acquisition of technological devices and systems.

The Uruguayan Ceibal en Inglés project

In Uruguay, the British Council is managing the Ceibal en Inglés project, which involves delivering lessons remotely via video-conferencing from other countries including Argentina, Colombia, Mexico and now The Philippines to classes in Uruguay. A YouTube clip *Ceibal en Inglés* provides a brief but graphic introduction to the Project. All the pupils have OLPC laptops and access to materials including games and songs from the LearnEnglish Kids website. In theory the pupils can continue their learning at home, and by making learning English fun we hope to motivate learners to acquire English language skills both inside and outside the classroom. Classroom teachers are taking an online language improvement course, LearnEnglish Pathways and their motivation levels are maintained by support via a learning management system, online discussion groups, e-moderation, and regular virtual meetings with the online tutor.

Key elements of the project in Uruguay are that every child has a laptop, and lessons are delivered by a remote teacher once a week using tele-presence technology. Uruguayan classroom teachers with only a limited knowledge of English organise two weekly 45-minute practice sessions. The whole thing has to be quite tightly scripted because of the class teachers' limited knowledge of the language content. It seems to be working: average scores on an achievement test after one term of instruction were 72 per cent.

So far, we have learnt that teachers need to be trained adequately, both in how to maximise use of the software on the laptops and how to manage a class where the pupils have laptops, for example, encouraging students to create their own simple blogs. Where laptops are to be used as part of a structured programme, materials need to be mapped to or created for the local syllabus. With young learners, not everything can be done on the laptops—they need to touch, feel, handle, move round the room and do things actively with other children. It is important that testing should test what the students have actually been taught.

The Ceibal en Inglés project is demonstrating that, with sufficient support, appropriate training for classroom teachers and appropriate materials for the pupils, learners are highly motivated, develop autonomy and achieve measurable results through lessons delivered via tele-presence technology and 1-to-1 laptops, supported by classroom teachers with only a very limited knowledge of English.

rphwoods@gmail.com

References

Ceibal en Inglés subtitulado. (Retrieved from http://www.youtube.com/watch?v=hNBhEv_4ZpU)

The *Economist*, April 2012. 'Education in Peru, error message: a disappointing return from an investment in computing'. (Retrieved on 11 June 2013 from http://www.economist.com/node/21552202)

7.9 Literature strikes back! Teaching literature with technology

Chryssanthe Sotiriou *and* **Dimitris Primalis** *Doukas School, Athens, Greece*

IATEFL Learning Technologies SIG Diana Eastment Scholarship winners

Technology has become an indispensable part in the daily life of the younger genera-tions and over the last few years concerted efforts have been made to integrate it into the syllabus. The emphasis on digital literacies and the development of 21st-century skills seems to have overshadowed literature, which seems to be losing ground. Since 2009, our school has adopted the one-to-one (one computer to one student) model in which students use electronic coursebooks and multimedia material. Hence the following questions arose: Do we need to teach literature in class? If so, how? Should technology rival literature or can there be a synergy to the learners' benefit?

Why literature?

Comparing fairly similar genres on the Web and literature, it is noticeable that the former rely heavily on visual and audio elements (i.e. video, photos or audio files) and the length and range of lexis used are limited, especially on social media. For example, a story narrated on Facebook will have few words, accompanied by a photo or video. Therefore, exposure to a wide range of lexis is limited. This is where literature can help students enrich their language.

Literature relies upon lexis as well as grammar to narrate stories. To a generation that has been raised with gadgets and short texts, attacking a page with a story full of words—often without visuals—can be frustrating. A teacher's role is to initiate the learners to the world of words and help them decipher the pictures, feelings and messages conveyed on and between the lines. In this battle the educator often has to fight prejudice, while stimulating the learners' interest and imagination. The best ally to achieve it is though technology! Firstly, students feel familiar with technology. Secondly, it can stimulate their interest in the activities mentioned below. Finally, it can be used to encourage the creative use of the language following Bloom's tax-onomy.

A jigsaw activity and flipped classroom

The following split viewing/listening activity aims at stimulating students' interest and encouraging them to read the next chapters of the story. The class is divided into two groups (viewers and listeners). Listeners leave the classroom while viewers watch the first two minutes of the film without sound and take notes. Then viewers leave the room and compare notes to reconstruct the story while listeners enter the room and listen to the first two minutes of the film with the monitor turned off. They also compare notes and reconstruct the story. Finally, the learners work in pairs. Every pair has a listener and a viewer; their task is to come up with a version of the story by combining snippets of information to bridge the information gap. The video used at the conference was from *Rebecca*, based on the book by Daphne du Maurier. For homework, students read the first chapter(s) of the book and compare their story to the plot of the book.

This activity can also be used as a 'flipped classroom' activity, by assigning the viewing and listening of the video as homework. Reconstructing the story is a motivating activity which can be completed either within the classroom environment or by posting it on educational platforms, such as *Edmodo*. Tweeting the story is also an attractive means of narrating which is especially popular among teenagers. Skype provides opportunities to contact authors of books and then have them 'visit' your classroom and discuss the book with them.

Internet and Web 2.0 tools

The learners' interest can be stimulated by listening to sounds described in extracts taken from the book. The sounds can be downloaded from the Internet and bring to life parts of the text. Sounds also help the pre-teaching of vocabulary.

A very interesting Web 2.0 tool that promotes collaborative writing is the virtual notice board *Lino-it*; students are invited to contribute with their views on the characters of the story. *Tagxedo* is another tool which allows students to create word clouds. Younger students are encouraged to create their own cloud with groups of words related to the characters or plot of a story.

Conclusions

Literature enriches the EFL class with exposure to different genres. Technology can be a powerful ally when teaching literature. Even though it is not a panacea, it can stimulate learners' interest in extensive reading.

dprimalis@gmail.com
x.sotiriou@doukas.gr

8 English in tertiary education around the world

English for Academic Purposes (EAP) is truly a global endeavour, and this chapter takes us on a journey to universities around the world. The opening paper is by **Edward de Chazal**, who argues that authentic material can and should be used by lower-level students. **Jianying Du** then presents her findings from a Chinese study in which instruction in critical thinking skills was integrated with language instruction. Moving to listening skills, **Jody Skinner** demonstrates tips for engaging the audience in large lectures, in this case in a German university. Next, **Kirsten Dofs** points out the importance of developing learner autonomy though material designed for use in the self-access centre of a New Zealand university. The next set of papers in the chapter address aspects of academic writing. First, **Partha Sarathi Misra** describes the development of another kind of centre, this time a writing centre in an Indian university. The following two papers deal with abstracts and summaries respectively. **Tanja Psonder** outlines a technique for teaching abstract writing that she uses with her Austrian students, while **Natalya Eydelman** introduces several activities using Flickr toys which she has used successfully with her Russian students. Still in the realm of technology and writing, **Ania Rolinska** discusses the potential for new types of text within academe, using a multimodal approach to text creation. Finally, the need for global scholars to publish internationally is highlighted by **Shih-Chieh Chien**, who addresses this issue with reference to academic writers in Taiwan.

8.1 EAP at lower levels: authentic texts, scaffolded tasks, realistic outcomes

Edward de Chazal *Independent, Lulworth, UK*

Rationale

Authentic texts may be associated with higher levels, but they can be used successfully at lower levels (for example, B1) with appropriately staged and scaffolded tasks. EAP students can then build their confidence and competence in approaching new academic texts, increasingly independently. In this workshop I argued for such an approach using generic tasks which work with a wide range of academic texts.
Level
   In ELT, level is generally taken to mean language level, yet in EAP cognitive level is also highly relevant. A student's language and cognitive levels may not be closely related. In principle, as Grellet (1981: 8) argues, we can grade tasks rather than texts, thereby enabling students to effectively access key information in texts above their language level.

Materials: texts and contexts

Materials, in the form of texts, are all around us, but these need careful selection and integration into task sequences with clear learning outcomes. We worked with texts from an IB (International Baccalaureate) textbook, developed as published materials in *Oxford EAP Upper Intermediate B1+* (de Chazal and Rogers 2013: 13–14). This genre presents information designed for its target audience of IB students aged 16–18, and is appropriate and accessible for lower-level EAP students. As an authentic route into the text, we 'navigated' the whole text, starting with the textbook cover, publication details, and contents page. Students need to notice such information to contextualise the information in the text extract itself, and record the publication details (author, date, place of publication and publisher) to subsequently use whenever citing the text.

Essential elements

Academic texts like the IB texts are comprised of *essential elements*. These express the purpose of the text; for example, an *argument* in an essay or report needs the support of *citation* in the form of *evidence* and *exemplification*, which needs some *explanation* and then *evaluation*. Other frequently occurring essential elements include analysis, cause, definition, effect, problem, process, solution and summary. For Nesi and Gardner (2012), recount is also significant, for example, when recounting the method in a lab report. To understand a text, EAP students need to identify the essential elements and work out their purpose.

Perspective

Also essential to academic texts are perspectives. Perspectives reflect how we look at the world, and are associated with objectivity and analysis. Frequent perspectives include economic, environmental, geographical, global, historical, political and technological. Participants identified the perspectives in the first text: psychological, cognitive, behavioural, linguistic and mathematical. Such perspectives again express the purpose of the text by expressing the ways in which the writer approaches and analyses the topic and material.

Meaning

All the above aspects of a text inform its meaning. Participants learnt how to apply straightforward questions to determine the topic, purpose and main idea in a text: first at text level, then at paragraph level. Initially students need given choices for their questions, for example, 'What is the text about?' (a) people's experiences; (b) cognitive processing and psychology. Although much of the text was about people's experiences, these constituted the essential element of exemplification to help the writer explain the actual text topic: cognitive processing and psychology.

Language

The meanings in a text are conveyed by language. We examined sentence patterns which typically moved from the **topic** of the text as grammatical subject, through *generic academic language*, to the <u>new information</u> in the text, for example, **Cognitive**

psychology *is concerned with* <u>the structure and functions of the mind</u>. Participants could see the frequency of this pattern in the text: it was repeated in five out of six sentences which presented new information on the topic. The exception was the opening sentence of the text, in which the pattern was reversed to gain the reader's interest.

Generic questions

We then considered the set of questions for students to apply to any academic text:

• *'GAP'*: What are the genre, audience and purpose of the text?
• *Context*: What are the publication details, background and essential elements?
• *Topic*: What is the text about?
• *Perspectives*: What are the main perspectives?
• *Meaning*: What are the main points?
• *Stance*: What is the author's stance?
• *Citation*: How clearly does the citation support the content?
• *Language*: What language can I use?
• *Critical thinking*: How can I evaluate the content?
• *Next steps and independence*: How can I use the text?

The first five of these can be answered objectively and unambiguously, while the rest are more challenging and potentially subjective.

Conclusion

We concluded with the observation that repeated scaffolded generic tasks based on authentic texts enable students to become effective independent learners.

Edward@emdechazalconsulting.co.uk

References

de Chazal, E. and L. Rogers. 2013. *Oxford EAP Intermediate /B1+ Student's Book*. Oxford: Oxford University Press.

Grellet, F. 1981. *Developing Reading Skills*. Cambridge: Cambridge University Press.

Nesi, H. and S. Gardner. 2012. *Genres across the Disciplines: Student Writing in Higher Education*. Cambridge: Cambridge University Press.

8.2 Teaching critical thinking in EAP classrooms: an empirical study

Jianying Du *Huazhong University of Science and Technology, China*

Introduction

Compared with decades of English language teaching, EAP courses are relatively new, and the teaching of critical thinking in the EAP classes is an even more recent practice. There is a lack of empirical studies on pedagogically oriented language-and-thought integration.

On the basis of the four-step model (Halpern 2006) and theme-based instruction (Brinton *et al.* 1989), a theme-based cognitive approach is proposed, which integrates critical thinking in EAP teaching. Themes and topics in general EAP coursebooks are used not only for linguistic study but also as the basis for discussions. It is presumed that the integrative approach is effective and efficient if it enhances the learners' critical thinking without hindering their linguistic development.

The study

An 18-month experimental programme was conducted at a Chinese university. Participants were 102 medical freshmen and two EAP teachers. Student participants were evenly grouped according to similarity in age, gender, English language proficiency and cognitive maturity. The experimental group was distinguished from the control group through the use of the integrative approach.

A combination of critical thinking disposition inventories and critical thinking essay tests (Finken and Ennis 1993) was used to measure students' critical thinking abilities. Regular English tests arranged by the university were used to examine students' language skills. Questionnaires and interviews were administered to determine students' general reaction to the programme.

Findings

Results of the experiment confirmed that teaching critical thinking in the EAP class aids learners' development in criticality. At the end of the programme, students in the experimental group showed a noticeable growth in critical thinking skills and disposition. The control group, by contrast, experienced a dramatic drop in critical thinking disposition along with little improvement in critical thinking skills. Throughout the programme, no significant distance was detected between the two groups in terms of English language proficiency. This, nonetheless, does not necessarily indicate linguistic progress in either of the groups.

Qualitative data elicited from questionnaires and interviews revealed students' perceptions of and problems with the language-and-thought integration. Over 90 per cent of the experimental students reported enjoyment and cognitive benefit from the integrative approach. But nearly half of them recalled that they did not realise the helpfulness until a very late stage in the programme. Over one third of the students complained about the high cognitive demands and asked for extra instruction in linguistic items.

Discussion and implications

This empirical study suggests that formal instruction helps to foster students' critical thinking skills. Limitations and implications of the study, however, are not to be overlooked. Because of the focus on the experimental students and their cognitive growth, the study revealed but failed to explain the noticeable drop in critical thinking abilities of the control group. Longitudinal research is, therefore, needed to see whether the cognitive gap between the control and the experimental students will continue to grow or eventually fade away throughout their university years. The findings of such research may provide us with a clearer picture about the long-term effect of the integrative approach on students' cognitive development.

Efficiency is another concern. Firstly, integrating instruction in critical thinking naturally reduces the teaching time devoted to language, hence the possible linguistic disadvantage of the experimental students. In fact, despite the extra language instruction received, the control group did not achieve greater linguistic improvement than the experimental group. This means the cognitively oriented approach is hardly more, or less, effective than other EAP models in fostering linguistic ability. Or rather, the effectiveness of language instruction in these models is to be questioned.

Secondly, the development of critical thinking requires teaching, training, practising and monitoring. It also takes time for the students to get used to this unconventional approach and to acknowledge its positive impact. A major challenge raised in the integrative programme concerns teacher development. For the integration to be successful, teachers need to create a comfortable and friendly classroom atmosphere so as to encourage critical thinking. They should also allow and value silence in the classroom. In fact, a reasonable period of silence provides students with the opportunity to ponder the information they receive and formulate an adequate response, before sharing this with their teacher and fellow learners.

Therefore, teaching critical thinking is concerned more with *how* rather than *what* to teach. Conceptual knowledge and practical capability of critical thinking are a prerequisite for an effective language-and-thinking integration. Formal training, along with self-development, is needed for EAP teachers to understand and teach critical thinking.

dujianying@hust.edu.cn

References

Brinton, D. M., M. A. Snow and M. B. Wesche. 1989. *Content-Based Second Language Instruction.* New York: Newbury House.

Finken, M. and R. Ennis. 1993. 'Illinois critical thinking essay test'. (Retrieved on 25 November 2012 from http://faculty.education.illinois.edu/rhennis/documents)

Halpern, D. F. 2006. 'The nature and nurture of critical thinking' in R. Sternberg, R. Roediger, and D. F. Halpern (eds.). *Critical Thinking in Psychology.* Cambridge, Mass.: Cambridge University Press.

8.3 Reaching the audience: tips for making large lectures successfully unique

Jody Skinner *Universitaet Koblenz, Germany*

During my early years as a TEFL instructor for students pursuing education degrees at German universities I managed to avoid what many colleagues have to do much earlier in their careers: teach very large courses usually designated by the ominous term 'lecture'. But then it was my turn to create an introductory lecture to Anglo-American cultural studies with topics ranging from history and geography to education, political life, minorities, religion, the environment and the arts. The audience: between 80 and 250 students with varying levels of English competence. After my first panic attack, I thought back to all the fantastic lectures I'd experienced at IATEFL conferences over the years, remembered some of my favourite teachers, and soon began to relish the new challenge.

I started with a technique I'd applied many years earlier to my very first very small language courses: learning as many student names as quickly as possible. With enrolment lists and the help of Word, I could easily generate an alphabetical list of all first names. I decided to structure the lectures in as varied a way as possible, learning how to dim and turn up the lights to create a theatre-like atmosphere at the right moments, to speak with and without a microphone, to insert video and audio sequences into PowerPoint. Using my IATEFL and Hollywood role models (like the teachers in *To Sir, With Love* and *Dead Poets Society* and *The Mirror Has Two Faces*), I thought of anecdotes to make the content more personal and hopefully more memorable for the audience. The goal: keeping the students' interest throughout each of the dozen 90-minute lectures per semester. Since the lecture topics were wonderfully broad, I could choose clips from all sorts of British and American television documentaries, from movies, songs, news interviews to emphasise and focus the content of each lecture. The clips shouldn't last longer than a few minutes each with a total of not more than 20 per cent of the lecture to be multimedia, spread judiciously throughout the entire time and also giving my voice and legs a break (sitting as part of the audience for the clips). To create a recognition effect and establish a familiar ritual, most but not all of the lectures started with a collage sequence or brief clip, and many ended with music relevant for the content of the lecture just completed.

I made use of the anonymous feedback tool within our virtual learning environment platform Open-OLAT (Online Learning and Teaching) for student response to each and every lecture. And I explicitly mentioned and used their recommendations to tweak the lectures as the semester continued. If only we had had the technical possibility of using simultaneous electronic voting tools … but at least I could call out old-fashioned questions using student names as often as possible. I encouraged response by awarding points to those willing to participate, a daunting task for students in a foreign language in a large lecture hall, but a task which all seemed to enjoy, turning the lecture briefly into a game show. To make sure that the participants realised how much I valued their contributions—which supplied in effect some of the content I would've otherwise had to give myself—I created an honour roll of all students who'd got points with a summary of the content they'd shared and then uploaded the file to OLAT for all to benefit from. I also uploaded detailed handouts for the content of each lecture in key words and a list of all sources for each illustration, video and audio clip used as well as the academic sources with further information about the topic of each lecture.

In the very last lecture I tailor-made the content to fit both the topic—the arts—and each semester's different individuals. Laura and Hannah, to give just two examples, seemed surprised and delighted to hear their names sung by Johnny Mathis and Ella Fitzgerald, and everyone learned something about important popular American singers and composers 'just for fun'. Surprise, delight and fun were important goals in my attempt to make each lecture a unique live and never-to-be-exactly-repeated experience carefully timed and structured with content, with audience participation both spontaneous and planned, with multimedia clips, and with detailed handouts afterwards for those who didn't want to take copious notes.

The lectures needed more preparation than normal classes, but the investment paid off with applause and the term 'lecture' becoming auspicious for me and hopefully for my students too. Tips are summarised in Figure 8.3.1.

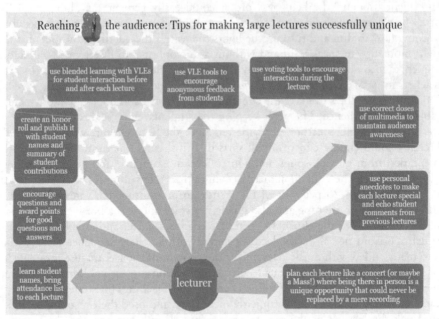

Figure 8.3.1: Tips for making large lectures successfully unique

jody@uni-koblenz.de

8.4 Autonomous study guides: bridging classroom and self-access centre learning

Kerstin Dofs *Christchurch Polytechnic Institute of Technology (CPIT), New Zealand*

Introduction

It is well known that all learners come with their own background and sets of needs and goals. Therefore, the pertinent question for anyone working in education is, how we can best meet the needs of all learners? Another closely linked area of enquiry is how we can assist learners so they become life-long learners. The answers to these questions may be found by exploring the concept of autonomous learning and teaching.

Benson and Voller (1997) state that over the years, autonomy has been viewed in terms of the following: situations where learners are studying on their own; a set of skills to be learned and applied in self-directed learning; as an inborn capacity; the exercising of learners' responsibility for their own learning; and a right for learners to determine and take control of the direction and content of their own learning.

However, as shown by Hornby and Dofs (2006), educational institutions have a particular responsibility to support autonomous learning development by

• providing timely support for learners and teachers for autonomous learning;
• providing suitable facilities which enable and allow this development; and
• teaching necessary skills and strategies for this to happen.

Besides, as pointed out by Dofs and Hobbs (2011), learners studying in self-access centres (SACs) benefit from both the range of easily accessible resources and the learning support they receive.

Background

In order to foster autonomous language learning (ALL), at Christchurch Polytechnic Institute of Technology (CPIT), all learners in the School of English are scheduled for one hour per week of supported self-studies in a Language Self-Access Centre (LSAC). Several research projects conducted by the author in recent years show a need for ALL support for both learners and teachers. Therefore, a set of ALL guides was created in conjunction with experienced teachers and their learners. The guides enable a flexible and supportive approach to ensure learning takes place at a deeper level. They assist with ALL, both inside and outside the classroom, as they help bridge the gap between the two study situations. They target three levels of English: pre-intermediate, intermediate and upper intermediate.

The student guide supports students in taking ownership of their own learning using quotes, tips and ideas for self-study. Study strategies and resources are recommended for improvement of reading, writing, speaking and listening skills, as well

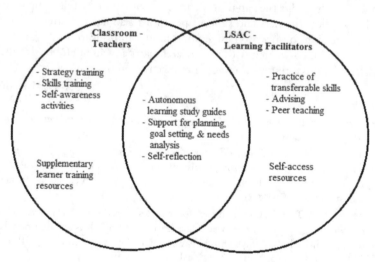

Figure 8.4.1: The CPIT self-study model

as for increasing grammar and vocabulary knowledge. The teacher guide contains the student guide and additional explanations, ideas, and instructions for teachers. This guide also has awareness building exercises for classroom use on self-knowledge, motivation, style, strategies and evaluation.

The model for utilising these guides and bridging the gap between the classroom and the LSAC combines transferrable skills and strategies practice in the classroom with supported self-studies in the LSAC (see Figure 8.4.1). All learners are provided with a planning document, for initial planning in the classroom and later for organising the self-study time in the LSAC in more detail. Students also have access to a range of self-study resources in the centre.

Research

The study guides were rewritten in 2012 to suit other institutions, and a research project was set up at CPIT in Christchurch and at Unitec in Auckland to trial and evaluate the benefits of the guides.

The results indicate that students learnt about useful resources, learnt how to study and learn, and they said they improved both language skills and ability. Some students pointed out that they felt like more active learners and they became more aware of their learning styles and their weak and strong language areas. Moreover, they said they received useful help with planning, organising and focusing on their preferred self-studies. Finally, they learnt to keep a record of what they had done so they could recognise and monitor their progress.

The ALL guides seem to fulfil some of the needs for autonomous learning support that teachers and students may require. However, some measures are needed to maximise the benefits of using them. For example, students need time set aside for self-study and a thorough induction to the self-study time, while teachers need to commit to the scheme and schedule time on learner training activities in the classroom, and actively bridge the gap to students' self-study time by following up on their out-of-class studies. Teachers and support personnel also need to attend professional development sessions on how to best support autonomous learning.

This summary is co-written with my research partner, Moira Hobbs, from Unitec, New Zealand, and is a result of on-going research collaboration.

kerstin.dofs@cpit.ac.nz

References

Benson, P. and P. Voller (eds.). 1997. *Autonomy and Independence in Language Learning.* Harlow: Pearson Education.

Dofs, K. and M. Hobbs. 2011. *Guidelines for Maximising Student Use of Independent Learning Centres: Support for ESOL Learners.* Christchurch and Auckland, New Zealand: Ako Aotearoa. (Retrieved from http://akoaotearoa.ac.nz/ako-hub/ako-aotearoa-southern-hub/maximising-student-use-of-ILCs)

Hornby, M. and K. Dofs. 2006. 'Horses for courses or courses for horses: Uptake of autonomous learning opportunities by staff and learners in English as an additional language programmes at Christchurch Polytechnic Institute of Technology'. Conference Proceedings, CLESOL 2006 Conference, Napier, New Zealand.

8.5 The university writing centre and academic writing in English

Partha Sarathi Misra *Azim Premji University, Bangalore, India*
IATEFL Ray Tongue Scholarship winner

Introduction

Though postgraduate students studying in Indian universities are generally required to write term papers and dissertations in English, there is no support system for enhancing their academic writing skills in English. Responding to the needs of the students, a newly established Indian university located in Bangalore started a Writing Centre in 2011 with the objectives of (a) familiarising its students with the relationship between the forms and practices of disciplinary genres; and (b) empowering them to articulate their ideas and perspectives as per the norms of academic writing in English. As I was associated with the Writing Centre since its inception, I will highlight the strategies I used to enhance the academic writing skills of the students who reported to the Centre for help.

Developing academic writing skills

Students reporting to the Writing Centre wanted help with English writing skills required for writing assignments, case studies and term papers. They did not know how to write academic papers as they had never been taught how to present and organise facts, opinions, thoughts and ideas in a writing style that is acceptable in western universities. In order to instil confidence in the students, I started to familiarise them with genre-specific written discourses. As a facilitator, I believed that non-native learners of English could acquire academic writing skills in 'developmental stages, through practice, through reading, and through exposure to models' (Casanave 2012: 289).

Using stylistics to explore academic texts

I asked the students to identify the lexical chain of genre-specific lexical items, to identify the topic sentences, to identify the cohesive devices, to analyse the narrative structure of the text and to identify the point of view of the author. A search for these stylistic features prompted them to read a given text not to locate specific information but to determine the ways of thinking about the subject matter discussed in a particular text. I also asked them to find out how a text worked and the kind of reasoning the particular text employed to arrive at a conclusion. While interacting with the students, I prompted them to produce relevant ideas by aligning what others had said on a particular topic with what they thought on that topic (Graff and Birkenstein 2010).

Teaching writing as a process

Though the students coming to the Writing Centre viewed academic writing as a product, I started to tell them that it was a process to be nurtured over a period of time. Instead of providing guidelines for improving their skills in academic writing in English, I prompted them to write a draft, to revise it and to produce a final version. One-on-one conversations with me gave the students the required space to develop their writing skills without suppressing their critical perspective. During my sessions, I worked with them to enhance their capacity to analyse, plan, write and revise their assignments in English. I never revised or edited their work; I created capacity in the students to identify and address the problems in their writing and develop their own style. While giving feedback, my approach was 'enabling rather than gate-keeping' (Alexander *et al.* 2008:18), and the students accepted it gracefully.

Conclusion

A stylistic approach to genre-specific texts sharpened the language sensitivity of the students and made them aware of the intermingling of *what* was said and *how* it was said. With many students, structuring their ideas in writing was more problematic than structuring their paragraphs, and it was often noticed that the lack of linearity in processing the thought content affected the processing of the writing output. The most challenging task faced by the students coming to the Writing Centre was the challenge of cohesion, thematic as well as linguistic. Often, there was a mismatch between the coherence of thought and the coherence of language. Again, even when some students were competent enough to develop an argument in English orally, they were confused about doing so in writing. Proficiency in speaking in academic English did not guarantee proficiency in academic writing. As they were not familiar with the conventions of academic writing, they needed mentoring and scaffolding.

A genre-specific stylistic analysis of academic texts and a constructivist pedagogy helped me a lot in helping the students to improve their academic writing skills. The experience of the Writing Centre will help me in designing a course in academic writing for non-native learners struggling with English in non-native contexts.

Partha.misra@azimpremjifoundation.org

References

Alexander, O., S. Argent and J. Spencer. 2008. *EAP Essentials: A Teacher's Guide to Principles and Practice*. Reading: Garnet Publishing Ltd.

Casanave, C. P. 2012. 'Controversy and change in how we view L2 writing in international contexts' in L. Alsagoff, S. L. McKay, G. Hu and W. A. Renandya (eds.). *Principles and Practices for Teaching English as an International Language*. New York: Routledge.

Graff, G. and C. Birkenstein. 2010. *They Say I Say: The Moves That Matter in Academic Writing*. New York: W.W. Norton & Company.

8.6 Abstract writing for advanced students in a technical discipline

Tanja Psonder *FH JOANNEUM University of Applied Sciences, Graz, Austria*

Background

Advanced students of a technical discipline in the obligatory English classroom in tertiary education are exposed to different written genres in English. One genre they are frequently confronted with is abstracts. They need to be trained carefully in the ability to read texts, to process the information and to write abstracts, as abstracts should be a compelling but very brief introduction to a subject. For this purpose, abstracts have to be fully self-contained although they convey as much information as the text that follows them. In order to guide students in writing compelling and well-structured abstracts, a six-step structure is applied that should help them filter out problematic areas in content, terminology and structure.

Task

In the classroom the students are asked to read some sample abstracts to recognise the format, the structure and the organisation of abstracts that precede papers in a technical discipline. In general, abstracts should be concise, descriptive and clear to the reader. Therefore, writers have to carefully select which words are necessary to convey the meaning of the long text. Hence, careful reading and the visual highlighting of the main message form an important introduction into this topic. Further reading of the abstracts should, of course, develop a deeper understanding and offer the students the possibility to focus on terminology and specific keywords.

Following this introduction to the topic of abstract writing, the students select one discipline-related text. The texts vary between four and six pages in length and are taken from current technical magazines. Once they have decided on a text, they must read it thoroughly and then discuss the content and the ESP-relevant terminology in small groups of three students each. To ease their preparative work in the selection of the relevant content and terminology they are provided with a six-step structure, as follows:

- Why do you care about the problem(s) and the results? [motivation/problem statement]
- What problem(s) are you trying to solve? Why are you carrying out this project or study? [purpose/aim]
- What did you do to solve or to make progress on the problem(s)? [methods]
- What are your findings so far? [results]
- What are the implications of your findings? [discussion/evaluation]
- What do the findings mean? Which conclusions can be drawn? [conclusion]

The students' task now is to follow these six questions, which should enable them to select the main content of the long text by answering them in chronological order. With the help of these pieces of information the students should pursue their main task, to write a concise paragraph or two that mirrors the message of the original text and entices the reader to learn more about the subject.

Accompanying aspects

The actual abstract writing process often entails other difficulties for the students such as the appropriate use of transitions within paragraphs, or between paragraphs in longer abstracts, so that the abstracts are cohesive and clear for the reader. Besides, the suitable choice of verbs and phrases that really express what writers want to say need to be considered. Factual knowledge includes the discrete facts and basic elements that experts use when communicating about their discipline, understanding it, and organising it systematically; there is little abstraction to factual knowledge (Pickard 2007). For this purpose, they should use measurable verbs and phrases which are free of ambiguity and vagueness. This aspect comes along with another feature of academic writing, hedging, which could be seen as a contradiction to the previous point. Hedging is a concept of cautious or vague language use that is intended to soften and modify the statement made by the author. A typical feature in academic writing, it needs to be introduced to the students to raise their awareness of a probably higher frequency of modal verbs, modal adverbs, introductory verbs, that-clauses, etc. Although academic writing is seen as factual writing that conveys facts and figures, writers nonetheless make a decision about their personal attitude towards a particular subject.

Conclusion

Students have difficulties in producing a clear, cohesive and coherent text; consequently, they should be trained in writing abstracts that are reader oriented, logically structured and linked, and that convey the relevant information while using the appropriate terminology. Albert Einstein says 'life should be as simple as possible, but not one bit simpler' (n.d.) and the same could be said about abstract writing. The mere reduction of words does not result in a good abstract. It is the selection of the relevant information that counts.

tanja.psonder@fh-joanneum.at

References

Pickard, M. J. 2007. 'The new Bloom's Taxonomy: an overview for family and consumer Sciences'. *Journal of Family and Consumer Sciences Education* 25/1: 45–55. (Retrieved on 13 May 2013 from http://natefacs.org/JFCSE/v25no1/v25no1Pickard.pdf)

Vallin, R. W. n.d. 'A Guide to Writing an Abstract'. *The Mathematical Association of America.* (Retrieved on 15 September 2011 from http://www.maa.org/students/writing%20abstracts.pdf)

8.7 Creative summary writing activities with technology

Natalya Eydelman *Novosibirsk State University, Novosibirsk, Russia*

My presentation was devoted to the discussion of a number of activities aimed at making summary writing more motivating for my students. They are majoring in teaching or translation studies and mostly have an intermediate to upper-intermediate level of English. One of the purposes of suggesting that students complete the described activities in this format is to demonstrate that writing can be an enjoyable and engaging activity—not simply something that the learners have to do to meet the course requirements.

There is a considerable body of research into the issues associated with motivation; in this case I looked into what can motivate students to write. According to Pintrich and Schunk (2002), learners' involvement and participation are more likely to be higher if they find a task more interesting and significant in terms of what it can help them to learn to do. Based on this assumption, I have developed a number of activities using Flickr toys (http://www.pimpampum.net/toys/); this is a set of tools associated with Flickr (http://flickr.com), a photo- and video-sharing website. The use of these tools can make the process of writing more creative and motivating. The choice of these tools was conditioned by the fact that they match some of the objectives of the writing class I teach; in addition, these tools are comparatively easy to use and are free.

Summarising is an essential skill for EAP students; thus, activities aimed at mastering this skill are typical in the language classroom and are offered to learners at different levels of instruction. Since they are quite common, they can become rather mechanical or even boring. I took this into consideration when designing the activities described below using Flickr toys.

All three Flickr toys described in my presentation use a selection of photos as their source material. These photos can be searched by either keyword or tag search and then associated with a phrase, sentence or a whole story, depending on the chosen tool.

- The first Flickr toy, Phrasr (http://www.pimpampum.net/phrasr), is an application which matches a phrase with images from Flickr, with one image corresponding to one word in the phrase. I have asked students to use Phrasr to write one-sentence summaries of their reading. A variation of this activity is thinking of a proverb that best summarises an article or a story. Writing one sentence summaries can help students to express their ideas more concisely and with greater precision.
- The second Flickr toy, Bubblr (http://www.pimpampum.net/bubblr), allows students to create comic strips. Creating a Bubblr is similar to creating a Phrasr, except that instead of writing a word or phrase matching the image, a story is created. It can consist of a single photo or a set, with one or more speech bubbles representing what the characters in the image say or think. Again, I used this tool to ask students to summarise their reading or create comic strips connected with the topics we discussed. In addition, Bubblr can be used to create presentations which are visually more appealing and engaging.
- The third Flickr toy, Bookr (http://www.pimpampum.net/bookr/), is used to create digital books based on Flickr images. I suggested to my students that they use this tool to write extended summaries of their reading. In addition, it can also be used to write a story or an article or create a presentation.

Using Flickr images to accompany academic writing can make learning this skill more engaging for students. They can be asked to compare their versions of summaries and choose the best one. Summary writing can be done individually or in groups; it can be followed by a discussion of summaries created by different (groups of) students, addressing, for example, how well they are written and which one has more visual appeal for learners.

Judging from the informal feedback my students gave me, they found mastering their summary writing skills with the help of the described tools more motivating. As a result, they became more engaged in their writing process, which made writing easier and more enjoyable for them. To quote one of my students, 'I have never imagined that I will immerse in the process of writing […] so deeply.

eydelman.natalia@gmail.com

Reference

Pintrich, P. R. and D. H. Schunk. 2002. *Motivation in Education: Theory, Research, and Applications* (second edition). Englewood Cliffs, N.J.: Prentice Hall.

8.8 Going multimodal: a design approach to writing

Ania Rolinska *Freelance, Glasgow, UK*

Contemporary times strongly feature visual artefacts, technologies and practices of production and consumption. This visual turn provides creative possibilities for designing new kinds of texts. The fact that designing such texts involves more than writing a logically structured linear composition might have certain implications for education.

Traditionally, creating multimedia artefacts is associated with leisure-time activities, i.e. home-based literacies (Carpenter 2009). Tertiary-level non-arts students are hardly ever expected to present their research in any form other than a written report. There is a fear that the Internet might undermine academic values by tainting them with what is deemed to be home and pop culture oriented. Such fears are not new. Socrates thought that writing 'will create forgetfulness in the learners' souls, because they will not use their memories' (469–399 BC). Yet one could argue that, over centuries, writing has instigated higher cognitive functions, creating analytic thought unknown in the solely oral culture.

So, although caution is needed, such fears might not be fully justified. The Internet as a medium of learning creates new possibilities for academic writers because the logic of digital texts is different. Technology democratically supports numerous modes, allowing one to 'write' with image, video, audio and layout, in addition to words. The underlying assumption here is that meanings are made, distributed and interpreted through many representational and communicational resources, of which language is but one (Kress and van Leeuwen 2001). All the modes are considered equal and partial in regard to constructing meaning, requiring that attention is paid to all of them. This is called a multimodal approach to communication.

A multimodal text makes use of a number of modes, and each of them actively participates in the meaning-making process. This means that images, for example, do not merely serve the purpose of 'reinforcement' or 'elaboration' (i.e. are inferior to the word); instead, they might create new layers of information by separating or linking different domains, or by juxtaposing texts to create tension, critique, similarity or contrast. To comprehend this better it is worth comparing the underlying logic of word and image. The former involves the presentation of time and sequence, the latter space and simultaneity. Therefore, visuality foregrounds the arrangement and display of elements, and as a result salience and connection whereas textuality relies on clause structures and sequencing.

Consequently, multimodal configurations often interrupt and fragment the genres and forms of texts, making them more flexible and fluid. This might threaten common understandings of authorship, knowledge of academic concepts and discourse. For example, a notion of an academic essay becomes problematic unless it is explored from the perspective of the genre theory elaborated on by Carpenter (2009) for digital environments. He looks at genre systems as operating within activity systems, thus shifting focus from form to function. A genre is not seen as a static category of discourse that displays certain formal and formalised features but a dynamic process that operates within, between and among users (writers and readers) and systems (Internet and academia).

Arranging modes into a coherent whole on the screen requires experimentation and risk-taking. It reconceptualises practices of writing, reading, learning and being literate. It requires that literacy, or rather literacies, are seen as practices rather than isolated sets of competences. This enables the student to negotiate a broader range of text types, including multimodal ones. These new practices of production and consumption offer new possibilities for identity formation, including areas of scholarship and academic discourse. Designing a multimodal assignment often resembles an intellectual/creative crisis, but being an engaging process, it instigates various cognitive processes involving creativity in finding alternative solutions and multiple strategies for tackling the task, dealing with tension due to manoeuvring across the boundaries, which overall helps the student become more autonomous.

Of course there are also numerous issues here. In regard to production, some students might feel disadvantaged because of a lack of technical expertise or visual sensitivity. There is a fine line between a conscious design and random choices of aesthetically pleasing visuals used for the sake of embellishment only. Kolb (2004) indicates that multimodal compositions often feature strong introductions but conclusions tend to be weaker or even non-existent. Since digital writing might lead to weaker argumentation, a question arises at what stage in education such experiments could be introduced. Another thing to explore is assessment as there might be a discrepancy between the author's intention and the assessor's interpretation, being it over- or under-interpretation.

annarolinska@yahoo.co.uk

References

Carpenter, R. 2009. 'Boundary negotiations: electronic environments as interface'. *Computers and Composition* 26: 138–48.

Kolb, D. 2004. 'The revenge of the page'. (Retrieved on 11 April 2013 from http://www.dkolb.org/fp002.kolb.pdf)

Kress, G. and T. van Leeuwen. 2001. *Multimodal Discourses: The Modes and Media of Contemporary Communication.* New York: Oxford University Press.

8.9 Writing for scholarly publication in English for Chinese researchers

Shih-Chieh Chien *Taipei Medical University, Taiwan*

Background

In an era of globalisation, in which professionals need to communicate effectively across languages and cultures, the importance of writing for scholarly purposes has increased in EFL settings. Studies of publication in English by non-native speakers (NNS), particularly in the field of humanities and social sciences (for example, Curry and Lillis 2010; Li and Flowerdew 2009), and of scholars who work with NNS (Jenkins *et al.* 1993) reveal that many NNS need to work even longer and harder to write, publish and get promoted in their careers. In Taiwan, issues related to publishing in international English-language journals by NNS have recently attracted considerable attention from Taiwanese government authorities, as well as from universities and researchers. Most universities in Taiwan have started to provide both 'carrots' and 'sticks' to encourage researchers to publish internationally. 'Carrots' (incentives) are in the form of financial aid for researchers to publish internationally, and 'sticks' (pressures) are in the form of more rigorous requirements for senior researchers to get promoted unless they publish internationally. Given the importance of this issue, this study aims to expand our understanding and to explore issues of writing for scholarly publication in English for Chinese researchers in the field of arts and humanities in higher education, and to inform some practices in writing for scholarly publication.

Research design

This study sought to answer the following questions:
- What are researchers' perceptions of publishing in English in the field of arts and humanities?
- What are their problems with publishing in English?
- What are their needs for successful publishing?

Participants in the study were 30 academics in the field of arts and humanities, including linguistics, literature, translation, philosophy, drama, musicology, fine arts, history and anthropology, from six universities in Taiwan. The investigation comprised in-depth semi-structured individual interviews with them in order to establish a broad understanding of the issues concerning their perceived needs regarding scholarly publication and their experiences of learning to write.

Findings

Three salient themes emerged through the study: the need to publish in English; difficulties in writing in English (vocabulary, grammar, discourse organisation and tone); and the need for academic writing support.

The first major theme emerging in the present study is the need for publication in English. As indicated by the researchers, scholarly publication is crucial for anyone wishing to work in academia: success or failure to publish can determine a researcher's career prospects. A further theme is the difficulties Chinese researchers experience in trying to get their work published in English. First, they must write in a second language for the purpose of convincing their peers. Second, they are required to write with lucidity and coherence, in accordance with the format and organisation required by certain authorities, such as journal and book editors and reviewers. Third, there are cultural differences among themselves and their peer readers which may lead to misinterpretation. Finally, researchers may have a rich knowledge in their field of study, but they still need assistance in applying that knowledge, particularly in cases where their first language is very different from English.

Conclusion

The findings reveal that publishing in international journals has become a requirement for researchers, but that they regard themselves as disadvantaged due to their limited proficiency in English compared with native English speakers. They do not have sufficient vocabulary, and they find it relatively difficult to construct a good argument for their research in English. The needs analysis framework offers an important insight: NNS are motivated to learn to write for publication despite their perceived English language incompetence. They are motivated to remedy the situation because English plays a role in their research, and they hope to improve their own English writing. In the Chinese EFL context, such as Taiwan, in the present study writers in the field of arts and humanities, as academics themselves, have documented their attempts to negotiate a path between the limited resources of the education sector and the growing publication demands placed upon them. Academic writing is an important issue that needs great attention and support from the academic community.

chien.paul@gmail.com

References

Curry, M. J. and T. Lillis. 2010. 'Academic research networks: Accessing resources for English-medium publishing'. *English for Specific Purposes* 29/4: 281–95.

Jenkins, S., M. K. Jordan and P. O'Weilland. 1993. 'The role of writing in graduate engineering education: A survey of faculty beliefs and practices'. *English for Specific Purposes* 12: 51–67.

Li, Y. and J. Flowerdew. 2009. 'International engagement versus local commitment: Hong Kong academics in the humanities and social sciences writing for publication'. *Journal of English for Academic Purposes* 8: 279–93.

9 Preparing learners for the workforce

English for Specific (Academic) Purposes is a growing area in ELT, and the papers in this chapter represent approaches to career-specific ELT around the world. The scene is set by **Michael Carrier, Mike Milanovic, David Nunan and Kathleen M. Bailey**; in the opening paper they summarise current approaches to curriculum, assessment and the use of technology. This is followed by six papers, all of which address ELT for specific careers. **Jana Jilkova** presents activities she has used with her marketing and PR students in the Czech Republic, while **Glória Regina Loreto Sampaio** outlines the very specific training needs of future interpreters in Brazil. Urban planning is the focus of **Rhoda McGraw**'s paper, in which she describes courses she has developed for French learners. **Adrian Millward-Sadler and Annette Casey** then describe the effect on motivation of using model kits. The final two papers in this chapter address English for business communication. **Barry Tomalin** offers tips to help non-native speakers deal more successfully with conference calls in business settings; and **Adrian Pilbeam** presents practical activities designed to improve the intercultural communication skills of those involved in business.

9.1 English for the 21st-century workforce: challenges and solutions

Michael Carrier *Cambridge English Language Assessment,* **Mike Milanovic**
  Cambridge English Language Assessment, **David Nunan** *Anaheim University,*
  Calif., USA and **Kathleen M. Bailey** *Monterey Institute of International*
  Studies, Calif., USA

As teachers of English for 21st-century workforce personnel, we face particular challenges that demand creative solutions. This panel presentation focused on those challenges, especially in curriculum, assessment and technology.

The panellists were volunteer Board members of the International Research Foundation for English Language Education (TIRF), a foundation started by TESOL in 1998. TIRF's mission includes generating research, applying research to practical problems, disseminating information on language teaching and learning and influencing policy with research findings.

Curriculum (David Nunan)

A major outcome of TIRF's recent study of workforce English (Fitzpatrick and O'Dowd 2012) is the identification of a paradigm shift in workplace education. Those authors argued that English is a tool to help people carry out their daily workplace practices, integrated with other skills needed in the 21st-century workplace.

Three key curricular issues emerged from that study. First, task- and project-based approaches differ from 'traditional' approaches to curriculum development in that they are learner- rather than subject-centred. Second, text authenticity in language teaching entails using written and spoken texts that were not produced for pedagogical purposes, but rather for natural communication. Task authenticity has to do with the extent to which a pedagogical task mirrors the communicative acts that people carry out in the world beyond the classroom. Third, just-in-time learning refers to putting effort into learning something now because of a need for it tomorrow. Workers and employers must meet the challenge of setting realistic learning goals.

Language assessment (Mike Milanovic)

Assessment should be considered at the outset and not as an afterthought. One of the greatest challenges in workforce language assessment is the form it should take. It is important to think about the methods of assessment, how the test results will be used and the desired impact of the test.

Another main challenge has to do with deciding what to test (the construct to be measured). It is important to determine the purpose of the test and the real-world linguistic demands that are placed on employees while they are doing their work. Part of the decision-making in this phase concerns appropriate levels of difficulty used in the assessment procedures. Lastly, it is important to ensure that test specifications are met in practice. This goal can be accomplished by confirming that the assessment criteria and the test format have been appropriately defined. Additionally, the item writing must be managed effectively. The test materials must be appropriately pretested and calibrated. Next the test must be administered, marked, and graded appropriately. Finally, an effective monitoring system must be in place for supporting future improvements in the assessment system (for example, determining test performance, detecting bias, etc.).

Technology (Michael Carrier)

English is a global tool for education, employment and mobility. Over one billion people are learning English, and they realise the economic value of having high levels of proficiency. Possessing English skills can improve salary levels by 20 to 40 per cent (Pinon and Haydon 2010).

Online courses for business and professional staff, and courses or apps for vocational learners such as taxi drivers and those in the tourism industry, can help learners improve their workplace skills even when traditional classes are unavailable or unfunded. The added value of technology for workforce learners is that they can study anytime and anyplace without interrupting work routines.

The use of technology requires new and innovative pedagogical models such as the 'flipped classroom': here, much of the preparation and cognitive learning takes place *outside* the classroom, using technology.

It is also possible to use video-conference technology to develop remote learning models, such as Uruguay's Plan Ceibal, where the teacher is in a different city from the students and connected by video link. Student devices are used for software-based activities.

Employers must ensure that workers have access to appropriate technology tools and learning materials so that they can continue to develop their language skills in and out of the workplace. Providing online language programs is significantly less expensive than providing face-to-face learning programs.

Conclusion (Kathi Bailey)

To address these challenges, TIRF has published a series of *Key Questions* papers that address important, unanswered questions regarding English policies and practices in the global workforce (for example, Fitzpatrick and O'Dowd 2012; TIRF 2009). The Foundation is trying to address people beyond the language teaching profession. For instance, TIRF published an article for international business educators. There are Chinese translations of two of the commissioned studies, published by *English Career* magazine in Taiwan. TIRF's website also provides other resources about English for the 21st-century workforce.

davidcnunan@gmail.com
Milanovic.M@cambridgeenglish.org
mcarrier@btconnect.com
kbailey@miis.edu

References

Fitzpatrick, A. and R. O'Dowd. 2012. *English at Work: An Analysis of Case Reports about English Language Training for the 21st –century Workforce.* Monterey, Calif.: TIRF. (Retrieved on 10 June 2013 from http://www.tirfonline.org/wp-content/uploads/2012/04/TIRF_EnglishAtWork_OnePageSpread_2012.pdf)

Pinon, R. and J. Haydon. 2010. *The Benefits of the English Language for Individuals and Societies: Quantitative Indicators from Cameroon, Nigeria, Rwanda, Bangladesh and Pakistan.* London: The British Council & Euromonitor International.

TIRF. 2009. *The Impact of English and Plurilingualism in Global Corporations.* Monterey, Calif.: TIRF. (Retrieved on 10 June 2013 from http://www.tirfonline.org/wp-content/uploads/2010/09/TIRF_KeyQuestionsWorkforcePaper_Final_25March2009.pdf)

9.2 Activities to develop students' language skills while supporting their careers

Jana Jilkova *Charles University, Prague, Czech Republic*

The world around us changes, so old professions die out and new ones emerge. The Faculty of Social Sciences at Charles University has reacted to these developments and offers a course specifically aimed at future workers in marketing and public relations (PR). The goal of the newly introduced two-semester course, *English for Marketing*, is to give students insight into the field and support their ability to communicate in this area in their native language and at least one foreign language. To enable maximum profit from the course (compare *SurveyLang*), the linguistic items, marketing content and techniques used should reflect the students' varied histories of language learning, awareness of marketing and learning preferences.

In the first year the course took place in two groups of almost 50 students with vastly differing backgrounds (English B2 to C2, and zero-to-expert knowledge of the field), in a room with poor acoustics and with desks fixed into rows. These disadvantages challenged me to look for more effective ways to teach. A curriculum was established, based on Ericksen's statement, 'Students learn what they care about and remember what they understand' (1984: 51), and an e-learning platform was created to offer material for study and to enable the publication of student work.

SISI

The SISI approach (Something Important, Something Interesting) helped to further increase student motivation and interest. The aim was for students to deal regularly with topics from our subject area, assess them and reflect on them. Students prepared at least three new marketing-relevant press releases every semester (80–110 words each, sources attributed). A brief space for discussion on those currently published was included in every lesson. This task both extended the students' knowledge of the field and increased their vocabulary. At the same time, the accuracy of the language structures used was monitored and, depending on their importance and frequency of occurrence, additional exercises to remove errors and drill the correct use of English were carried out.

Personal SWOT

The students showed great interest when given the task of carrying out self-evaluation with the help of a SWOT analysis. The SWOT analysis—a standard tool in marketing—identifies strengths, weaknesses, opportunities and threats, with regard to future possible developments. Students were required to carry out a SWOT analysis of their relationship to the field and to the study of foreign languages; they were given the choice of making their work accessible to other students, or limiting

SWOT analysis of my personality

STRENGTHS
- Focused
- Scrupulous in labour issues
- Communicative
- Friendly

WEAKNESSES
- Sometimes lazy
- Procrastinating things at the last minute, especially at the school when I am bored.
- Moody

OPPORTUNITIES
- Working in PR agency and after studies work full-time
- Be a part of organization team of MISS UK
- To finish my studies soon

THREATS
- Too many things doing together (three jobs and school)
- Little time for school

Figure 9.2.1: Example of a SWOT analysis

access to just the tutor. It was a challenge to get an overview of the students with whom I subsequently worked for two semesters. See Aneta's work in Figure 9.2.1.

At the end of the semester, an activity was included in which students reflected on their SWOT analyses, evaluated them and carried out up-to-date versions. A number of them greatly appreciated this reflection, including the chance for discussion with fellow-students who provided additional points of view on their personalities. Martin H. said:

> If I look at myself using the SWOT analysis, I can start to really develop my human and professional potential. From this point of view I consider SWOT analysis as a useful tool how to critically reflect my personality. So that here is my attempt of personal SWOT analysis.

Application

For practical work, accurate communication, time management and teamwork are also important. These skills were developed using an international cooperative project called *Advertising across Europe*. The aim was to share and compare information and opinions about marketing in participating countries. Students prepared presentations using interesting video ads and shared their personal and expert opinions on how the ads worked and their effectiveness. The project can be accessed at http://e4marketing.pbworks.com.

A significant part of the course was an introduction to presentation techniques and the preparation and implementation of students' own presentations, which were also evaluated by their fellow students. A presentation formed part of the final evaluation of each student, together with a written test, an essay and the evaluation of other activities.

Conclusion (and the job market)

The course showed how activities which develop general and expert competences play an important role in preparing students for their future careers. These activities enable their active involvement, the application of their own experience and opinions and the sharing of these with others; they not only provide motivation but can also significantly support their relationship to their field of activity and society and improve their chances in the job market.

(Uncorrected student work published with their permission)

jajilkova@gmail.com

References

Ericksen, S. C. 1984. *The Essence of Good Teaching: Helping Students Learn and Remember What They Learn*. San Francisco: Jossey Bass.

SurveyLang: First European Survey on Language Competences. (Retrieved on 1 November 2012 from http://dokumenti.ncvvo.hr/ESLC/Final_Report_Eng.pdf)

9.3 Listening and speaking skills: the case of interpreters-to-be

Glória Regina Loreto Sampaio *Pontifical Catholic University of São Paulo, Brazil*

Competence in interpreting encompasses grasping the sense of a given oral text and providing an oral rendering of it into another language immediately afterwards. To achieve the necessary level of competence, future interpreters should fulfil a series of basic requirements, which include high-level listening, speaking and oral translation skills. At a further stage, they will have to develop specific skills in the different interpreting modes: consecutive interpretation, sight translation and simultaneous interpretation.

Experience shows that students of interpreting are more frequently than not at a threshold level; that is, they are reasonably close to satisfying the basic requirements and, in the initial stages of the training period, they must devote considerable time and effort to developing and honing their oral skills. In other words, from that threshold level, listening skills must achieve a level of excellence so that the sense of any given oral text is thoroughly grasped, taking into account linguistic and paralinguistic elements intrinsic to the expression of the message. Speaking skills, in turn, should achieve a level as close as possible to that of a public speaker, bearing in mind factors such as clarity of expression, precision, coherence, cohesion, attention to prosody, idiomatic use of language and consideration of the target public.

What is more, in between these two basic skills lies competence in re-expressing what was understood in one language in the linguistic and cultural framework of another language: oral translation skills. There is no doubt that for some, this is a great challenge, if not a rather daunting task.

Considering the specificities of the profession they are about to embrace, in the first stages of their training interpreters-in-the-making should be given suitable opportunities to develop the necessary fundamental skills. Proper methodology with well-devised exercises and activities will help to boost and refine listening and speaking skills, with room for preliminary oral translation skills. Thus the initial training will represent the stepping stones to the next stages, when specific interpreting modes will be tackled.

To achieve this, the process should necessarily include the following:

1 *Active listening*, which means listening attentively and processing information with a clear mind, namely, being able to re-express the sense, intention and content of the text, either in the same language or, at a further stage, in another language. It also implies observing the way the text is structured and the type of discourse, and detecting the main and secondary ideas with due attention to cultural elements.

2 *Note-taking*, which helps re-expression, once again requires processing information. Essential for discrete elements of the text, note-taking can be done intuitively at first, and then by following some basic guidelines (main ideas/examples/key words/discourse markers).

3 *Shadowing* the oral text, that is, reciting it concomitantly in the same language, as you listen to it, helps to improve pronunciation, intonation, stress patterns and

prosody. Being a dual-task cognitive activity, shadowing paves the way for simultaneous interpretation.

4 *Speaking, re-expression* or *message reformulation* can be done initially in the source language (by paraphasing or summarising), and later in the target language (gist interpretation), with special attention to a series of factors, including completeness of sentences, quality of voice, rhythm and fluidity.

In between active listening and re-expression in the target language lies oral translation competence or competence in interpreting, which implies being able to reformulate a given oral message in another language, not only considering grammar, lexis, register, type and tone of discourse and target audience, but also and most importantly, doing it idiomatically.

Throughout the process, trainers should also provide motivation, exposure to a wide variety of topics, intensive practice with authentic audio and video materials, clear aims and evaluation criteria, constant guidance and feedback on the progress made, extra class study and skills practice, and contact with professionals. Moreover, students should be constantly reminded that success in interpreter training will depend mostly on their commitment, self-discipline, willpower and effort.

Dealing with listening and speaking skills in the early stages of interpreter training is a crucial methodological component. Firstly, it will enable students to re-assess their skills and capabilities, with proper guidance and time to make a move in the right direction if necessary. Secondly, it will provide a gradual introduction to oral text re-formulation. Thirdly, through it students will learn about and do public speaking, gain self-confidence and learn how to keep emotional control.

Above all, dealing with these fundamental skills will provide a solid basis for the development of the specific interpreting modes in the subsequent phases of the training process.

gloria_sampaio@hotmail.com

9.4 Cities as a global issue

Rhoda McGraw *Ecole des Ponts ParisTech, Paris, France*

The rapid growth of urban areas all over the world is a strong trend with major social, environmental, and economic consequences (LeGates and Stout 2011; Worldwatch Institute 2007). And urban themes are often of local as well as global interest for English learners and teachers. In this presentation, I discussed my experience of designing and running content-based English courses about urban planning and development.

In my work as an English teacher in French higher education, I first used urban issues in the developing world as the subject of a course for non-specialist students. Over the years, as I became increasingly interested in cities and planning myself, I began to work more with present and future urban planners. I now teach specialist students, at master's level or above, as well as practitioners. While most of these learners are preparing for careers in France, they use English for international projects during their studies and later on.

I began the session by suggesting that the global issue of cities may serve as particularly appropriate content for English learning, providing a coherent framework for studying many other important topics. Some obvious ones are agriculture, community development, energy, heritage, housing, transport, sanitation, water supply and urban sprawl. Yet many larger issues, such as youth and aging, poverty and conflict are also relevant.

I then talked about how I organise 20–30-hour courses for groups of 12 to 25 students with mixed language levels. Sources of material include ideas and questions arising from learners' work or studies, research centres, government agencies, non-governmental organisations and the news media, as well as films, television series and literature. Classroom tasks are intended to focus on learners' personal, academic, or professional experience of urban issues along with their responses to the materials, and to promote the effective use of integrated skills. Activities may be as simple as interviews, reports and debates. However, they always give priority to learners' contributions, focus on response rather than mastery, provide time to plan for speaking and allow choice about participation. Outside class, learners are required to write regularly, and they are helped and encouraged to engage in as much extensive reading and listening as possible.

Session participants mentioned a wide range of reasons for attending, and they brought diverse perspectives to the discussion. Two of them, who work in private language schools in Switzerland and the UK, appreciated the fact that urban issues affect all learners locally in some way, giving them experiences to share. Three other audience members, working on educational projects related to international development in China, sustainable development in Germany and tourism in Uzbekistan, found that the presentation offered concrete information and suggestions that they could use in their own settings. Another participant, teaching on a UK-based master's program in urban planning, said that he had discovered new ways to engage his language students within a prescribed curriculum.

My main aim in offering the presentation was to focus on a global issue which concerns all teachers and learners and interests many of them. I also tried to both describe and demonstrate a way of working with content which depends heavily on learners' engagement and interaction. Students in one of my classes have even told me that they see our way of working as a model for public participation in urban planning projects. Thus I was pleased that those who attended the conference session were eager to communicate with each other and to make their own contributions.

rhoda.mcgraw@mail.enpc.fr

References

LeGates, R. T. and F. Stout (eds.). 2011. *The City Reader* (fifth edition). New York: Routledge.

Worldwatch Institute. 2007. *State of the World 2007: Our Urban Future*. New York: W.W. Norton & Company.

9.5 Getting hands-on: using model kits in the ESP classroom

Adrian Millward-Sadler *and* **Annette Casey** *FH JOANNEUM, University of Applied Sciences, Graz, Austria*

This paper sits at the overlap between language teaching and engineering education and reports on an action research project conducted with the intention of improving student motivation for language learning. Model kit internal combustion engines (ICE) were purchased and used to teach English for Specific Purposes (ESP) vocabulary and writing skills to undergraduate automotive engineers in their third semester. Using Project-Based Learning (PBL) as a framework to implement these into an engineering ESP course, this paper highlights the already known benefits that such an approach can bring (Casey 2012).

Rationale

The use of hands-on activities as an effective teaching method which engages students is well known (Satterthwait 2010) and is a useful method in scientific teaching. Yet, in the field of ESP teaching of technical subjects, it is often underused, as students are taught using more traditional linguistic activities, which may not be suitable for them (Millward-Sadler *et al.* 2011). By increasing the 'hands-on' nature of language production and vocabulary acquisition, it will be argued that student motivation was raised and as a result their language learning enhanced. Furthermore, the aim was to provide the students with an opportunity to practice their technical writing and documentation skills as well as to encourage authentic team interaction.

Methods

This activity was designed in accordance with the PBL approach within an action research framework. To gauge language production, instructors took field notes during the monitoring phases of the activity and also videoed volunteer student groups. To further assess the success of the project, a questionnaire was circulated amongst participating learners to ascertain the learning outcomes and motivating effects of the activity. The results of this feedback loop will be discussed briefly later.

Activity

Two instructors team-taught an intensive series of lessons over a three-day period. Students were introduced to ICE using a number of lead-in activities to ascertain their current knowledge of engine-specific vocabulary and to review some of the basic working principles of internal combustion engines. Groups of two or three were then given ICE model kits and were asked to catalogue all parts before embarking on the actual assembly. During this phase, instructors circulated, providing both language and technical (!) assistance. Students photographically documented the entire construction process, assessed the quality of the original set of instructions and produced a written report of their work. It is worth noting that great efforts were made to ensure L2 production was not eschewed in these generally monolingual groups in favour of simply constructing the model kits. Among the various measures taken were, for example, instructions to document all of the components into engine systems prior to assembly as well as the removal of a vital engine part, which students were required to identify and request from instructors before their building could begin.

Learner feedback

In the paper-based questionnaires completed by the students (n=50) after the final session, the majority reported having acquired not only engine-specific vocabulary but also valuable experience in teamwork. A considerable number stated that they had, in addition, acquired knowledge about the workings of internal combustion engines. Constructing the models themselves was mentioned as the most enjoyable aspect overall, whereas writing the documentation, unsurprisingly, was mentioned as the least popular.

In order to determine any influence on motivation, students were requested to rate a series of statements concerning the motivational effects of the activity using a five-point Likert scale. As can be seen from the summary of student responses to these statements in Figure 9.5.1, the majority of learners strongly agreed that they had been motivated by using and assembling models. Similarly, the majority appear to have been motivated to engage with the subject matter in general. Just over 75 per cent of the respondents claimed that their team colleagues contributed positively to the overall motivational effects.

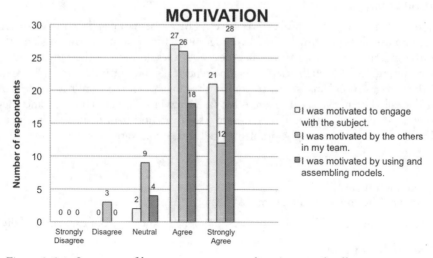

Figure 9.5.1: Summary of learner responses regarding (perceived) effects on motivation

Conclusion

Although the activity and feedback cycle has only been completed once, meaning any conclusions to be drawn can merely be of the most tentative nature, statements from the questionnaires certainly seem to indicate positive student motivation for the activity. Furthermore, field notes suggest that L2 production was high and authentic in the model construction phase, while the submitted written assignments show that students engaged with the target vocabulary. While another cycle is planned to further assess the impact and validity of the approach, we may cautiously conclude that the integration of PBL and hands-on activities can contribute to language learning and motivation, at least in our ESP classrooms for engineers.

adrian.millward-sadler@fh-joanneum.at

annette.casey@fh-joanneum.at

References

Casey, A. 2012. 'Using project-based learning in English for Specific Purposes courses for automotive engineering students' in D. Tatzl, A. Millward-Sadler and A. Casey (eds.). *English for Specific Purposes across the Disciplines: Practices and Experiences.* Graz: Leykam.

Millward-Sadler, A., A. Casey and D. Tatzl. 2011. 'A study of engineering students' learning preferences: a multiple intelligences approach'. *Professional and Academic English* 37: 8–15.

Satterthwait, D. 2010. 'Why are "hands-on" science activities so effective for student learning?' *Teaching Science* 56/2: 7–10.

9.6 Make your meetings work

Barry Tomalin *Culture-Training.com, London and Reigate, UK*

Introduction

I work with non-native speaker executives. Their international face-to-face meetings opportunities are now limited by budget limitations, security concerns and the need to minimise time away from their desks. As a result, most of their international communication is through telephone conference calls, often called 'conf calls'. One of their biggest problems is how to control meetings when there are native-speakers on the call. The native speakers are often fast, they talk across each other, and they dominate the conversation. The non-native speakers find it difficult to participate. Here's a short summary of the problem. I call it the 'non-native speaker's lament':

- think;
- translate;
- open mouth; and
- too late! (the conversation has moved on)

How can we help non-native speakers intervene in and run conf calls successfully?

Three training tools

I run meetings seminars for my students, and I introduce three tools: the agenda, meeting control strategies and intervention tips. I recommend learners think of the agenda as the spine of the meeting, the control strategies as the ribs and the intervention tips as the limbs to help them run or participate in a successful conf call.

Tool 1: the agenda

A clear agenda helps order the discussion. I teach a fairly formal agenda, divided into two stages. Stage 1 includes welcome, introductions, minutes of last meeting and matters arising. Stage 2 includes agenda items, AOB (any other business) and date of next meeting. I get students to practise the language that goes with each stage by running mini-meetings in class or the training room.

Not all countries are consistent in the use of agendas. I explain that agendas are important as they provide a structure for the meeting. Many non-native speaker executives complain it is difficult to intervene in a fast-moving meeting. I suggest that to get space to talk, they request the agenda beforehand, identify the point they wish to talk about and call or email the convenor to say they wish to contribute on a particular point. That way, the convenor will call on them to contribute at the appropriate point, which gives them space to speak.

Tool 2: control strategies

If a non-native speaker is the convenor of the meeting, it is vital to establish control at from the start and re-establish it at each stage. I recommend that non-native speaker convenors follow these simple principles:

- Don't take the minutes yourself. It is hard to control the conversation and write minutes at the same time. Get someone else to do it.
- Establish control immediately. Welcome, ask for brief introductions, and introduce each agenda item and the person who will present it.
- Thank the presenter and solicit other contributions.
- Decide what to minute. Use phrases like, 'Let's minute that ...'
- Keep the action points tight. Action (what will happen), Owner (who is responsible) and Time (when the action point will be completed) are usually sufficient. Often the minute reads, 'Report at next meeting.'
- Conclude the meeting, summarise key action points and fix the date of the next meeting.
- Review the minutes before circulating. Remember, 'Who controls the minutes controls the meeting.' Make sure the minutes reflect what you expect before they are sent out.

Tool 3: intervention tips

You also need ways of controlling people who go too fast, digress, talk too much and become aggressive. Stock phrases taught and practised will help, for example:

- Slow down: 'Excuse me, I'm not a native speaker. Can you slow down a bit please?' (Note that 'Could you slow down?' often achieves no result; adding 'I'm not a native-speaker' often does.)
- Get repetition: 'Sorry, I didn't catch that. Can you say it again, please?'
- Interruption: 'Can I just come in here? Can I interrupt briefly?'
- Stopping interruptions: 'Just let me finish.'
- Digression: 'Can we keep to/get back to the agenda, please?'
- Time: 'We are short of time. Can you sum up briefly, please?'
- Aggression: 'Let's discuss this outside the meeting.'

Some teachers find these expressions clichéd. Actually, they work; that's why they are popular. However, it is important to get trainees to practise them in class to ensure they use them correctly.

Conclusion

Teach the techniques of agenda setting, control strategies and intervention tips to your non-native speaker professional learners at CEFR B2 and C1 levels, and they will thank you. You have made a difficult part of their lives much easier.

barrytomalin@aol.com

9.7 Activities to help learners improve their intercultural communication

Adrian Pilbeam *LTS training and consulting, Bath, UK*

At IATEFL 2010 I gave a presentation entitled 'Understanding the role of culture in international business'. In Liverpool, I wanted to describe some activities that can be used to improve intercultural communication. The aim of my talk was to answer the following questions:

- What is intercultural competence and effective intercultural communication?
- How can we develop effective intercultural communication in our learners?
- What are some activities we can use to do this?

After some audience discussion, I presented my 'definition' of intercultural competence: 'having the knowledge, attitudes, awareness and skills to communicate effectively with cultures other than your own'. It comes from a presentation I once attended in the USA by Robert Kohls, an American intercultural specialist.

Activities to develop knowledge about other cultures

A first step in acquiring knowledge about other cultures is to know some facts and figures about another country. One good way to achieve this is to use a quiz. My example was India, with questions such as 'How many official languages are there?', and 'What is the official religion?' Another activity is map completions, putting in the main cities and provinces.

It is also useful to learn about typical behaviour in other cultures. In a multicultural group you can ask people to describe a typical behaviour in their culture Ask them to explain why this behaviour is important, and what the reaction would be if a foreigner behaved differently. Some examples could be ways of greeting (shake hands, kiss, hug, etc.); forms of address (with titles, by surname, by first name); ways of requesting things using direct or indirect language; ways of dressing for different occasions; how close it is comfortable to stand to someone, and so on.

Activities to develop awareness about how we react to other cultures

An activity I often use to develop intercultural awareness is a simulation called the Visitor Game, in which members of a group have to find out more about visitors from another culture by asking a series of yes/no questions. They don't know that the visitors have very specific rules in their culture about who they can talk to and when they say yes or no. After a while, the hosts start to get confused and even annoyed at their visitors' apparently inconsistent and even impolite behaviour. In the debrief phase, the visitors' rules are revealed and the mistaken assumptions of the hosts are discussed. The learning point is that what is normal to us may not be normal in other cultures because different rules often apply. This is followed by asking the learners for examples of 'normal' behaviour in their culture, and examples they have found of 'normal' behaviour in other cultures, but which they considered different or even strange.

A good way to avoid making assumptions before you are better informed is to follow the DIE process. When you encounter behaviour which is different or even strange to you, you should:

1 *Describe* what has happened without judging.
2 *Interpret* what the behaviour or action probably means, or what influences it.
3 And only then, consider *evaluating* the behaviour—whether it is polite, friendly, rude, etc.

Activities to develop skills to communicate more effectively with other cultures

Developing skills is the hardest part of intercultural training. One activity is to ask people to write an email to a team member whose first language is not English. The task is to tell them you need to produce a report by a certain date, and you need some input (facts, figures, etc.) from them to include in your report. The skill is pitching the tone of the email to balance friendliness, clarity and a sense of urgency.

Another activity, this time for speaking, is to get a group to participate in a problem-solving discussion based on a short case. They are given no guidelines about how to hold the discussion other than a maximum duration of 20 minutes. You appoint one person as an observer, and this person has to give feedback about turn-taking styles, whether some people dominated the discussion because of personality or better English, whether quieter participants were invited to comment or were just ignored, whether good English speakers took account of less good speakers, and ultimately, if it was a successful meeting.

I concluded by recommending two websites: www.dialogin.com and www.absolutely-intercultural.com, two books (see References), and I mentioned a train the trainer course that we have run since 2005 at LTS in Bath, called *Developing Intercultural Training Skills* (www.lts-training.com/ICTTcourse.htm).

adrian.pilbeam@lts-training.com

References

Gibson, R. 2002. *Intercultural Business Communication* (*Oxford Handbooks for Language Teachers* series). Oxford: Oxford University Press.

Schmidt, P. 2007. *In Search of Intercultural Understanding*. Vienna: Meridian World Press.

10 Technology in ELT: in the classroom and on the move

Does digital technology enhance language learning? This is the question posed by **Kalyan Chattopadhyay**, whose paper opens this chapter; the author's response to this question is based on research carried out in India. Subsequent papers in this chapter address different aspects of technology, both inside and outside the classroom. **Handan Kopkalli-Yavuz and Debra Marsh** report on another study, this one carried out in Turkey, into the effectiveness of online learning—with some unexpected results. **Isabela Villas Boas** then describes her own experiences as a novice online teacher charged with transforming a face-to-face course into a blended course. The use of handheld, portable devices for 'mobile' learning is attracting much attention, and the next group of papers address this topic. First, **Nicky Hockly** demonstrates some activities designed to exploit the use of handheld devices in class; then, **Simon Williams** provides an analysis of students' use of mobile devices and attitudes towards them. Three papers from specific contexts follow. **Jon Parnham** reports on the questions raised when implementing iPads into classroom instruction in Hong Kong; **Svetlana Titova** outlines the challenges of teaching 'mobile natives' in Russia; and the team of **James Simpson, Richard Badger, Atanu Bhattacharya and Sunil Shah** introduce a research project aimed at investigating the use of mobile technologies in a rural region of India and the extent to which mobile technologies may be used to counter inequality.

10.1 Does digital technology as instructional tool enhance language learning?

Kalyan Chattopadhyay *Bankim Sardar College, University of Calcutta, India*

Introduction

There is now an increased use of digital technology in language teaching in India. It is believed that the use of such technology allows learners to learn and practice language independently or collaboratively, and to become more autonomous (Larsen-Freeman and Anderson 2011). It is also believed that the use of technology provides brings learners in contact with real language, allows them to explore language in use, and motivates them to produce more language (Stanley 2013). There is evidence that the use of digital technologies leads to enhancement of learning (Vai and Sosulski 2011), but there is little evidence that the use of digital technology as instructional tool enhances *language* learning. I hypothesise that if the use of digital technology improves learning then it enhances language learning. To validate this hypothesis, I conducted a study among two groups of students enrolled in a certificate course in

Communicative English in the English Language Centre and addressed the following research questions:

- Does instruction through digital technology make any difference in language learning outcomes?
- Does instruction through digital technology lead to any other learning outcomes?

Method

Each group consisted of 20 learners aged 18–19, with a pre-intermediate level of proficiency. They received lessons for two hours, twice a week for three months. For Group 1, devices like interactive whiteboards, laptops, tablets and smart TV were used to design and present materials for different activities and to facilitate interaction. Students completed activities and assignments using those forms of technology. For Group 2, no such technology was used for instruction and interaction. Students received instruction through printed materials and completed pen-and-paper activities and assignments.

The data collection measures included learners' pre-course and end-of-course proficiency test scores to identify learners' current knowledge of syntax, vocabulary, rhetorical organisation, cohesion and formal register as evidenced from the use in the context specific tasks, classroom observations and oral feedback. Classroom observations were conducted to record interaction between the instructor and learners, and to record learners' classroom practices. Observation was followed by interviews with the three top students from each group.

Discussion

Pre-test and end-of-course test scores for both groups showed enhancement in knowledge about English and in skills in using English. However, Group 1, which received instruction with digital technology, showed a marginally greater improvement than Group 2. The classroom observation data reveals that, at the end of the course, the learners in Group 1 increased their level of confidence in the use of technologies, the Internet and English; they also showed more interest in completing interactive activities and a greater willingness to collaborate and learn on their own than the learners in Group 2. The learners in Group 2, however, increased their level of confidence in the use of English only. They lacked confidence to learn on their own and collaborate. They were less inclined to learn beyond the lesson, but they were interested in reading and writing with the use of technology.

The data received from interviewing learners was correlated with information from both learner test scores and classroom observations. I specifically looked at classroom practices and found that certain practices were more closely correlated to learner performance than others. The learners in Group 1 believed that the use of digital technology helped them gain confidence in using technologies and English in different situations; they also believed reading and writing through technologies would help them secure new-age jobs. On the other hand, the learners in Group 2 believed that a lack of exposure to technology had affected their performance and future prospects as job-seekers; they thought that even after the course, they lacked technological competence and the ability to read and write through technologies.

Limitations

This study, however, had some limitations. The most obvious limitation was that it was controlled action research. Another serious limitation of this study was that no attempt was made to understand whether competencies of the language instructors in the use of digital technologies affected any of the test scores or the classroom practices of the learners. No case studies were conducted; otherwise, I would have richer descriptions of the learners' classroom practices to generalise.

Summing up

Previous research had indicated that the use of digital technologies as instructional tools significantly enhanced language learning, and learning outcomes. However, my research shows that the use of digital technology need not necessarily lead to the enhancement of language proficiency, but that it significantly influences the level of motivation, and ease of use of technologies, and that it promotes collaborative engagement and self-directed learning. The marginal improvement noticed in the performance of the learners in Group 1 that received instruction with digital technologies could be due to the increased level of motivation.

profkalyan@gmail.com

References

Larsen-Freeman, D. and M. Anderson. 2011. *Techniques and Principles in Language Teaching.* Oxford: Oxford University Press.

Stanley, G. 2013. *Language Learning with Technology: Ideas for Integrating Technology in the Classroom.* Cambridge: Cambridge University Press.

Vai, M. and K. Sosulski. 2011. *Essentials of Online Course Design: A Standards-Based Guide.* New York and London: Routledge.

10.2 Self-study language learning: providing a learning structure to encourage and support student participation

Handan Kopkalli-Yavuz *Anadolu University, Turkey and* **Debra Marsh** *Cambridge University Press*

Background

Anadolu University is the largest university in Turkey offering distance education programmes and provides self-study English language programmes to over 200,000 students. In 2009, recognising the need for independent language learners to have access to a wide range of materials and resources in order to benefit from self-study (Nielson 2011) and the role multi-media content can play in maintaining interest and motivation, Anadolu University partnered with Cambridge University Press to provide students with a rich set of learning content, including online materials accessed through a learning management system (LMS).

The research

Every new technology offers 'unlimited promise to learning' (Luckin *et al.* 2012), but the question remains: to what extent does technology help improve the learning experience and outcomes? In 2012 Anadolu University, in collaboration with Cambridge University Press, initiated an ambitious research project to be carried out over a number of years. The principal objective of this project was to understand how learners were using the multiple components of the course, and in particular, to assess the impact of introduction of the online element on the learning experience and outcomes.

Results

Participants in the research were 3,256 students, and the analysis of this data revealed some unexpected results. Contrary to all expectations, the online content did not appear to increase student engagement, and more students reported a preference for using the print components rather than the online course. When asked to rate the effectiveness of the language material, the students feedback was, on the face of it, disappointingly negative.

However, when questioned further, the students' provided more detailed feedback which revealed that the real issue had nothing to do with the content or the medium itself, but with their lack of knowing *how* to learn English independently, and by extension the need for a guided learning structure.

In retrospect, the concluding results may well appear self-evident. But all too often, there is a tendency to forget the pedagogical fundamentals when introducing technology into the learning process. Clearly from our research we can conclude that digital content and the use of technology alone do not necessarily ensure increased student engagement, and just as in any other self-study context, the 'online' learner needs appropriate guidance and support.

The learning structure

As a direct result of this research a learning structure consisting of a central website, SMS alerts, weekly study plans, and weekly webinars has now been put in place. Encouragingly, student engagement has increased significantly with the introduction of each new component of the learning structure. The first circle on the graph below

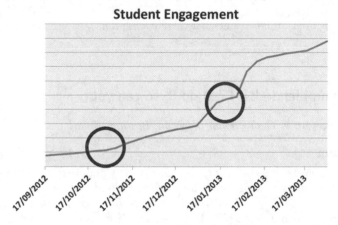

Figure 10.2.1: Student engagement

represents the introduction of the weekly study plans and the second circle represents the introduction of the SMS alerts and central website—see Figure 10.2.1.

Conclusions

Technology is an important part of our daily lives and without a doubt has a role to play in education and the learning process, but it is important to remind ourselves that '… no technology has an impact on learning in its own right; rather, its impact depends on the way it is used' (Luckin *et al.* 2012: 90).

Our research has shown that certain pre-conceived assumptions about the learning preferences of our 'digital native' students do not necessarily hold true. As has also been concluded in research elsewhere (Kaznowska *et al.* 2011), today's generation of 'digital natives' still prefers to have physical resources available to them, and is still '… far from preferring to be immersed in a digital world of self-directed learning' (page 17).

It is also important to remind ourselves that, as identified in research elsewhere (Johnson and March 2013), 'the confident *digital native* is not necessarily a confident *digital learner*', and just as in all learning contexts the distance students need appropriate guidance and support in order to manage their learning to best effect.

In the words of Luckin *et al.*, 'Learners … have to draw upon on a range of resources beyond the technology itself in order to make that technology work' (2012: 9), and it is up to us to provide these resources in the form of appropriate guidance to the self-study learner.

dmarsh@cambridge.org

References

Johnson, C. and D. Marsh. 2013 'The Laureate English Program taking a research informed approach to blended learning'. *Higher Learning Research Communications* 3/1. (Retrieved on 7 June 2013 http://journals.sfu.ca/liu/index.php/HLRC/article/view/103)

Kaznowska, E., J. Rogers and A. Usher. 2011. *The State of E-Learning in Canadian Universities, 2011: If Students Are Digital Natives, Why Don't They Like E-Learning?* Toronto: Higher Education Strategy Associates. (Retrieved from http://higheredstrategy.com/wp-content/uploads/2011/09/InsightBrief42.pdf)

Luckin, R. B. Bligh, A. Manches, S. Ainsworth, C. Crook and R. Noss. 2012. *Decoding Learning: The Proof, the Promise and Potential of Digital Education*. NESTA (Retrieved on 7 June 2013 from http://www.nesta.org.uk/library/documents/DecodingLearningReport_v12.pdf)

10.3 Going blended: if I can do it, so can you!

Isabela Villas Boas *Casa Thomas Jefferson, Brasilia, Brazil*

Introduction

Transforming an existing course into a blended variety may seem a daunting task, but my experience with a writing course for teachers showed that it's possible to develop this expertise. The Composition Course is a 32-hour module, part of a 360-hour Teacher Development Course (TDC), the goal of which is to improve student teachers' writing and provide an authentic experience with the process approach.

Preparation

Having no previous experience with online course development, I prepared myself to develop online activities on MOODLE by exploring various tutorials about the platform on YouTube and Slideshare, reading books on online course design, such Vai and Sosulski (2011), and taking an online course myself, through an e-teacher scholarship programme with the University of Oregon. These experiences were essential in providing me with the knowledge and skills to create a rich and effective online learning experience closely connected to the face-to-face encounters.

The crucial aspect of developing a blended course is choosing the blend—in other words, deciding what to do in class and what to do online. In the writing course that I piloted, half of the course hours were accomplished online and the other half in class. The course supervisor and I decided to continue using the same course book as in the traditional class, *Greater Essays* by Folse and Pugh (2009). However, we didn't restrict ourselves to the book, but rather, used its organisational structure as a springboard for additional, authentic resources focused on the topic of learning and teaching EFL. Thus, authentic models of the different types of texts were provided.

A sample lesson: classroom and online activities

A lesson on the narrative essay illustrates the choices of face-to-face and online activities. Students started working on the lesson online, as theoretical material and more mechanical exercises (for example, reading the introductory remarks on narrative essays, checking topics appropriate for narrative essays, and suggesting additional topics) are examples of tasks that students can easily perform independently. Hence, the students were asked to read the introductory pages, take a quiz on the topics appropriate for narrative essays provided in the book, and post additional topics on a forum. They were also asked to read an authentic narrative and relate it to the information in the book and in an additional online resource on narrative essays, provided on their MOODLE course page. Specific guidelines on what to comment on in their post and minimum and maximum number of lines were also provided.

They were then ready for the following face-to-face class. We started out by commenting on the forum posts regarding the narrative text, and then moved on to an analysis of the suggestions of topics for narrative essays, provided by students in another forum post. Following that, students selected their narrative topics, performed a 'free-talking' activity aimed at generating ideas for the essay and wrote an outline. Next, students gave each other feedback on their narrative essay outlines, using a form provided in the course book. They were thus ready to go home and write their essays. One of the next batch of online activities consisted of a peer review of the narrative essays, using the wiki available on MOODLE. Students received an essay by email with a number and had to post their answers to the questions in the peer review form in the book. The wiki page served as a collective online space for the peer reviews.

As the cycle of activities above shows, the work with narrative essays began online, continued in the face-to-face class, and culminated in their again online work, writing the essay and giving feedback to each other. The online and face-to-face activities were closely interrelated, forming a course unity. In addition, all levels of thinking in the revised version of Bloom's taxonomy (Anderson and Krathwohl 2001) were included in the course activities.

Student feedback

For their final assignment, students wrote an argumentative essay in favour or against the blended model for the TDC. Eleven defended the blended course, highlighting its flexibility, the deeper levels of thinking they had to engage in, and how it contributed to developing their digital literacies. The two who argued against it said they preferred the face-to-face interaction with the teacher and reported difficulty managing their time online. Blended learning thus showed to be effective for most students, but not everyone had the necessary self-discipline to conclude the tasks on time. However, seeing the students once a week allowed me to encourage them to perform their tasks and to solve difficulties face-to-face.

isabela.villasboas@thomas.org.br

References

Anderson, L., and D. Krathwohl. 2001. *A Taxonomy for Learning, Teaching and Assessing: A Revision of Bloom's Taxonomy of Educational Objectives*. New York: Addison, Wesley Longman.

Folse, K. and T. Pugh. 2009. *Great Writing 5: Greater Essays*. Boston, Mass.: Heinle Cengage Learning.

Vai, M. and K. Sosulski. 2011. *Essentials of Online Course Design: A Standards-Based Guide*. New York and London: Routledge.

10.4 Moving with the times: mobile literacy and ELT

Nicky Hockly *The Consultants-E, Barcelona, Spain*

From games and apps to augmented reality and moblogging, mobile (or 'handheld') devices are now part of the fabric of daily life. In this workshop we explored practical classroom-based activities to help develop learners' English language skills *and* an increasingly important 21st century skill—mobile literacy. Workshop participants were encouraged to bring their own devices to the session.

We tried out several activities with mobile devices, mapped against Ruben Puentedura's SAMR model (2010). The SAMR model proposes four increasing levels of complexity in the use of technology tools: *substitution, augmentation, modifications* and *redefinition*. At the simplest level, 'substitution' means that the technology simply substitutes or replaces a traditional tool. At the highest level, 'redefinition' means that the tool allows learners to carry out a task which would have been previously inconceivable. Although Puentedura's model focuses on the use of technology tools in general, it is a model that can usefully be applied to the use of mobile devices to help the teacher identify whether his or her use of the device for a particular activity is simply at the level of substitution, or whether it is towards the other end of the scale, requiring modifications or redefinition. In the workshop, we looked at practical activities illustrating a number of these SAMR levels, and participants used their own mobile devices to carry these out.

Activity 1 (substitution)

This was a letter dictation activity in which workshop participants took down the dictation in the text message, or note-taking function, of their phones. The letters formed two different questions related to the use of mobile devices, which participants then discussed. In an activity like this, the use of a mobile device simply substitutes pen and paper.

Activity 2 (substitution)

This was a photo-sharing activity in small groups, with group members needing to find and share six photos from their mobile phones, on a number of themes. This simple discussion activity allows personalisation, and the activity requires no preparation.

The reason for starting the workshop with two 'substitution' activities was to show participants that it is very easy to carry out simple communicative classroom activities with mobile devices. Both activities work with feature phones, and smartphones are often not required for 'substitution' activities. For teachers unclear about how to integrate the use of mobile devices into their teaching, or worried that using devices means doing new, complex or 'technical' things they don't feel confident with, starting at this level of 'substitution' is a good way in.

Activity 3 (augmentation)

This real-time online polling activity required participants to use smartphones with an Internet connection. The first poll allowed participants to choose one of several options, and the second required them to send in short messages. Polls like this substitute a show of hands, or replace brainstorming items on the board, but there is potential enhancement to the activity in having a digital record of these polls. The polls can be shared electronically with students and/or embedded into blogs or websites, etc. So we have moved up one level in the SAMR model with this activity, to 'augmentation'.

Activity 4 (modifications)

Participants with a QR code reader on their smartphones were asked to read one code and to follow the instructions. QR codes can be used in treasure hunt activities, with both teacher and students creating them. Again, we move one level up in the SAMR model with this type of activity, to 'modifications'.

Activity 5 (redefinition)

Geo-location and augmented reality, both of which are affordances of high-end mobile devices such as smartphones or tablets, enable us to produce completely new tasks for language learning; these take us to the level of 'redefinition' in the SAMR model. We looked at augmented reality apps such as Wiktude, and discussed geo-tagging activities with Woices. We also briefly discussed the movement towards wearable technology as (literally) embodied in the Google glass project.

nicky.hockly@theconsultants-e.com

Reference

Puentedura, R. 2010: *SAMR*. (Retrieved from http://goo.gl/1zuNK)

10.5 Mobile devices and learner interaction inside and outside the classroom

Simon Williams *University of Sussex, Brighton, UK*

In the last decade, mobile technology has proliferated in the hands of language learners. Most have a mobile phone and many also bring to the classroom other portable devices, discretely using them as dictionaries, messaging systems and search tools. An observer might wonder why, despite having quite powerful mini-versions of the classroom PC and interactive whiteboard in front of them, the learners are not working with their devices more openly and collectively. Is it because their incorporation would be at odds with the here-and-now activity of many language classrooms? This presentation explored the tensions between mediated interaction and group language learning and suggested that learner interaction may take place around rather than through the devices and applications.

Background

In the presentation, I used the term Mobile Assisted Language Learning (MALL) to refer to mobile devices, applications and related activities. There is a small but growing body of research on mobile devices and learner interaction in the language classroom. In their survey, Kukulska-Hulme and Shield (2008) observe that 'the activities … rarely allow for collaborative learner interaction' (page 280). The vast majority of applications are text based, product oriented, and characterised by more formal contexts and by one-way teacher–learner interaction. In contrast, uses that promote process-oriented communication and interaction are characterised by less formal contexts, and by teacher/learner–learner interaction in which learners define their own learning or provide materials to other learners—see Table 10.5.1.

MALL	Product-oriented learning materials	Process-oriented communication and interaction activities
Context	more formal	less formal
Interaction	teacher–learner	teacher/learner–learner
Typical learning situation	learners study alone	learners define own learning/ provide materials to other learners
Problem	text-based	existing opportunities for collaborative learner interaction are rare

Table 10.5.1: Comparison of MALL applications and activities

The few exceptions identified in Kukulska-Hulme and Shield's (2008) survey illustrate the mobile affordances identified by JISC (2005), i.e. the enabling of interactive learning and fieldwork evidence gathering. Mapping the various MALL activities onto Bowers' (1980) model of learner interaction and teacher involvement in the language classroom (Table 10.5.2), it is clear that the majority of MALL activity, while offering feedback, occasions no genuine interaction, while the scant process-oriented activities encourage unmonitored interaction.

Direct teacher involvement	1 Teacher presentation	2 Teacher / student question and answer	3 Class conversation and discussion	4 Teacher / student conversation	5 Interpersonal group with teacher as member
	6 Dictionary Cooney & Ceogh (2007) Supervised individual seatwork	7 Headway Class and group drills and exercises	8 Woices JISC (2005) Problem-centred group activity	9 Twitter Communication games	10 Shakespeare Free dramatisation and role-play
	11 Vocab learning, quizzes & surveys Haiku Individual self-access study	12 Pemberton et al (2010) Ogata & Yano (2003) Individual self-access study with interactive (audio) support	13 Lan et al (2007) Wise Judge Controlled simulation and role-play	14 Business interviews Student / student conversation	15 Turkish news Ros I Solé et al (2010) Interpersonal group without teacher as member
Indirect teacher Involvement					
Whiteboard photo	No genuine interaction				
Tree photo					Genuine interaction

Table 10.5.2: Learner interaction vs. teacher involvement (based on Bowers 1980)

Reflection

As an EAP teacher experimenting with MALL, I wanted to encourage my foundation-level students to socialise because they often worked alone, adopted a passive learning style and seldom used English outside the classroom. Together, the MALL activities I tried tick all the boxes in Bowers' model and go beyond it. The activities could be categorised as student-initiated or teacher-initiated, inside or outside the classroom. Inside, I asked learners to use their mobile phones do the following:

• photograph themselves in tableaux from four of Shakespeare's tragedies;
• tweet messages in character from Davis and Rinvolucri's running dictation *The Messenger and the Scribe*;
• access the university blackboard via the campus wireless network; and
• surf the web for answers to general knowledge questions posed in their course book, *Headway Academic Skills* (OUP).

The results suggested that MALL encouraged these learners' creativity, enabled social relationships, permitted repeat attempts and fostered self-confidence.

I asked new learners to go outside to do the following:
• record audio interviews with local business people;
• photograph themselves in tableaux from *The Messenger and the Scribe*;
• roam the campus and photograph unusual architecture to accompany their own haiku; and

- record audio interviews with passers-by on campus and upload the results to the application Woices.

Despite occasioning a great deal of negotiation when uploading the results, in discussion afterwards it became clear that learners felt self-conscious about approaching strangers and using the target language; they expected to face rejection, and they did not want to use recording devices.

Learners' spontaneous use of mobile devices was both utilitarian and subversive. Inside the classroom, they photographed board work for later upload to their web-based blackboard site; checked the pronunciation of unfamiliar words; and watched rolling news in their first language on web-based media channels. Outside, as we were walking between classrooms one day, one learner took a dramatic photograph of the felling of a healthy sycamore tree in the centre of campus; back in the classroom it formed the basis for a lively discussion on ecology. It is these spontaneous learner uses that go beyond Bowers' model.

Comment

Balancing the affordances and constraints of MALL, it is ironic that the unique strengths of the technology—its portability and social interactivity—may be a disincentive for some learners. While MALL provides a lifeline for the shyer learner, it breaks the pattern of teacher-dominated classroom discourse, and learners from some cultures might find that discomforting. It seems that only by encouraging its use on learners' own terms can the disincentives be overcome and learner-produced material harvested outside the classroom provide a resource for group-based learning inside.

S.A.Williams@sussex.ac.uk

References

Bowers, R. 1980. 'Verbal Behavior in the Language Teaching Classroom'. Unpublished PhD Thesis, University of Reading.

JISC. 2005. 'Innovative practice with e-learning: a good practice guide to embedding mobile and wireless technologies into everyday practice'. HEFCE. (Retrieved on 2 June 2013 from http://www.jisc.ac.uk/media/documents/publications/innovativepe.pdf)

Kukulska-Hulme, A. and L. Shield. 2008. 'An overview of mobile assisted language-learning: from content delivery to supported collaboration and interaction'. *ReCALL* 20/3: 271–89.

10.6 Implementing iPads in the classroom: a project in Hong Kong

Jon Parnham *British Council, Hong Kong*

The British Council Hong Kong bought 33 iPads for its Teaching Centre in June 2012. This paper draws on some of the key findings that arose while preparing for and starting to implement them in the classroom.

Setting up

From the start it was crucial to get input from teachers on their thoughts and ideas about using iPads in the classroom. To do this we set up an iPad special interest group

(SIG). We found that building a team of teachers with knowledge and expertise in integrating iPads in the classroom was essential to get buy-in and support. This is reflected in the literature of recent iPad deployment in schools in other parts of the world (Burden *et al.* 2012).

Having established the SIG, we asked ourselves questions to research and discuss. Two important points included (a) what apps and tasks would work well in the classroom to help develop and support language learning, and (b) what challenges we might encounter using iPads in lessons and how we could overcome them. I will now highlight some of the findings we made in answering these questions.

Apps and tasks to help develop and support language learning

We found that iPads are a very good tool for developing collaboration and creativity. Apps which can get students working on speaking fluency include *Morfo*, which allows students to record a voiceover for an animated talking head, and *Puppet Pals,* where students can work together to produce animations. Also, having students produce comics and posters using *Comic Life* was found to be an effective way of helping learners to work together on their writing skills. Another useful task was related to creating media-rich mind maps using *Popplet*, which is a tool for brainstorming using text, drawings and images.

Apps that enhance the assessment for learning process have also proved to be a major advantage of using iPads. For example, the app *Socrative* allows teachers to set questions and get instant feedback from students. This helps teachers find out where all learners currently are with their understanding of a topic.

Finally, engaging students using social networks was found to be a positive way of encouraging students to use English outside of class. The website and app *Edmodo* was one useful tool for teachers to develop an online community that is safe and secure for learners to interact with each other, allowing them to share documents as well as view, discuss and give feedback on their peers' work.

Challenges of using iPads in the classroom

One main concern was around e-safety. As tasks using iPads can involve uploading and sharing text, pictures and video online, ensuring learners are doing so appropriately was extremely important. To deal with this we found it crucial to establish rules about appropriate behaviour using iPads and communicating online when first starting to use the device in class.

An important factor we initially overlooked was having adequate WiFi. Many tasks involving iPads require a fast Internet connection. We found that both students and teachers become frustrated if tasks cannot be completed due to slow Internet speeds. Some teachers may be put off using iPads again if they have to spend more time solving connectivity problems rather than on the language content of the lesson. Therefore, a fast WiFi connection is key to successful iPad implementation in a school.

A further challenge was saving students' work and getting it off the iPad. In our context, our iPads are shared between classes, which means that the iPads could move from a class of young learners to a class of adults. This means that student work, especially if it involves pictures and video content, must be taken off the iPad at the end of each class. Teachers need to plan for this and build it into their lesson procedures.

The final issues concern time and the role of the teacher. We found that students need time to explore apps and see what they can do. This can result in tasks taking a lot longer than expected and teachers need to take this into account when they first use iPads. Also, the teacher's role can change as learners take control of their learning and make discoveries through the apps themselves. As learners develop confidence and expertise using the technology, teachers need to be comfortable stepping back and not knowing everything about the iPad. This may be one of the main challenges teachers will face as we continue to go further with integrating iPads into the classroom.

jon.parnham@britishcouncil.org.hk

Reference

Burden, K., P. Hopkins, T. Male, S. Martin, and C. Trala. 2012. *iPad Scotland Evaluation*. Hull: University of Hull.

10.7 Teaching 'mobile natives' in Russia: challenges and perspectives

Svetlana Titova *Lomonosov Moscow State University, Russia*

Introduction

Mobile devices and technologies are becoming pervasive and ubiquitous in many modern societies. They can enhance learning experience in many ways: they provide instant feedback and better diagnosis of learning problems; they help to design new assessment models (Traxler 2009); they enhance learner autonomy (Kukulska-Hulme 2010); and more. These facts put enormous pressure on universities that are not yet ready to communicate with their key audience using mobile devices. In order to implement a new device or technology efficiently, it is necessary to investigate its didactic potential.

Objectives of the project

A long-term research and evaluation project, *Mobile Devices in the Language Classroom: Theory and Practice*, was launched in 2011 at the Department of Foreign Languages and Area Studies, Lomonosov Moscow State University. Its aim is to evaluate learners' and instructors' preparedness to integrate mobile technologies into foreign language classroom and to incorporate m-learning strategies into the teaching process. This project included the following objectives: analysis of students' preparedness to implement new technologies and possible strategies of mobile learning through the eyes of our learners; setting up a moblog for educators to share their experiences of mobile teaching; establishing the syllabus for a distance education professional development course for foreign language teachers; and determining ways to deliver mobile content to our students. Methods for investigation included questionnaires, interviews, focus groups, lesson observations, audio and video recordings, informal face-to-face discussion groups, online forum discussion and online blog discussion.

Research results

The results demonstrate that the majority of the students have very advanced mobile (ICT) competence and skills because they can download an app (95 per cent); record a presentation (80 per cent); save multimedia and text materials on their device (84 per cent); write a commentary in a moblog and share links with group mates (84 per cent); and search the web via mobile access (98 per cent). As for their mobile learning experience outside the classroom, every day 95.6 per cent of students use mobile devices on their own to access reference materials (dictionaries, encyclopedias); 65 per cent use them for multimedia material playback; 68 per cent use mobile devices as a means of interaction with group mates via Twitter, moblogs, email, etc.; and only 12 per cent use apps designed for learning foreign languages.

When it comes to using mobile devices for learning, 80 per cent employ them both in class and outside class on their own every day, 16 per cent use them twice a week, and only 1 per cent never use mobile devices. Regarding possible ways of integrating mobile technology, almost 60 per cent said that they would like to use it for academic interaction and material sharing, 52 per cent for educational mobile apps, 42 per cent for the course mobile syllabus apps created by their instructors, and 38 per cent for recording and filming presentations and speech production tasks. According to our students' answers, their instructors implement mobile devices (mostly tablets) at least once during a semester for communication outside the classroom (72 per cent); for multimedia presentation of teaching content in class (52 per cent), for sharing educational content (50 per cent), and for voice recording (12 per cent); 30 per cent never use mobile devices.

Conclusions

To sum up, students today are technologically and psychologically ready to use mobile devices on a regular basis, both in the classroom and for autonomous work. The students surveyed use mobile devices and apps more frequently outside the class on their own, rather than in classroom work; they use mobile devices predominantly as means of access to reference materials, as multimedia material playback and as a means of interaction. They very rarely use in-class educational mobile apps for ELT to do exercises; they don't use mobile devices for production or for collaborative activities (for example, such as digital storytelling, web projects, etc.).

Unfortunately, today our instructors are often unwilling to employ mobile devices in their teaching experience. This survey shows once again that the pressure towards the use of mobile devices is coming from students themselves, and that it is necessary to work out certain steps and strategies of mobile technologies implementation into the traditional classroom to avoid undesirable consequences of mobile devices misuse in learning.

This survey encouraged us firstly to design some m-learning activities focused on authentic real-life situations for developing communicative skills; secondly to create collaborative learning activities based on Google Maps, Geo-Everything, mind mapping and other apps; and thirdly to employ smart phones to elicit students' immediate feedback during lecture courses via a free mobile application, Student Response System. The next stage of our project involves working out methodological strategies on how to implement mobile technologies into the traditional classroom and making the decisions necessary to take advantages of these new technological opportunities in professional development courses for foreign language teachers.

stitova3@gmail.com

References

Kukulska-Hulme, A. 2010. *Mobile Learning for Quality Education and Social Inclusion.* Moscow: UNESCO IITI.

Traxler, J. 2009. 'Current state of Mobile Learning' in M. Ally (ed.). *Mobile Learning: Transforming the Delivery of Education and Training.* Edmonton: Athabasca University Press.

10.8 Mobigam: language on the move in Gujarat

James Simpson, *University of Leeds, UK*, **Richard Badger**, *University of Leeds, UK*, **Atanu Bhattacharya**, *Central University of Gujarat, India and* **Sunil Shah**, *HM Patel Institute of English Training and Research, Gujarat, India*

Our IATEFL conference presentation described the Mobigam initiative, currently funded by the British Academy, and focusing on the use of mobile technology in Gujarat, India. Mobigam is a partnership between academics at the University of Leeds, Central University of Gujarat and HM Patel Institute, also in Gujarat. The name Mobigam is a composite of 'mobile' and 'gam', a 'rural area' in Gujarati.

Our collaboration began when we identified these issues:

1 Mobile technologies potentially contribute to digital inclusion in India through their relative cheapness, *but* how users interact with them is barely researched in the Indian context.

2 Rapidly evolving mobile technologies have enormous potential for language use and language learning, *but* neither their contextually situated use nor the factors that influence their use are especially well understood.

Our overall objective is to address these gaps in understanding. In 2012 we were awarded a grant from the British Academy's Academic International Partnership and Mobility Scheme. Our activities under this scheme comprise:

• knowledge exchange and research training workshops across Gujarat; and
• the development of a proposal for a large-scale study of mobile technology use across the state.

The rest of this report focuses on the development of this large project. The scope of our proposal encompasses our first objective, to examine the potential of mobile technology for digital inclusion in Gujarat. Mobile and wireless technology (phones, tablets, etc.) has enormous potential to extend peoples' networks and to change relationships, to the extent that it can affect patterns of inequality. We can gain insights into this potential through a study of language use and mobile literacy practices amongst people who themselves are in some way on the move in Gujarat.

Our aim

• To ascertain the potential of the use of mobile and networked digital technology to disturb, interrupt and otherwise challenge the established patterns of marginalisation, including educational marginalisation, among migrants in Gujarat, India.

The overarching research question

• How are mobile technologies implicated in current digital literacy and language practices amongst migrants across interconnected social and spatial dimensions in Gujarat?

Our research is located in the Indian state of Gujarat but speaks to other development contexts nationwide and worldwide. Governments make mobile networks accessible, enabling participation in practices involving, for instance, phone calls, text messaging, engagement with social media and the Internet. In India, mobile telephony has expanded rapidly: Gujarat has shared this development and has reached a tele-density (telephones per 100 inhabitants) of over 85 per cent.

Although governments, which put in place the infrastructure for mobile communication, primarily invoke the benefits to economic growth, this is often also done with a nod to social inclusion. Yet it is well established that simple access to hardware or to infrastructural networks cannot of itself address inequality. What is under-explored, and what this research seeks to examine, is the actual nature of people's interactions using mobile technology—their situated mobile digital literacy practices—and how these might contribute to enabling them to counter the inequalities which abound in India and in Gujarat. These relate to material and economic concerns, and to other key issues including the caste system, landlessness, urban–rural distinctions, educational marginalisation and gender. In our research this will be addressed through the examination of case studies of people who have migrated to and within Gujarat. Migration is often associated with aspiration, the desire for a better future life. At the same time, migrants are subject to loss of capital of various kinds as a concomitant to the migration process. This leads us to consider mobility of *people* as well as technology in our research.

The consequences of using mobile devices for inter- and intra-state migrants are diverse and can be unexpected. Our own research will examine mobile interaction amongst migrants to uncover patterns of mobile use and whether (if at all) they challenge aspects of the established status quo. Our case studies include seasonal labourers, migrant workers in the diamond-polishing industry, female students who travel from rural areas to study, ex-nomads working in the handicrafts industry and mobile pastoralists. For each case we will carry out broad brush survey work, qualitative work including analysis of written and spoken mobile interaction and accompanying interviews, and critical linguistic ethnographies involving in-depth study of mobile literacy practices and events.

We aim to begin this study in mid-2014. In the meantime, you can contact James Simpson: j.e.b.simpson@education.leeds.ac.uk, visit our blog: mobigam.wordpress.com, join us on Facebook: facebook.com/mobigamgujarat and follow us on Twitter: @mobigam1.

j.e.b.simpson@education.leeds.ac.uk

11 Issues in feedback and assessment

This chapter explores issues related to giving feedback on course work and evaluating performance through formal testing. We start with writing. **Martina Elicker and Ulla Fürstenberg** investigate whether or not code marking is an effective method of giving feedback. The next two papers, both from Switzerland, address the evaluation of oral skills. **JoAnn Salvisberg** questions whether the time and effort required to organise a practice exam is justified by improved performance, and **Maggi Lussi Bell and Kirsten Rudin** describe an approach to oral evaluation at a Swiss university. We then turn our attention to formal written tests. **Russell Whitehead and Shakeh Manassian** provide guidelines for teachers engaged in writing tests, and the Pearson Signature Event, reported by event chair **David Booth**, explores current issues in testing and ways in which testing can be made more efficient and effective. The final paper in this chapter looks at a different form of assessment—the assessment of schools, rather than of individual students. **Maria-Araxi Sachpazian** describes some of the challenges related to school assessment and suggests improvements to the process.

11.1 Feedback in student writing: a closer look at code-marking

Martina Elicker *and* **Ulla Fürstenberg** *University of Graz, Austria*

The project

Students of English at university level are expected to achieve a high level of proficiency and accuracy in their writing. The feedback that we as teachers provide is an essential element in this learning process. It is therefore crucial to establish what kind of feedback is most helpful and efficient.

In a study carried out at the English Department of the University of Graz from 2010 to 2012 involving 264 students, this question was investigated regarding the use of a marking code in a process writing approach, since this is the established form of written feedback at the department.

The respondents completed a three-part questionnaire. In Parts 1 and 2, they were asked about their experiences with feedback on their written work and how well they understand certain grammatical concepts (for example, tense, aspect, verb complementation, syntax). In Part 3, they had to correct a short text which had been constructed on the basis of frequent student errors. For this part of the questionnaire, respondents were randomly split into three groups: for the first group, errors were underlined and code-marked; for the second group, errors were indicated by underlining; and for the third group, errors were not identified at all.

The main objective of the project was to determine whether code-marking significantly improves students' ability to correct mistakes, compared to a simple indication of errors by underlining. Another point we addressed was the relationship between students' self-assessment and their actual performance in a correction task.

Results

Code-marking and error correction

The results of the correction task (Part 3 of the questionnaire) seem to indicate that code-marking does not contribute significantly to the successful correction of errors; it appears to be less relevant than the indication of the error as such. In fact, students often do better when the error is only indicated by underlining than when the error is indicated and code-marked. The results for errors of tense, as shown in Table 11.1.1, are typical in that respect.

Errors code-marked	Errors indicated by underlining	No indication of error
88.7%	92.3%	68%

Table 11.1.1: Tense: error appropriately corrected

Code-marking and awareness of grammatical concepts

The relationship between self-assessment (i.e. how students rate their own understanding of grammatical concepts and their ability to correct certain types of error in part two of the questionnaire) and performance (i.e. students' performance on the correction task in part three of the questionnaire) is complex. Unsurprisingly, students have great difficulty correcting errors when they are not familiar with the grammatical categories indicated by the marking code. In this regard, the error categories concerning the verb, i.e. the tense–aspect–verb complementation cluster, are of particular interest. Of these three error types, tense is the only one that students say they understand clearly.

It is, however, not possible to have a clear understanding of the concept of tense, but not of aspect and verb complementation, since—to put it simply—all three concern the verb, so that if students misunderstand one of them, it automatically affects their understanding of the other concepts. If the marking code points them to a concept they understand imperfectly, it is hardly surprising that they will experience the code as confusing rather than helpful.

On the other hand, types of error that are perceived as easy to correct by the students also often cause problems. Errors of syntax are a case in point: most students report a good understanding of the concept and consider errors of syntax easy to correct. However, as Table 11.1.2 shows, the results of the correction task tell a different story:

Errors code-marked	Errors indicated by underlining	No indication of error
15.3%	19.3%	9.7%

Table 11.1.2: Syntax: error appropriately corrected

Practical implications: looking beyond error correction

While code-marking does not seem to be the most efficient type of feedback when it comes to simply improving student texts, it has other advantages. Most crucially, it promotes 'the practice of metalinguistic reflection' which 'encourages and facilitates L2 development' (Simard *et al.* 2007: 510). While this is beneficial for all learners, especially advanced learners like our students, we believe it to be essential for future teachers to develop teacher language awareness, i.e. 'knowledge of grammar terminology, classifications and rules and an ability to apply this knowledge, for example in identifying learner errors and providing useful explanations to students' (Svalberg 2012: 383).

We will, therefore, continue to use the marking code with some adaptations, focusing on those concepts that students find particularly challenging and continually monitoring the results of this approach.

martina.elicker@uni-graz.at

References

Simard, D., L. French and V. Fortier. 2007. 'Elicited metalinguistic reflection and second language learning: Is there a link?' *System* 35: 509–22.

Svalberg, A. M.-L. 2012. 'Language awareness in language learning and teaching: a research agenda.' *Language Teaching* 45/3: 376–88.

11.2 Formative assessment of oral skills: does the end justify the means?

JoAnn Salvisberg *Lucerne University of Applied Sciences and Arts, Switzerland*

Introduction

This workshop, given during the TEA SIG programme day, was based on action research performed in the classroom on formative assessment of oral skills. The underlying rationale was to find out whether all the effort to organise practice (mock) exams, plus giving personal diagnostic feedback to each individual student, produces improvement in student performance on the final semester exam.

One might ask, what does testing have to do with teaching and learning? My personal experience has shown that nothing gets students' attention and involvement better than knowing that what they are doing is directly related to the exam. Given all the work involved, one might also ask, why bother with formative assessment? Adcock (2012) explains that mock exams are a good thing because they offer students consolidation of material learned, help keep them on the right track, provide feedback, and offer the chance to work on specific exam techniques they need.

In designing practice tests, or mock exams, while the specific content will obviously differ, the test should resemble the types of material, topics, grammar and lexis that students have had in class. In Harrison's words:

> The content of a diagnostic test is quite specific, referring back to recent classwork. It is intended to have positive results for the student by encouraging him with success or pointing out exactly what he needs to do to improve, and it should therefore be based on further examples of the kind of material which has been used in class (1983: 49).

Background

The students in this study are enrolled in the bachelor's programme and will graduate with a degree in finance and banking, communication and marketing, or a similar subject. Each student's acceptance is based, among other things, on having at least a B2 level of English, and some of their constraints comprise stakeholders' expectations, individual study challenges, commuting and their course load.

Case study

The focus of the action research was based on two classes taking Module 3 English, which focuses on human resources management (HRM), including topics such as employees, teams, meetings, leadership and recruitment. While Modules 1 and 2 are evaluated by written exams, Module 3 has an oral exam. During the semester students read and discuss texts and hone their oral summarising skills.

The focus of the mock and exam is to summarise an HRM text, and then link it to similar texts, videos and topics covered in class. Marking criteria focuses on language, oral skill (for example, pronunciation, fluency), text comprehension and how well students relate their exam text to other class material. The justification is that they are building useful skills for future employment.

Workshop participants listened to recordings of two students, noting their language, pronunciation and fluency. A discussion of each then ensued with participants giving their input as to what they had noted and the feedback they had received based on the above criteria. In comparing the two candidates, everyone agreed that whereas one was stronger linguistically, the other was better able to link the text to other HRM topics and texts they had discussed in class.

Evaluation

We then returned to our original question: does the end justify the means? Organising the mocks involves the following:
• scheduling;
• preparation of appropriate material;
• acquiring and checking equipment;
• recording;
• transcribing and typing individual feedback;

- photocopying; and
- giving feedback and answering questions.

An average of the grades showed a slight improvement from 4.7 to 4.9 (highest score 6.0). Some made significant progress, and others digressed. Although the data does not unequivocally prove that the mock significantly influenced all the students' grades on the final exam, feedback from the students was overwhelmingly in favour of the mock exam. They felt it not only gave them a real *feel* for what the exam would be like (including timing), but they also really appreciated the personal feedback on their language and skills performance.

Conclusion

While many teachers have to administer exams, as in this tertiary-level institution in Switzerland, not all are required or even encouraged to organise mock exams. Due to the intensive and often unpaid work involved in organising oral mock exams, it is not difficult to see why many balk at the idea of initiating these in their teaching situations.

Each teacher, however, is responsible for offering the best possible preparation to the students to meet the course objectives and exam criteria. Although we cannot equivocally say that Effort + Feedback = Improvement, particularly in high stakes situations where exam failure means no graduation and possibly limited employment possibilities, the end does very definitely justify the means.

joann.salvisberg@hslu.ch

References

Adcock, J. 2012. 'Mock exams: Why they are a good thing.' (Retrieved on 6 September 2012 from http://www.kbs.org.uk/news/2012/01/09/mock-exams-why-they-are-a-good-thing)

Harrison, A. 1983. *A Language Testing Handbook*. London: Macmillan Press Ltd.

11.3 Using academic oral presentations for assessment purposes

Maggi Lussi Bell *and* **Kirsten Rudin** *Zurich University of Applied Sciences, Switzerland*

Introduction

Not only are academic oral presentations highly relevant to study programmes in higher education, where they are used in a variety of subjects (from science to the arts), but they are also an effective and efficient means of assessment (Sundrarajun and Kiely 2009). The aim of this talk was to provide an example of their use as an assessment tool at a university of applied sciences in Switzerland. It also drew on a small-scale study to give students' perspectives of issues relating to the exam.

Background

Before considering the academic oral presentation (AOP) exam itself, we described the teaching context in which it is used. In this situation BSc students (of Life

Sciences or Facility Management) have four semesters of compulsory English as part of their degree programme. The courses are designed to assist the students with the English needed for their studies as well as to prepare them for professional life or post-graduate studies. As student intake level varies greatly, the courses are taught at three different levels and are intended to bring students to between B2 and C1 on the CEFR. Both general English as well as specialised English (in particular, English related to the students' fields of study) are taught and tested each semester. To complete semester 4, students take a written test and give an assessed AOP, each of which count as 50 per cent of the final mark. Throughout the courses, students are given input on presentations as well as numerous opportunities to practise their presentation skills.

The AOP exam procedure

In the AOP exam, a time slot of 10 minutes is allowed for each student; longer exams have been considered but currently cannot be accommodated by the university's intensive exam timetable. Each student is required to give a 6–7 minute presentation on a topic related to their field of studies, which is followed by a 3–4 minute question phase. The specific topics are chosen by the students (for example, a biotechnology student might choose to give a presentation on lab-grown meat or 3D printing). The students are examined in groups of three or four to give some sense of audience and to reflect possible future situations in the world of work. A small-scale study carried out in 2009 found that the majority of students (90 per cent) were not disturbed by the presence of their peers during their AOP exam.

Two examiners are present: the interlocutor, who is responsible for the timing of the exam and for interaction in the question phase, and the assessor, who completes the score sheet.

The question phase

Although students are required to specify the topic chosen in advance of the AOP exam, the content details are unknown to the examiners prior to the presentation. The questions asked by the interlocutor are, therefore, unscripted as they need to reflect the specific subject matter and content of each student's presentation. Students are asked to give their presentations at a level the examiners can understand, and the interlocutor's questions may hone in on any unclear areas or ask for expansion or different perspectives on certain points.

Scoring

During the exam the assessor fills in a score sheet by awarding marks for the following criteria (shown with weighting):

- Content, style and support materials (40 per cent of the final mark).
- Language (voice, vocabulary, grammar) (40 per cent of the final mark).

In respect of content, separate marks are given for the introduction, main part, summary/conclusion and question phase. Descriptor bands appropriate to the students' level of learning (for example, B2 or C1) are used for the language components, and the vocabulary and grammar criteria take both range and accuracy into account.

- To complete the scoring, a global mark is awarded by the interlocutor (20 per cent of the final mark).

As even the best criteria are open to interpretation, rater training is considered essential and carried out prior to an exam session at each level. The examiners complete score sheets for entire AOPs which have been videoed in previous years and discuss the marks awarded to achieve an appropriate degree of consensus. This contributes to the reliability of the assessment process.

Conclusion

We have used AOPs for around five years and found them to be an efficient, effective means of assessment, which promotes independent learning and develops important abilities. Not only do AOPs involve speaking skills, but also reading (to prepare the AOP), writing (of the supporting visual material) and listening (to the interlocutor's questions). The marking scheme described takes these different aspects into account and promotes reliable scoring of the exam.

luma@zhaw.ch
kirudin@gmx.net

Reference

Sundrarajun, C. and R. N. Kiely. 2009. 'The oral presentation as a context for learning and assessment'. *Innovation in Language Learning and Teaching* 3: 1–17.

11.4 How to write a good test

Russell Whitehead and Shakeh Manassian *Language Testing 123, Cambridge, UK*

This workshop focused on the issues that teachers need to bear in mind when developing tests for use in the classroom, whether they be for formative purposes or for summative purposes.

What is a test?

The workshop covered three key issues:

- what a test is;
- what the purposes of testing are and why this is such an important consideration; and
- what the elements of a good test task are.

The workshop encouraged participants to work together at certain points during the presentation, to compare experiences and to pool knowledge and understanding about testing. This began with a discussion of what a test is: an organised set of tasks, where the organisation is based on the purposes of the test, and these purposes affect the selection of the material to be included in the test as well as the format of test tasks. We continued by trying to identify the characteristics of a 'good' test: A *tool* that allows you to *collect evidence* from the student in order to make a fair *evaluation* and/or *judgment.*

Why have tests?

The discussion then moved onto the purposes of testing, and again the participants were encouraged to reflect on their own contexts. Answers provided included selection, diagnosis, feedback, future action and so on. It can be argued that some of these decisions may be made by teachers without resorting to testing. However, testing does provide teachers with certain elements that reflect real life situations in a way that the classroom cannot. The test allows us to collect a sample of student performance at a certain point in time (usually at the end of a learning period), under certain conditions that apply to everyone being tested, and where errors can have serious consequences, which is so often the case in real-life situations. This is very different from the classroom, where student error does not have a huge impact on the student.

What is a good test?

It is very important that the tasks in the test allow teachers to sample the correct kind of performance so that they make fair judgments based on the performances of their students. Testing tasks thus need to be based around a variety of task types, in order to collect a range of evidence from students. Tasks also need to make sure that the tasks focus on what the student can *do* more than on what the student *knows* about language, making best use of the time available. Testing tasks also give us insights into the student's communicative competence: how well the students can use what they know in order to communicate. As test writers, we aim to make testing tasks contextualised, meaningful and purposeful where appropriate: we want to mirror the kinds of real-life activities students may need to carry out in the L2. Learning tasks, on the other hand, tend to be repetitional, their main purpose being to help students understand and practise, and generally they tend to focus on a single element of language at a time—vocabulary or structure.

Not wide of the mark

One final element that test writers need to consider is the way marks are allocated to each task and performance. Mark allocation needs to represent our purposes, how much we value each element that we are testing, and the cognitive processing that the student undertakes when completing the task and answering the question(s).

So...

This session therefore highlighted some of the issues that need to be taken into consideration when teachers begin to develop their own tests. Test writing is a complex activity. It must be based on careful consideration of the purposes and a clear understanding of the outcomes required in order to make fair judgments about the performance of our students and their next steps.

russell@languagetesting123.co
shakeh@languagetesting123.co

11.5 Pearson Signature Event: Testing in a 21st-century paradigm—measuring students' progress using appropriate technology and integrated skills testing

David Booth *Pearson*

Introduction

With students becoming ever more results oriented, there is more pressure on teachers to be able to define a student's level of English and to provide evidence of the progress that students have made during their English course. But what does it mean to accurately measure a student's level of English and to identify the progress that a student has made across all four language skills, and how can we avoid teaching and learning for the test? The Pearson IATEFL Conference Signature Event brought together experts in the field of learning and testing to answer questions related to progress testing and the way forward in the 21st century. The panel discussed ways to test progress and debated the pros and cons of discrete versus integrated skills testing and the role of technology in future developments.

The panel was chaired by David Booth, Director of Test Development at Pearson English. Speakers were Dave Allan, Director and co-founder of NILE; Zeynep Urkun, Assessment Coordinator at Sabanci University, Istanbul; Raquel Villanueva Bergasa, Language Coordinator, Ceste, Zaragoza; and John de Jong, Professor of Assessment at VU University Amsterdam, President of EALTA, and Senior Vice President, Standards and Quality Office, Pearson.

Question for the panel

What are the current limitations in the testing of students' progress?

In summary, there are different interpretations of levels. Traditional labels such as 'elementary' and 'intermediate' are not particularly helpful. CEFR levels have gone some way to address this but they are still not granular enough to give a clear idea of progression. Similarly a CEFR level is a stretch, so the label 'B1' does not tell you where in the B1 range a student is.

To test progress there needs to be two points of measurement; Dave Allan noted that the length of time between these two points can sometimes be too short to observe any meaningful progress. The expectation that it takes a few weeks or 100 hours of instruction to move a level is a widely held misconception. It takes a long time to move through levels, though clearly it is quicker to move through lower levels than higher levels.

In addition the assessment instrument must be sufficiently accurate to give a meaningful measurement. We need more modern approaches to testing, including the use of adaptive testing.

Curriculum and courses can have a great deal of content, of which much is important. Selecting what to test is a challenge that classroom teachers face. Related to this is the issue of assessment literacy. Zeynep Urkun pointed out that teaching methodology courses, teacher training courses and longer degree courses have very little content relating to assessment. What they do have tends to be theoretical and not practical; however, teachers will often find they are asked to prepare tests, including progress tests, in their work.

Audience responses

Members of the audience raised the point of unrealistic expectations in academic and general language contexts. One member of the audience gave the example of IELTS courses where students are expected to move a half or a whole band on the scale. The audience member felt this was unrealistic, especially in terms of vocabulary knowledge. The panel member agreed that it is not possible to raise students' level significantly over a very short period of time. Assessment literacy was also cited again as a barrier to implementing appropriate and realistic progress tests.

Question from the website

What are the advantages of technology in testing, in particular, in testing speaking?

Practical experience shows us that it is more and more important to integrate technology and assessment. The context is wider though; it relates not only to assessment but also to learning in, and indeed outside, the classroom and across all skills. Students expect technology in the classroom and as language professionals we need to keep up with the times.

Audience responses

In response to an audience question the panel gave examples of where technology has been implemented to overcome practical issues such as the location of candidates. The panel also discussed how the careful use of technology can add significant value to the validity of tests by allowing us to test real language in real time. The panel also stressed the value of a profile of scores which technology can help to produce more accurately.

The way in which automated scoring of spoken and written items is carried out was explained by John de Jong. He explained, in simple terms, how the technology uses comparisons with other responses which had been marked by very experienced assessors in conjunction with other tools such as speech recognition and corpus data analysis.

Question from the website

How can we (teachers and institutions) design integrated skills tests to diagnose students' levels effectively and accurately?

It is not realistic to expect teachers to develop the skills to do this without proper training. With training and investment in terms of time money and effort, it is very possible for teachers to develop the skills to design and develop integrated tests of English.

Trends in education now are going further than just integrated skills. A wider range of skills, sometimes called 21st-century skills are needed across a range of subjects including reading and listening, reading and maths, problem solving giving presentations, and other 'soft' skills.

Question from the website

Do students do better when they know they are being tested?

It depends on the student. Raquel Villanueva Bergasa pointed out that some students are happy if they pass an exam rather than if there is proof of improvement. Sometimes the focus is too much on results rather than progress. Teachers try to present topics which are interesting to students and work across a range of skills, which helps motivate students. They can be motivated, for example, by computer games where they can 'save the princess' or win points or stars. We need to replicate this in language learning. Critical to good assessment is a balance of different assessment procedures which allow us to build a profile of a student's skills to get the best possible sample so that we are fair in our assessment. Problem solving skills also have a role in testing as they foster achievement. The successful solving of a problem has a positive effect on learning which, in turn, can lead to progress in language learning.

Teaching and learning

The conceptual framework which underpins effective progress testing is Assessment for Learning—the idea that testing should inform and support teaching, and also be informed and supported by teaching, in a continuous feedback loop. There is considerable academic evidence for the potential of Assessment for Learning to not only demonstrate outcomes but actually improve them.

In 1998 the Nuffield Foundation commissioned Professors Paul Black and Dylan William to evaluate the evidence from more than 250 studies linking assessment and learning. Their analysis was definitive; that initiatives designed to enhance the effectiveness of assessment in the classroom can raise students' achievement. They showed that linking assessment and learning can improve student's achievement more effectively than other interventions.

Speck and Knipe (2001) showed that teachers who are supported to collect and analyse data in order to reflect on their practice are more likely to make improvements as they learn new skills and practice them in the classroom. Through the evaluation process, teachers learn to examine their teaching, reflect on practice and evaluate their results based on student achievement. Other researchers have also shown that ¬teachers can adapt instruction on the basis of evidence, reflect and make changes that will yield immediate benefits to student learning.

In summary, the most effective approach to learning and assessment is to align the formative and summative elements so they are seen to measure the same concept i.e. student progress.

Conclusions

The Pearson IATEFL conference signature event brought together experts in the field of learning and testing to answer questions related to progress testing and the way forward in the 21st Century. There was general agreement on the challenges in using technology in testing and giving teachers the tools and the assessment knowledge and skills to effectively promote real learning and progress in students' language ability.

The organisers would like to thank all members of the panel and the knowledgeable and attentive audience for making the event a great success.

david.booth@pearson.com

References

Black, P. and D. William. 1999. *Assessment for Learning: Beyond the Black Box.* University of Cambridge School of Education.

Council of Europe. 2001. *Common European Framework of Reference for Language; Learning, teaching, assessment.* Strasbourg: Modern Languages Division, Council of Europe.

Speck, M. and C. Knipe. 2001. *Why Can't We get it Right? Professional Development in our Schools.* Thousand Oaks, Calif.: Corwin Press, Inc.

11.6 Assessing the unassessed or the unassessible: issues of school evaluation

Maria-Araxi Sachpazian *Input on Education, Thessaloniki, Greece.*

The debate regarding school assessment

If seen superficially, any discussion on school assessment seems unnecessary as professionals know the strengths and weaknesses of the schools at which they teach. Quite contrary to this emotional take on the issue, systematic assessment of our practices, which can render quantifiable data, is the only means available to us in order to initiate change and improve the work of the school.

Unfortunately, there are many obstacles standing between school assessment and the formation of clear conclusions related to the efficacy of the school. First of all, assessing schools is not straightforward as schools are complicated organisations (White *et al.* 2008), with many of their features remaining either *unassessed*, because they slip under the assessment radar, or *unassessible* because they are too qualitative to be quantified. Secondly, the definition of 'a good teacher' or 'a good lesson' is hard to standardise (Coleman and Earley 2005). Even the tools used in school assessments (observations, questionnaires, interviews) are highly subjective and can easily give us a misleading idea of what actually happens in the school *after* the assessment is over. Finally, when school assessment is carried out by external inspection teams, educational issues cannot be fully understood in the limited time available. An internal assessment, which might solve this problem, may suffer from another problem: lack of objectivity.

Confusion made worse

Many think that through school assessment we can identify policies of excellence, which can then be applied by other schools in an effort to create 'recipes' for effective schools. While that sounds promising, only indications of what has worked in other schools can be given, not exact practices that can be duplicated. (Harris 2002: 7)

Others have related school assessment solely to accountability and the upward or downward movement of the staff. This has discouraged the employees from actually investing in the assessment and has created a contradiction: although the assessment is supposed to take place for the benefit of the school, the staff tends to be less than excited about it. Relating assessment closely with accountability means that the element of change, which is what teachers hope to get out of an in-depth assessment of the school practices, is removed. Therefore, the assessment seems to be irrelevant to the real issues that touch upon the teaching reality of that school; this explains why the staff members do not invest emotionally in it.

Another area of confusion is that of relating the success of the students with the efficacy of the school. Contrary to the opinion of non-experts, student achievement cannot account for the efficacy of the school, as student intake is carefully scrutinised so that only high scorers are accepted (Coleman and Earley 2005). Student achievement is an indicator of school efficacy but we cannot rely on it to evaluate the actual process of teaching. The area that might render useful data might be that of the actual effect the school has had on the lives and personalities of the learners, but this is far too difficult to study (Coleman and Earley 2005).

Towards a self-regulated model of SA

So far we have seen school assessment as externally imposed and top-down. Undoubtedly, this mode of assessment is significant but hopefully in the near future assessment will be more closely associated with continuing professional development; it will be considered an agent of change rather than a means of firing or promoting. In that case school assessment ought to become part of the reflective practice of the school with the staff determining what is assessed and the criteria to assess it. Ideally, the only real way of assessing whether such an assessment has been successful would be to check the extent of sustainable change that it has inspired and the progress the entire school has made.

Conclusions

The obvious benefit of this self-regulated model of school assessment is that the staff would feel more connected to the assessment process, since it would emerge as a need from within; in other words, it would be more closely related to the real issues that matter to those involved with the school. Moreover, a comparison of the findings of external and internal assessments would enable the school administration to rate data that has so far remained either unassessed or was considered unassessible; this would help administration reach more reliable conclusions regarding the kind of change that needs to be initiated.

sachpazian@input.edu.gr

References

Coleman, M. and P. Earley. 2005. *Leadership and Management in Education: Cultures, Change and Context.* Oxford: Oxford University Press.

Harris, A. 2002. *School Improvement. What's in It for Schools?* New York: Routledge.

White, R., A. Hockley, J. Van der Horst Jensen and M. Laughner. 2008. *From Teacher to Manager. Managing Language Teaching Organisations.* Cambridge: Cambridge University Press.

12 The developing teacher

One of the key themes at IATEFL 2013 was that of teacher development; some of the papers presented are included in this final chapter. The chapter begins with **Deniz Kurtoğlu Eken**'s plenary, in which she reports on her research into teacher perceptions of the effectiveness of ELT in specific contexts, as well as their motivation as educators. This is followed by **Alan Waters**' thought-provoking paper on the similarities between concepts found in George Orwell's *Nineteen Eighty-Four* and the discourse of ELT. Next, **Peter Watkins** presents examples of 'bottom-up' teacher development activities; **Sarah Milligan** encourages teachers to take chances and experiment in their teaching; and **Andrew Walkley** appeals for an emphasis on language in teacher development activities. Next, **Chris Baldwin** discusses the benefits of using e-portfolios as a tool for professional development. The following papers describe research and professional development projects carried out in various contexts around the world. **Barbara González** reports on research carried out in Mexico on the influence that trust, respect and pride have on teacher development, while **Daniel Xerri** questions the extent to which Maltese teachers use social media for professional development. **Ekaterina Shadrova** reports on a CPD project for novice teachers in Russia; and finally, **Jane Cohen** describes a school-based professional development programme for teachers in Israel.

12.1 Plenary: The ELT weather forecast: perceptions on effectiveness and teacher motivation

Deniz Kurtoğlu Eken *Sabancı University, Istanbul, Turkey*

Introduction

> Thinking is like the weather: in itself it is neither good nor bad. However, when people project their own needs and feelings on to the weather, then the weather can become 'good' to one person and 'bad' to another: a farmer who is crying out for rain will see the persistent sunshine as 'bad', while the holidaymaker will see the same sunshine as 'glorious' and the dark clouds as 'bad'. Similarly, thoughts in themselves have little power to influence how people feel about themselves, or others, or life; it is the emotions which infuse them that are powerful. (Humphreys 1996: 27)

What is the weather like in ELT today? What atmospheric patterns can we observe in our perceptions on effectiveness in different areas in our energy field: in methodology, research, curriculum, assessment, technology, learner development, teacher training and development, management and professional networking? What low and high pressures exist in our professional contexts? What about teacher motivation? We know our well-being matters, that it affects all aspects of our lives, and that our health, energy, happiness and inner peace are prerequisites for greater effectiveness in our professional work. So how are we doing on the motivational front in our work places?

Based on a qualitative research study on our own perceptions of effectiveness and motivation in a variety of ELT contexts across the world, this paper explores how we perceive 'the weather' (c.f. extract from Humphreys above) in ELT in terms of effectiveness in different professional areas; discusses patterns that seem to emerge with respect to our understanding and expectations of teacher motivation; and presents findings on what the ELT forecast seems to call for in the near future.

Background and research

The research was carried out through an online survey sent out in January 2013 to a wide range of networks across the world, for example, IATEFL associate members, EAQUALS members, members of various other language associations, European language project networks, various professional networks, etc.; it was also promoted through several social media networks. The survey consisted of two demographic, two Likert-scale and six open-ended questions focusing on participants' perceptions on the effectiveness of ELT in a variety of professional areas in the countries and contexts where they worked as well as their views on personal and professional development and teacher motivation.

A total of 290 responses were received from language professionals in 51 different countries. Table 12.1.1 below presents the top five countries according to the number and percentage of respondents who completed the survey.

Country	Number of respondents	Percentage of respondents
Turkey	54	18.62
The UK (England 24, Scotland 11)	35	12.07
The United Arab Emirates	28	9.66
Argentina	23	7.93
Spain	15	5.17

Table 12.1.1: The top five countries with highest survey response rates

The remaining 46.55 per cent of the responses were from the following countries listed according to response rates from high to low: Austria, Malta, Hong Kong, Ireland, Japan, Switzerland, Greece, Estonia, Italy, Australia, Bangladesh, Canada, Croatia, Germany, Oman, Serbia, the USA, China, Pakistan, Bosnia-Herzegovina, Czech Republic, India, KSA, Kuwait, Nepal, Romania, TRNC, Uganda, Algeria, Belgium, Colombia, Honduras, Iceland, Israel, Korea, Macedonia, Namibia, Poland, Qatar, Russia, Senegal, South Korea, Taiwan, Thailand and Tunisia.

In terms of educational context, 56.90 per cent of the respondents were from higher education; 22.41 per cent from language schools, language institutes or adult education; and 20.69 per cent from primary and/or secondary education. With respect to teaching experience, 47.93 per cent of the respondents had over 15 years of teaching experience; 19.31 per cent between 11 and 15 years; 17.93 per cent between 6 and 10 years; and 14.83 per cent up to 5 years. Finally, Table 12.1.2 presents respondents' involvement in teaching and other professional responsibilities, in response to the question regarding what their 'current' work *mainly* involved at the time of the research.

Teaching	TTD	Management	Curriculum	Assessment	Other
60.34%	11.38%	15.17%	1.72%	0.34%	11.03%

Table 12.1.2: Respondents' main areas of involvement

What follows is a discussion of the findings based on the survey data, analysed through the use of descriptive statistics and qualitative analysis based on description, exemplification and cross data analysis.

The findings

A closer look at the respondents

[I am like] a tree—over the years developing strong roots and solid branches as well as lush leaves to provide a safe place for students to learn, rest and develop.

The demographic and factual information presented above is useful in terms of a general understanding of the respondents' backgrounds; what is much more revealing, however, is the qualitative data obtained through respondents' perceptions of where/how they see themselves with respect to their personal and professional development. This is revealed through their responses to the question: 'If you were to choose a metaphor for where/how you see yourself with respect to your personal and professional development, how would you describe it? What metaphor would you choose and why?' In this respect, although this section attempts to present in-depth data on the self-perceptions of survey respondents, it also acts as a bridge between the factual information and the findings which the survey data reveal. It was gratifying to see that although the question was an optional one, 81.4 per cent of the respondents chose to answer it. It was even more gratifying to observe the wealth of metaphors used, as is revealed in the graphic representation in Figure 12.1.1 (overleaf) attempting to highlight the most common concepts that were referred to in the 236 metaphors used.

Despite some highly positive metaphors related to respondents' perceptions of their own personal and professional development, such as those involving concepts of growth (for example, the extract of the tree metaphor in the introduction to this section), journey, progression, exploration and hard work, an overwhelming majority of the metaphors used involved concepts of challenge, struggle, mismatch in aims/

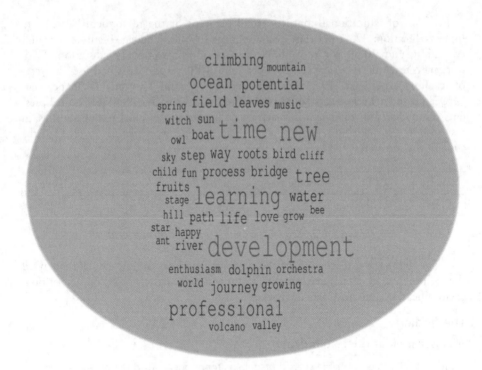

Figure 12.1.1: Metaphors for personal and professional development

expectations, frustration/helplessness, multitasking and untapped/unfulfilled potential. These metaphors are exemplified in Table 12.1.3 along with several key concepts
that each one appears to relate to.

Perceptions of effectiveness in ELT

Respondents were asked to comment on their perceptions of the overall effectiveness
of 12 different areas in ELT in two separate questions based on a four-point Likert
scale (4 = highly effective, 1 = not effective) as well as a 'not applicable' option:

- What is your perception of the *overall* effectiveness of the following areas in *the
country where you work*?
- What is your perception of the *overall* effectiveness of the following areas in *your
current work context*?

The 12 areas were as follows: language teaching methodology; curriculum development; language testing and assessment; technology-supported teaching and learning;
learner development; fostering student motivation; teacher training and development; fostering teacher motivation; professional networking; research in language
teaching and learning; academic management; English language teaching overall.
One of the questions focused on how respondents perceived effectiveness in a given
area in the country where they worked while the second question focused on their

Metaphor	Key concept(s)
I always think of myself as a plate spinner, trying to keep a number of plates spinning without letting of them fall. The plates are my numerous roles—wife, mother, teacher, examiner, writer, researcher, presenter.	multitasking frustration/helplessness
'A glorified secretary'—as the Director of the department, I seem to spend most of my days sitting in front of a PC or running around preparing ISO documentation for my teachers to use. I have very little/no time to teach or develop my own career.	frustration/helplessness
I see myself as continuously grasping for the apple on the tree—I can't always see it, I know it is there, but I just don't seem to be able to pick it. This is because ELT is continuously developing and it is challenging to keep up with all the new ideas and research. There's never enough time.	frustration/helplessness challenge/struggle
I see myself as the turtle in the race against the hare. A turtle has a protective shell which is needed as the academic environment can be sharply critical. At the same time, real scholarship and teaching development is a slow process by which results are not immediately seen. There are many hares leaping ahead but then they get complacent and rest which is when the turtles manage to win the race...	challenge/struggle untapped/unfulfilled potential
I am a caged bird. I want to soar in the open sky; I want to taste with newness. But I am compelled to follow what my masters—school, curriculum, textbooks, assessment system, etc. order me to do. I know the outside is open; I know I can grow ... when I go out of this cage ... I am confident I can travel far (give better results), but am helpless. I have no power ... to go out of this cage.	mismatch in aims/ expectations frustration/helplessness
The only description, and my colleagues would agree, would be that of slaves with no faces that can be thrown around like puppets, used and thrown at the bosses' convenience. Gaining more qualifications, or expressing a desire to improve in terms of professional development, would be thwarted, boycotted ... not acknowledged either in terms of responsibilities in the school or in terms of pay.	frustration/helplessness
I am an anchor on a lifeboat. The boat is desperately trying to flow with the current in the hopes of colliding with an inhabited island. The anchor is there waiting to be used and thirsty to catch onto something with strength, but no one wants to release it. They would rather float aimlessly in a vast ocean of ideas and theories.	mismatch in aims/ expectations untapped/unfulfilled potential frustration/helplessness

Table 12.1.3: Metaphors for personal and professional development

current work context. Figure 12.1.2 presents a comparative analysis of respondents' perceptions on effectiveness with respect to the 12 areas above, in the countries where they work and in their work contexts.

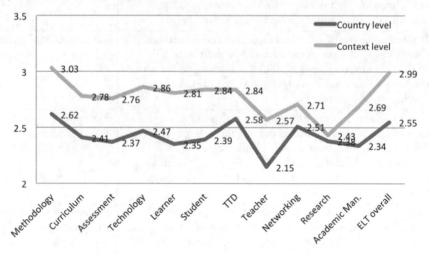

Figure 12.1.2: Perceptions of effectiveness in countries and work contexts in the given 12 areas in ELT

The areas of language teaching methodology and ELT overall were perceived among the top three areas in terms of effectiveness, both at the country level and in terms of effectiveness in the work contexts. Although in differing orders of effectiveness, the same applied to the areas of teacher training and development and technology-supported teaching and learning. It is worth mentioning at this stage that despite the fact that both areas were in the top five in terms of perceived effectiveness, fewer comments were provided by the respondents in terms of technology-supported teaching and learning than were for teacher training and development. The former focused on key factors such as the provision of technological equipment, budget and investment issues, access and software, training opportunities and integration into the curriculum. With the latter, i.e. teacher training and development, respondents appeared to express varying yet greater degrees of satisfaction—i.e. than they did for technology-supported teaching and learning—with what they appreciated the most in their countries and/or their work contexts:

- in-service training and staff development opportunities: INSET, developmental sessions, workshops, visiting speakers/guests, induction programmes;
- teacher training courses (for example, CELTA, DELTA, post-DELTA/post-MA opportunities, other training courses);
- Special Interest Groups (SIGs), teacher forums;
- research groups, institutional research projects;
- opportunities for lesson observation and feedback; and
- professional networking opportunities.

For greater effectiveness, what appeared to be common concerns in the area of teacher training and development were related to the frequency and practical applications of the opportunities provided as well as to the provision of funding opportunities.

Professional networking, fostering student motivation, curriculum development, learner development, language testing and assessment, and research in language teaching and learning were perceived to be effective in the work contexts but much less effective at the country level. In fact this seemed to be a common pattern in all the data received on the two Likert-scale questions on effectiveness (see Table 12.1.4); respondents almost unanimously expressed a (much) higher degree of effectiveness in their perceptions of effectiveness in all 12 areas at the work context level and a lesser degree of effectiveness at the country level.

Area	Country	Area	Work context (4-point Likert scale)
Methodology	2.62	Methodology	3.03
TTD	2.58	ELT overall	2.99
ELT overall	2.55	Technology	2.86
Networking	2.51	Student motivation	2.84
Technology	2.47	TTD	2.84
Curriculum	2.41	Learner development	2.81
Student motivation	2.39	Curriculum	2.78
Research	2.38	Assessment	2.76
Assessment	2.37	Networking	2.71
Learner development	2.35	Academic management	2.69
Academic management	2.34	Teacher motivation	2.57
Teacher motivation	2.15	Research	2.43

Table 12.1.4: Perceptions of effectiveness in countries and work contexts in the given 12 areas in ELT

The qualitative data obtained through the comments sections in both questions reveal a variety of factors that may have influenced the difference in respondents' perceptions in these two categories i.e. the country level and the work context level:

- differences in educational settings within the country;
- too many changes and/or experimentation with little time to observe the results;
- *ad hoc* policies and (rushed) decisions;
- high student population, class sizes and limited educational resources;
- differences in the way teachers are trained;
- public/state and private sector divide in education;
- involvement of persons with no ELT background or training in policy-making and educational design;

- time restrictions/constraints in implementation; and
- poor management of human and academic resources.

It is clear from the data that the above factors changed from country to country and from context to context. Yet, along with other factors that are discussed in the following sections, such factors also seemed to affect respondents' perceptions of the areas they perceived as the least effective at both the country level and in their work contexts.

Respondents were also asked the question, 'If you have rated any of the areas as "not (very) effective", what do you believe is needed the most to make it/them more effective in your current work context?' However, for the purposes of this paper and due to space limitations, we will only be focusing on respondents' comments in the two areas of fostering teacher motivation and academic management, which were rated as the least effective at the work context level and much less effective at the country level—see Table 12.1.4.

Feedback to managers

> [What is needed are] highly qualified, flexible and adaptable managers who can manage talent and different types of personality... This mainly requires a strong personality; [being] at peace with oneself, a facilitative and solution-oriented approach, willingness to share responsibility... and respect for initiative.

The findings in this section are a synthesis of the data obtained from the answers given by respondents on what they believe is needed most in the area of academic management to make it more effective, as well as responses to a separate question in the survey, seeking respondents' views on what feedback they may wish to share with the relevant group of professionals, i.e. academic managers.

A detailed analysis of the qualitative data reveals that respondents' needs and feedback in terms of (greater) effectiveness in academic management centre around the key sub-areas presented below with sample extracts from the data:

- Listening to teachers [more], for example, 'Seek feedback from your staff; listen to their feedback without offence.'
- Trusting teachers, for example, 'Trust teachers more and interfere less. Realise that teaching is a creative act, the results of which are not always quantifiable. What counts cannot be counted.' and, 'Treat teachers as professionals not as skilled workers in need of constant supervision.'
- Having a flexible and open-minded approach, for example, 'Please don't let technology become the be all and end all of ELT because it is not. Language is firstly communication, but using technology all the time is making the students passive and uncommunicative.'
- Involving teachers in decision making, for example, 'Involve your teachers in decision making; do not make unilateral decisions that affect the whole staff and learners.'
- Observing fairness, for example, 'The school leadership should be chosen based on academic and leadership efficiency, not on age and tenure basis.'
- Having a less top down approach, for example, 'No or less hierarchy please!'
- Encouraging people to work as a team, for example, 'Teachers need to communicate more and collaborate instead of self-promotion and back-stabbing.'

- A supportive, not authoritarian, approach, for example, 'Communicate more and better; smiling does not harm; be responsive and constructive; your positive attitude matters to us.'
- Balancing work and life for example, 'I love my work, but am also a mother, spouse and daughter, if not more...' and, 'Help teachers to develop and grow both personally and professionally.'
- Stronger and more decisive action, for example, 'Just say it or do it when we [teachers] cannot decide or it just takes too long and everyone has something different to say!'

The above data and extracts clearly reveal that an effective manager is someone who trusts and listens to his/her teachers, involving them in decision-making processes; who has a flexible and open-minded approach, observing fairness and equality as much as possible; who does not have a top-down approach, but is supportive and encourages teachers to work as a team, helping them to maintain a balance between their work and life; and who does not shy away from putting his/her foot down in cases of group/team indecision.

Fostering teacher motivation

> I am based in a large school and am just another number. More feedback and motivation needed.

Another survey question sought to receive qualitative data on key areas of teacher motivation and—if existed within the context—on teacher demotivation. Figure 12.1.3 is an attempt to capture a synthesis of the data on the former area, using *tagxedo.com* to create a visual word cloud where words are individually sized appropriately to highlight the frequencies of occurrence within the body of text.

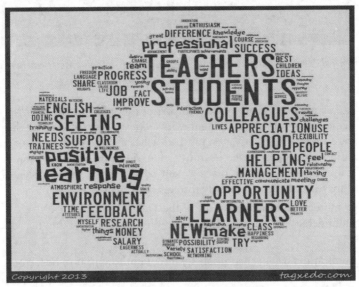

Figure 12.1.3: A data word cloud on what seems to motivate teachers the most in their profession

Data obtained from the non-compulsory and open-ended responses to the question, 'What motivates you most in your current work context?' reveals that students or learners themselves are one of the biggest sources of motivation along with teachers or colleagues who are ready and willing to support mutual learning processes through various forms of help, support, feedback and 'new' or different learning opportunities within the work environment. However, most of the qualitative comments in the data obtained also additionally refer to management support and appreciation as discussed in the previous section.

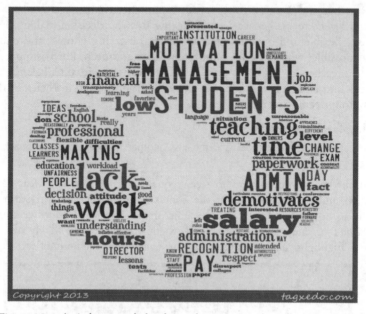

Figure 12.1.4: A data word cloud on what seems to demotivate teachers the most in their profession

Similarly, data obtained from the second part of the same question, 'What—if anything—demotivates you in your current work context?' seemed to reveal that students can also be a source of demotivation for the teacher if students themselves are lacking in motivation towards language learning. Alongside this data, however, are factors such as those discussed in the management-related issues in the previous section, expressed maybe even more intensely through data such as:

• Teacher motivation is sadly not part of the agenda in my context.
• Being considered like human beings instead of 24-hour working machines would be nice.

Less frequent in the data, yet additionally importantly, appear to be factors related to rewards (for example, better pay, financial rewards); better policies and approach; balance in workload; recognition, appreciation and praise; opportunities for promotion and advancement; and encouragement of creativity and experimentation.

So what is the weather like in ELT today?

The weather metaphor used by a research informant in terms of how s/he perceives her/his personal and professional development also appears to neatly summarise the findings of this research study with respect to effectiveness in different areas in ELT:

A partly-cloudy sky with the sun shining from behind the clouds; this metaphor describes how I see myself with respect to both my personal and professional development quite well because while I feel I can bring sunshine to the lives of others as well as to myself there are too many dense clouds sometimes in my way.

As the data suggests, we seem to be doing well in a wide range of areas despite inevitable differences in the degree of effectiveness at the country level and in terms of our different work contexts. To use 'sunshine' in a positive perception, we can conclude that the sun *is* shining, yet there appear to be two 'dense clouds' which need our greater attention and thinking: academic management practices and fostering teacher motivation. This is also supported by research on effective exemplary schools where strong educational leadership stands out as a key area of need along with, professional autonomy, a clear intention to get the best out of every learner, a safe and orderly environment, and a healthy school climate (Scheerens 2000: 52).

The effectiveness of our school practices clearly depends on staff effectiveness, but this is not possible to achieve without a motivated group of individuals who approach their work in a positive frame of mind, knowing that their efforts and work are recognised. A frustrated teacher asks:

Do you feel the frustration I feel because almost all we are talking about is 'how to be better teachers' like everything else were just fine?

Teachers are our most important asset. We cannot have true development, enrichment and advancement without an investment in teacher motivation and teachers' personal professional development. A manager or school director clearly plays the biggest role in promoting and sustaining a positive and constructive work environment and an ethos of participation, engagement and responsibility. This, however, cannot be the responsibility of the manager or director alone; 'the sand of an entire shore is indivisible' (McTaggart 2002: 214) and every individual member of staff needs to be encouraged to contribute towards such a positive ethos and synthesis of energy:

Nothing is meaningful as long as we perceive only separate fragments. But as soon as the fragments come together into a synthesis, a new entity emerges, whose nature we could not have foreseen by considering the fragments alone. (Ferrucci 1982: 22)

Examples of motivational strategies that can usefully be practised by all parties include the following:

• Learning to thank ourselves and others; appreciating positive developments no matter how 'small' they may appear to be; 'little things' do matter and make a difference.
• Looking for progress rather than perfection in ourselves and others.
• Practising acts of kindness and learning to apologise to others.

- Adopting a label- and category-free mindset; avoiding social comparison; using constructive language and feedback with our colleagues (not only with our students).
- Developing collaborative strategies for coping with challenges and teacher burnout.
- Rather than dismissing ideas, embracing choices, alternatives, elements of surprise and some ambiguity in the work context.
- Looking after one's 'space'; creating opportunities for personal development (in addition to professional development) within the work context where individuals voluntarily offer sessions in an area of expertise or interest for example, jewellery making, dance routines, how to do self and other massage, the Tarot, chess or backgammon tournaments, effective breathing techniques, cooking, etc.

Finally and maybe most importantly schools can benefit from engaging in ongoing institutional research and development, seeking ways to enhance staff morale and motivation (Whitaker *et al.* 2009) and exploring perceptions of individuals in their own work contexts for example, by discussing perception-based questions such as, 'If you became your (own) manager for six months, what would you do?'

A copy of the survey used in the research study can be obtained from the author at the email address below.

kurtoglueken@sabanciuniv.edu

References

Ferrucci, P. 1982. *What We May Be: Techniques for Psychological and Spiritual Growth through Psychosynthesis.* New York: Jeremy P.Tarcher/Penguin.

Humphreys, T. 1996. *The Power of 'Negative' Thinking.* Warrington: Newleaf.

McTaggart, L. 2002. *The Field: The Quest for the Secret Force of the Universe.* London: Harper Perennial.

Scheerens, J. 2000. *Improving School Effectiveness: Fundamentals of Educational Planning.* No. 68. Paris: International Institute for Educational Planning.

Whitaker, T, B. Whitaker and D. Lumpa. 2009. *Motivating and Inspiring Teachers: The Educational Leader's Guide for Building Staff Morale.* (second edition). New York: Routledge.

12.2 'Orwellian' professional discourse in ELT: a threat to diversity

Alan Waters *Lancaster University, UK*

It is important that the ELT professional discourse (PD)—the main 'messages' in academic publications, and so on—represents its true diversity. Unfortunately, this is frequently not the case. A major reason for this state of affairs is the operation within the ELT PD of forms of 'thought control' similar to those in Orwell's novel *Nineteen Eighty-Four* (Orwell 2003).

In this novel, England is ruled by a dictator called 'Big Brother'. His repressive political ideology—'Ingsoc'—is based on three main concepts: (a) 'newspeak', (b) 'thoughtcrime', and (c) 'doublethink'. What each of these involves and how they also operate within the ELT PD is explained in what follows.

'Newspeak'

In *Nineteen Eighty-Four*, 'the purpose of Newspeak was not only to provide a medium of expression for the world-view and mental habits proper to the devotees of Ingsoc, but to make all other modes of thought impossible' (Orwell 2003: 312–13). Newspeak-like language also exists in the ELT PD, as in the use of terms such as 'authentic'. Texts within ELT are of two main kinds: 'naturally occurring' and 'specially written' ones. *Both* kinds have their pedagogical advantages and disadvantages. But the ELT PD uses the term 'authentic' only to refer to the former, whereas the latter are usually referred to as 'artificial'. In fact, however, no ELT text can be truly 'authentic' in this way, since it is not being used in its original context and for its original purpose. On the other hand, so-called 'artificial' texts can actually be regarded as 'authentic' in terms of their context of use and function. The PD usage in this respect therefore involves an (unwarranted) underlying bias in favour of 'naturalistic' and against classroom-based forms of language learning, a covert type of thought control.

'Thoughtcrime'

In Orwell's novel, holding views seen as contrary to the beliefs of Ingsoc is regarded as 'thoughtcrime', i.e. illegal. Compliance is enforced by the 'Thought Police'. This form of thought control also exists in the ELT PD with respect to, for example, Task-based Learning (TBL). Reviews of research on TBL, such as Swan (2005), show that it is ineffective 'as regards the systematic teaching of new linguistic material' and 'its exclusive use is particularly unsuitable for exposure-poor contexts where time is limited—that is to say, for most of the world's language learners.' (Swan 2005: 396–7). Nevertheless, as Prodromou and Mishan point out:

> There are forces in the native-speaker centre which would like to see the ... TBL focus applied more generally as a 'good thing', if not a best method ... Indeed in some local areas, the new methodological trends are accepted and adopted as 'correct', given the authority of native-speakers and academics based in prestigious Anglo-American ... and ... Australian universities (2008: 194).

As they go on to say, such attitudes result in what they refer to as 'methodological correctness', that is 'a set of beliefs derived from prestigious but incomplete academic research in the Anglo-phone centre that influences the decisions one makes regarding materials and methods in the classroom, even if those decisions are inconsistent with the local context and particular needs and wants of the students one is teaching' (2008: 194).

'Doublethink'

In *Nineteen Eighty-Four*, '"Doublethink" means the power of holding two contradictory beliefs in one's mind simultaneously, and accepting both of them' (Orwell 2003: 219). A representative illustration of the presence of this concept in ELT PD is in its attitude towards pedagogical models of English. For various theoretical reasons, the ELT PD tends to regard the 'English as a native language' pedagogical model as inappropriate. However, research shows learners tend to prefer it. That learners hold such views has therefore resulted in the ELT PD constructing them as 'victims' of 'standard language ideology'. But this contradicts a well-established professional principle, the concept of 'learner-centredness', i.e. the importance of basing pedagogy on learners' perceived needs.

Conclusion

As has been shown, by behaving in ways which resemble the methods of thought control used in Orwell's *Nineteen Eighty-Four*, the ELT PD frequently fails to represent the true diversity of views that exist within ELT. This is greatly to the detriment of a healthy, democratic professional 'ecology'. It is therefore important that those most closely involved in the construction of the ELT PD make it a good deal more inclusive by developing a considerably less 'repressive' and much more balanced, open-minded outlook.

a.waters@lancaster.ac.uk

References

Orwell, G. 2003. *Nineteen Eighty-Four*. London: Penguin.

Prodromou, L. and F. Mishan. 2008. 'Materials used in western Europe' in B. Tomlinson (ed.). *English Language Learning Materials: A Critical Review*. London: Continuum.

Swan, M. 2005. 'Legislation by hypothesis: the case of task-based instruction'. *Applied Linguistics* 26/3: 376–401.

12.3 Taking control of teacher development

Peter Watkins *University of Portsmouth, UK*

Introduction

The talk began by arguing that teacher development (TD) is a process and hopefully one that is ongoing throughout a teacher's career. This internal process of development can be supported by external programmes of workshops, observations, and so on. However, for some teachers there is no TD support. For others, that support reflects an external agenda imposed by an institution or government ministry; this agenda may not address the developmental interests of the individual teacher. The talk centred on practical ways in which teachers could create a bottom-up, collaborative TD programme that would reflect their own interests and needs and be available as and when it was required.

Core principles

There is widespread evidence that teachers value talking to other teachers (for example, Senior 2006). This should not surprise us because staffroom talk is characterised as being reflective, practical, non-judgemental, localised (in the sense that it relates to a context that we share) and empathetic (we understand the constraints and challenges faced by our colleagues). The very nature of conversation makes staffroom talk collaborative and reciprocal, allowing tentative ideas to be built on and developed by others. These are solid principles on which to base any TD programme.

Some suggested activities

Reflective teaching has become a dominant model of teacher learning and is usually traced back to the work of John Dewey in the 1930s. While reflection is sometimes conceived of as a solitary process, this need not be the case. Collaborative reflection can be facilitated through simple procedures. For example, teachers can make notes at the end of a lesson about something that went well, or perhaps something that was less successful. At an agreed time, working with a small group of colleagues they trust and respect, teachers can then explain in as much detail as they can what happened and use questions from colleagues to build up a rich description of the incident. The group can work towards deciding the extent to which successful sequences could be generalised to other classes and contexts, as well as possible alternatives for the things that worked less well. This is a simple way of systematising and giving a focus to the staffroom talk that we know is valued.

A similar process could be gone through with experimental practice. Based on the ideas popularised by John Fanselow (1987), teachers can experiment by breaking with the 'rules' of their usual teaching routine. To give just one example, a teacher may experiment with using silence to a greater extent and thereby encouraging more learner thinking time. Teachers could all try the same experiment, or each try different ones, before getting together and reflecting on the outcomes.

Observation is a central component of most TD programmes. However, when it is implemented in a top-down way it can lead to defensiveness and anxiety. This vulnerability may prevent teachers being observed from seeking guidance where they feel the most need and instead 'playing safe', demonstrating techniques in which they already feel comfortable. Peer observation with a negotiated agenda can help to alleviate some aspects of this although subsequent discussion suggested those audience members with experience of peer observation found it difficult to remove all judgement. Two solutions to this were suggested. One is to team-teach the lesson so that both people are observed and observer, removing the hierarchical structure of most observations. Another potential solution is to limit the role of the observer to collecting data, for example, counting and classifying teacher questions, timing student contributions, and so on. With an agreed agenda, this removes all judgement from the situation.

Setting up reading groups that discuss the relevance of articles and papers to the local context is another excellent way of promoting collaborative development. In addition, the more theoretical orientation of reading can support reflective practice as teachers strive to understand the theory that informs their classroom activity. Working collaboratively can give a focus and purpose to reading and be both motivating and rewarding.

Conclusion

TD is an internal process, unique to each teacher and as such, it cannot be measured in terms of workshops, observations, and so on. However, that ongoing process can and should be supported. A TD programme needs to address the needs and agendas of those it serves, and one way of achieving this is for it to be designed by the very people who use it. Hopefully the activities suggested above can help more teachers take control of their own development programmes.

peter.watkins@port.ac.uk

References

Dewey, J. 1938. *Experience and Education*. New York: Collier.

Fanselow, J. 1987. *Breaking Rules*. New York: Longman.

Senior, R. 2006. *The Experience of Language Teaching*. Cambridge: Cambridge University Press.

12.4 Do something you don't want to do, every day

Sarah Milligan *Macmillan Education*

I want to tell you about some excellent advice I was once given by a wise woman: do something you don't want to do, every day.

So, why should you bother to go against the grain or ruffle your feathers? Because the reason you don't want to do this 'thing' is that it scares you. I can hear you shouting, 'But Sarah, what has this got to do with teaching English?!' Well, whether you've been teaching for five minutes or five years, trying something challenging or new in your lesson will not only inspire your students but will also unearth a fresh outlook on teaching and liven up your day. Here are five things you don't want to do that you should.

Teach a topic that scares you

I used to avoid teaching pronunciation like the plague. I tried to persuade myself it wasn't important and that students would just pick it up, wouldn't they? No! Why should my students miss out just because I'm worried I might get something wrong or not know all the answers? So, I pledged to myself that I would learn about phonemes and tackle pronunciation in class. There had been no need to be afraid: I remained the expert on English. Teach the things you don't want to teach, and you will feel happy walking out of the lesson knowing you've done all you can to help your students learn English. The things that are hardest to teach are often the most important.

Let there be silence

Generally, during your teacher training courses you are taught to encourage discussion. However, when you're standing up in front of your class, asking them to talk to you, you might be given nothing in response. Complete silence! A common reaction is to continue talking at a million miles an hour and move swiftly on to the activity, but that would be cheating! Let there be a healthy few minutes of silence because your students might be thinking your question over. They might be pondering what to say. You can rephrase the question and give some suggestions, but show your class that they are the ones who need to practise their English, not you.

Use all the equipment you have

You might have an IWB, a projector, a computer lab, or a virtual learning environment. You might have all of those things, lucky you! I've seen how some teachers embrace the equipment they're given and how others hide away from it. The teachers that embrace new technology and opportunities tend to be the ones who are excited about teaching and open to developing their skills. Changing the way you give a class can really shake things up, and that is a sure way to engage your students. It doesn't have to be complicated, and you don't have to be a technical expert; there'll always be a student in your class that will be happy to help if something doesn't go the way you expected.

Change your lesson plan

You're comfortable; you know all the textbooks inside out and what you'll cover for each day. Well done; you're all set for the rest of your teaching days ... No wonder you don't feel the same way about teaching anymore. It's a lovely place to be when you can confidently walk into a classroom and teach a lesson seamlessly; however, your students will appreciate it if you add some personality to the lesson. They will notice if you add an extra activity that wasn't in the book or personalise an exercise. If you make the effort to give something extra, your students will give something extra back.

Ask your students for feedback and listen to their answers

Give them feedback forms to fill out and learn what they're thinking. If you get the same criticism more than a couple of times, there is almost certainly some truth in it. And, if you see that your students have gone all moody in the class, why not ask them what's wrong? It might be something really simple. It pays to ask and to take heed of their response. Happy students learn better.

There you have it: those were my suggestions. You might not have liked them; after all, they are things you don't want to do! Even if it's just one tiny, scary thing per day, do it and you'll feel a little bit tingly, but most importantly inspired.

s.milligan@macmillan.com

12.5 Language-focused teacher development

Andrew Walkley *University of Westminster, UK*

In *Thinking, Fast and Slow*, the psychologist Daniel Kahneman (2011) presents two systems of thought and decision making. The first is related to intuitive action and the second to more considered thinking. Fast thinking is a natural feature of our lives, but it is affected by a number of factors which lead to less-than-perfect decisions, even by those considered experts. Two of these factors—priming and the availability bias—have relevance to ELT especially in terms of lexical approaches, Dogme and Jim Scrivener's Demand High teaching (DH), as these approaches emphasise the provision of 'natural' examples, responding to students as people and language learners, and reformulating and teaching on the spot. The implications of this are that we need a very different approach to teacher education and development, if we believe such teaching is better.

Priming is how previous events and language experiences create subconscious networks that affect behaviour. In terms of the kind of teacher behaviour that fails to engage with students and language (Scrivener 2013), one can see primings from four-week training courses: short classes restrict opportunities for detailed teaching recommended by DH. Trainees are additionally exhorted to reduce teacher talking time, so trainees inevitably avoid situations where they need to speak (for example, correction). Due to limited language awareness (LA) of both 'L2' and native-speaker English, trainees may simply not hear or understand what students are saying, let alone notice 'gaps' in their knowledge. Yet post-cert teacher development, if it takes place at all, tends not to focus on LA, but instead more technique, activities and class management.

Regarding 'dogmeticians' and lexical approach practitioners, priming is also a challenge in the kind of language that is emphasised. Lexical views of language are frequently ignored entirely on initial training courses in favour of LA sessions focusing on verb phrases as 'McNuggets'. This priming may lead to teachers, when they do correct, focusing on simple issues ('I *going* to the cinema last night') rather than complex errors which may be discoursal or otherwise difficult to explain from basic rules because of a mix of grammar *and* vocabulary error.

The availability bias also has an impact on the language teachers choose to teach, the examples we give and the affordances we exploit. Kahneman (2011) explains how even experts overestimate the frequency of certain events because some examples are more easily recalled than others. In teaching contexts, this may lead us to overestimate the frequency of certain words and underestimate others: it will surprise many that 'blonde' is less frequent than 'arise', or 'nurse' than 'in terms of'. We can bring to mind more easily examples of the less-frequent word (we can all picture blondes) and furthermore can think of example sentences more easily as they fit a simple 'X is Y' pattern. Availability biases, therefore, mean we will fail to teach many useful words and will find it difficult to come up with natural examples. This might be of particular concern in ESP, EAP or CLIL contexts.

Kahneman gives the example of chess players who become spontaneous *and* accurate in decision making through thousands of hours of study and planning. By the same token, if we want teachers who are more lexical, Demand High or Dogme-like, we need a much broader education in LA in initial training, and post-cert language development needs to be ongoing throughout our careers. DH and Dogme actually run counter to this goal by suggesting the issue is just technical 'tweaks' (DH) or denying teachers materials to analyse and *plan* language teaching in a considered manner (Dogme). Paradoxically, moving towards Dogme might mean exploiting coursebooks *more* to begin with in order to build up a repertoire for teaching without material.

A restricted list of language-focused teacher development tasks to enable this teaching might be include preparation time focusing on:

- noticing useful language including examples not focused on by the course writers;
- thinking of natural examples of words in the book with co-text beyond sentence level; and
- thinking of questions that check language and generate ideas from students.

Teacher development sessions might include:

- quizzes testing knowledge of frequency;
- brainstorming sentences students might want to say in speaking tasks and/or writing a discussion, then discussing grammar and pattern teaching opportunities;
- writing vocabulary material (especially less 'available' contexts such as EAP);
- gapping listening texts to exploit chunks and useful language; and
- comparing photos of board work.

Staffroom discussions might include:

- something new I taught today; and
- what I learnt about my students today.

A.Walkley@westminster.ac.uk

References

Kahneman, D. 2011. *Thinking, Fast and Slow*. London: Penguin.

Scrivener, J. 2013. 'A proposal for active interventionist teaching' in T. Pattison (ed.). *IATEFL 2012 Glasgow Conference Selections*. Canterbury: IATEFL.

12.6 Exploratory practice in ELT: an opportunity to develop yourself

Mike Harrison *Bromley College of Further and Higher Education, UK*

A teacher embarking on his or her career may have only been exposed to a narrow range of teaching methodologies, approaches and techniques. Certain initial training courses are designed according to a particular methodology and some focus on training teachers how to best use different materials, such as coursebooks, authentic material and using different technological aides. However, a four-week training course, such as a CELTA, does not offer the time to explore these much.

Once a teacher has reached the stage of his or her career where it is desirable to pursue a higher level of training, such as an MA or Diploma course, the teacher may come across the metaphor of experimental practice. According to the dictionary, an experiment is 'the process of testing various ideas, methods, or activities to see what effect they have' and something experimental is 'using new ideas or methods that are not yet proved to be successful every time'. This has been a useful metaphor for me in thinking about trying different and new teaching practices.

However, a metaphor of exploration may also be useful, as what is experimental practice for one teacher may differ completely for another. If ELT is a territory to be explored, we can place ourselves on a kind of map of practice, based on our initial training and our teaching experience. Depicting the landscape of ELT as a map has been shown to be beneficial for reviewing and reflecting on practice (Hancock 2013; Waters 2009).

As teachers we can take charge of our professional development by engaging with aspects of ELT that we may be less familiar with, investigating them, thinking of ways to incorporating them into our teaching practice and reflecting on this process of experimentation. A metaphor of exploration and travelling can also help us to think through the stages that are necessary for effective experimental practice research, ensuring that we reflect thoroughly on the process and use it as a tool for our own development. The following questions can be useful:

Why explore ELT anyway?

'The history of language teaching has been characterized by a search for more effective ways of teaching second or foreign languages' (Richards and Rodgers 2001: viii). We can see that teaching does not stand still and stagnant; its development depends on exploring practice.

What areas can be explored?

There is so much to ELT that it can be daunting to think of all the possible things that could be explored. However, it is important to remember that any exploring is relative: what is experimental for one teacher may not be for another. Thinking about what you have and haven't done so far in your teaching can be helpful in planning what areas you wish to explore.

When is the best time?

The inexperienced teacher could be forgiven for thinking that he or she will never be ready to conduct experimental practice. However, as mentioned above, the areas that can be explored are particular to each individual teacher. In fact, as was mentioned in the talk, the beginning of a teaching career may be the best time to experiment and explore.

What are good things to do when exploring?

Someone who is exploring an area does not do so ignorantly; the explorer often takes snapshots of their travels, some even write journal entries. Exploring practice in ELT needs to be recorded: taking photos during an experimental lesson, writing notes to yourself, inviting someone into your classroom to observe, and asking your learners to fill in a questionnaire based on what they thought about it are useful tools to record.

What are good things to do after?

Similarly, when returning from a period of exploration, it is usual to share the experience in some way. People share photos that they took and tell others about their trips. The experience of exploration does not exist in a vacuum; rather, it develops in how the experience is shared and built upon. Similarly, the experience of experimental practice needs to be shared, by talking to colleagues, writing articles, through social media or by talking at conferences like IATEFL.

Final thoughts

I believe it is a shame that teachers often only come across the notion of researching, experimenting and reflecting on their practice later on in their careers. Instead, exploring and experimenting with ELT should be encouraged right at from the beginning, as a bedrock of reflective practice and self-directed action research. After all, if we don't experiment, how can we develop?

mjah84@gmail.com

References

Hancock, M. 2013. 'A map of ELT'. Paper presented at 36th Annual National Convention TESOL Spain 2013, Sevilla, Spain, 8–10 March 2013.

Richards, J. and T. Rodgers. 2001. *Approaches and Methods in Language Teaching* (second edition). Cambridge: Cambridge University Press.

Waters, A. 2009. 'A guide to Methodologia: past, present and future'. English Language Teaching Journal 63/2: 108–15.

12.7 E-portfolios for teacher development: a simple approach

Chris Baldwin *British Council, Hong Kong*

What are e-portfolios?

With a significant amount of our professional lives taking place online these days, it is becoming increasingly difficult to organise everything that we do. E-portfolios can help. What is an e-portfolio? At its most basic form, an e-portfolio is just a file store; the difference between a folder on your desktop and an effective e-portfolio is the tools that encourage reflection and different levels of sharing of 'artefacts' (the term used for anything in an e-portfolio). Effective e-portfolios are online tools to keep track of work, to share thoughts, reflections and materials with peers, to showcase your best work to potential employers and to store personal reflections. They can be used to build evidence of professional development over time as well as to create CVs. The main problem with e-portfolios for general CPD is that it's another thing for busy teachers to do.

As well as for general professional development, e-portfolios can be used in specific training courses as a reflective tool to keep track of learning as well as for formal assessment. Course assessment can be integrated into the e-portfolio, and reflective learning can be built into the whole course using the e-portfolio as a reflective tool to store personal reflections and to share reflections with the course tutor and peers on the course. Course-specific e-portfolio tools are much more successful than general CPD e-portfolios as teachers on a CPD course will already be using the online learning platform and will have a peer group to share reflections with.

Essential questions

If you are thinking about incorporating an e-portfolio system into your institution, there are a number of factors to think about. *PebblePad* (2011) gives a list of questions to consider, key points being:

- What type of e-portfolio do you want? Is it simply a file-store, or do you want a tool to support teachers' CPD, building in reflective tools?
- Who will build the e-portfolio? There are many e-portfolio tools on the market that you can adopt such as *Mahara* and *PebblePad*, or you could use a much simpler system such as a free blogging platform as an e-portfolio tool. Whatever platform you choose, it will need to be built and maintained.
- Can the system support all your needs? These may be for professional development, reflection and assessment while following your institutional processes.
- Who owns the content? Does the user have full control of his or her content? Is privacy fully respected? A system that allows users to export their artefacts to another platform is important here.
- Do you have the support to manage an e-portfolio system over time? Will the system be available long term? As e-portfolios are designed to grow with the user, a system that is not going to disappear overnight is important.

A simple approach

The British Council runs a programme of online teacher development courses using Moodle (see moodle.org). Course participants are typically mid-career state-sector English language teachers, many having relatively little experience with online learning. Our goal was to develop an e-portfolio system into our online courses in order to integrate assessment and reflective learning with a sense of ownership of learning outcomes.

In order to achieve this, we decided to develop an e-portfolio using only core Moodle tools in order to simplify the experience for our course participants as much as possible and also to avoid complications of maintaining an external e-portfolio platform. In order to do this, we created a 'Moodle course' as an e-portfolio with the following tools:

- Moodle internal blog, for self-reflection and reflection with tutor;
- forum, for reflection with peer group;
- course assignments, all integrated into the portfolio;
- reflective materials connected to the course; and
- a private files storage area.

While this functioned reasonably well, we found that course participants needed a way to take their work from across a whole course (built from several 'Moodle courses') and include this in their portfolio. There was no core Moodle tool that allowed this, so we commissioned a new Moodle plugin to allow exporting of any user-created 'artefacts' into the Moodle blog—either set to private for personal reflection, to share with the peer-group or to publish to the world. We have made this plugin available open-source to the community: https://moodle.org/plugins/view. php?plugin=portfolio_blogexport

The response from users was very enthusiastic. In the first month, it was used 2700 times, the vast majority of uses being private, indicating its use for reflection on their learning. In addition, the use of the public blog for reflection increased enormously. It has proved to be a valuable reflective tool in our online courses.

Chris.Baldwin@britishcouncil.org.hk

Reference

PebblePad. 2011. '10 essential questions to consider when choosing an eportfolio system'. (Retrieved from http://www.pebblepad.co.uk/essentialquestions.asp)

12.8 Key emotions in the transformation of EFL teachers' professional identities

Barbara González *Veracruz University, Mexico*

As language teachers we are all aware of the enormous pressures that may affect our sense of professional identity, as well as our teaching practice. However, perhaps our 'relevant others', such as our peers, students, parents and educational authorities—or even we ourselves—may not be as aware of how these translate into emotions that may influence our perception of professional-self, as well as our commitment, decision-making and practice as EFL teachers. If this emotional dimension of our profession is not acknowledged, recognised and paid attention to, then as Day suggests, it may 'act unnoticed and thus have unacknowledged negative or positive influences' (2007: 605) on our sense of professional identity, our actions within our working contexts, or both.

The study

This was a small-scale study regarding the perceptions of 18 Mexican EFL teachers who all work at different educational institutions, but who were all taking a professional development course during their MA in TEFL. An analysis of their written personal response portfolio submissions reveals teachers' self-reflexive answers to the questions: 'Who was I before?' and 'Who am I now?' and the influence that *trust, respect* and *pride* have on these answers; this analysis demonstrates the construction and continual transformation of their professional identities.

Trust

Two facets of trust emerged from the findings: self-trust and trust in others. Self-trust may be defined as 'self-confidence', characterised by 'faith in oneself' which, arguably, is the first secret to success. Why? Because we depend to a large extent on our own emotional, mental and physical resources to navigate the world in which we live. Teachers in front of a classroom of students question their inner resources every day. Having doubts about their abilities can negatively affect their sense of professional identity. However, once these doubts have been proven to be false, their sense of identity can be strengthened. Regarding trust in others, Hoffman *et al.*'s (2006) inquiry supports the view that when there is a climate of trust, teachers are more open when talking about their practices, as well as more prone to taking risks; both of these are considered as necessary for professional development and the transformation of their professional identity as teachers.

Respect

According to Heikkinen (2003), teachers need to feel recognised by their 'relevant others', that is their peers, students and the education authorities. This acknowledgement of their abilities and accomplishments at work signifies for them that not only do they have the right to exist, but that they are accepted for who they are as professionals. Thus, if they are successful at this level, they may achieve self-confidence, self-esteem, and therefore, self-respect, all of which help to transform their sense of professional identity. Perhaps even more importantly, when they feel respected by others, they feel a great sense of achievement.

Pride

Pride feeds off respect and recognition. Therefore, the different degrees to which teachers perceive they have achieved these may influence or affect the sense of their professional identities regarding their self-confidence, self-respect and self-esteem. More importantly, it may also influence their sense of commitment and their decision-making, as well as their teaching practice in their working context. In contrast, a perceived lack of recognition may contribute to teacher burnout. Fortunately, these particular informants are proud of their achievements.

In conclusion, I present an extract from the findings that appears to sum up how the pressures of a teacher's work translate into emotions that may influence their perception and the transformation of their professional-selves as EFL teachers:

> When I think of the work of a teacher, I picture an enormous rainbow in which each colour reflects a different emotion; I understand that all these emotions, as the colours in the rainbow, have to be together in order to function; it does not matter whether they are positive or negative, because they will produce a fantastic effect that would not be possible if one of them were missing. The work of a teacher will always be pointed out, so are rainbows, and yet, they are in the sky. The work of a teacher will take place no matter the circumstances; the same happens with rainbows that need the sun and the rain to exist. The work of a teacher is full of emotions that colour his professional-self. (Eric)

In sum, teachers' emotions have an undeniable impact on their work, their commitment and their relationships with other people which combined influence the continual transformation of their professional identity.

scholesbarbara@yahoo.co.uk

References

Day, C. 2007. 'School reform and transitions in teacher professionalism and identity' in T. Townsend and R. Bates (eds.). *Handbook of Teacher Education*. Dordrecht, Netherlands: Springer.

Heikkinen, H. L. T. 2003. 'Becoming a teacher: struggling for recognition'. Paper presented at ECER 2003, Hamburg, 18 September 2003.

Hoffman, S., D. Holden and N. Neggers. 2006. 'Educational networks: Structures for enhancing school leadership'. BC Educational Leadership Research. (Retrieved on 2 September 2008 from http://www.slc.edu.ubc.ca/eJournal/Issue6/articles/Educational_Networks.pdf)

12.9 PLN: teachers' use of social media for professional development

Daniel Xerri *University of Malta, Msida, Malta*

Benefits of a PLN

The concept of a personal learning network (PLN) is not new; however, over the past few years the reach, size and look of a PLN have changed due to the proliferation of social media. Thanks to social media, teachers are finding it much easier to create networks whose main purpose is to facilitate the process of continuing professional development (CPD). The benefits of social media like YouTube, Facebook and Twitter in allowing teachers to set up a PLN are widely recognised, and it seems that such 'cyber-enabled networks hold great promise for supporting teachers' development of new knowledge and practices' (Schalger *et al.* 2009: 87). One of the main benefits derived by teachers' use of social media for CPD is that of having access to shared knowledge that is specific to their own needs and interests. The immediate effect of a PLN is that teachers are able to dynamically contribute and share innovative ideas with a network of people that extends beyond the physical confines of their school.

Using social media for CPD

The concept of a PLN served as the basis of a small-scale study involving 60 teachers of English working in state secondary schools all over Malta. Its aim was to explore teachers' use of social media for CPD purposes. The teachers were asked to complete an online survey; subsequently, semi-structured interviews were conducted with eight participants.

The fact that for these teachers CPD is either 'very important' (65 per cent) or 'important' (35 per cent) shows that they value the benefits accrued from engaging in professional development activities. However, only 10 per cent of the teachers specified that for them the most effective form of CPD is using social media with the express purpose of attaining professional growth. This might suggest that most of these teachers have not yet fully embraced the idea that 'The digital era opens unprecedented opportunities to expand [their] traditional learning experience by participating in networked spaces where sharing and reciprocity are expected' (Nussbaum-Beach and Ritter Hall 2012: 13). Nonetheless, the majority of these teachers (63.3 per cent) spend between one and five hours per week accessing social media for professional development.

The two most common social media for CPD purposes amongst teachers are YouTube (81.6 per cent) and Facebook (40.0 per cent). These were followed by LinkedIn (10.0 per cent), blogs (10.0 per cent), Google Reader (7.0 per cent), and Twitter (3.3 per cent). YouTube seems to be a staple part of how some teachers acquire new knowledge and skills relevant to their subject and profession. However, the fact that the purposeful use of other forms of social media for CPD registered much lower percentages might suggest that there is not yet sufficient awareness among teachers about the potential of such tools. In fact, three of the interviewed teachers indicated that they never thought about using certain social networks for this purpose as they 'usually have Facebook to stay in touch with friends and family'. They also suggested that in-service training does not usually address this gap in their knowledge and skills.

The other five interviewed teachers claimed that they use social media for CPD on a regular basis because 'there is so much you can learn from others' and so much an individual 'can share not only with Maltese teachers but also ones abroad'. The 'sharing of information is essential' for them, as is 'the possibility to network with so many teachers from all around the globe for free'. These teachers value 'the network you create for your own particular needs' and which is used to 'learn and grow as a teacher'. Highlighting the inefficacy of current training, one interviewee suggested that 'a teacher needs to take the reins and learn how to do it ... it's not the kind of thing they show you in the in-service'.

Conclusion

A PLN allows connected teachers to be constantly in tune with the most recent developments in their field and enables them to share knowledge with their peers for the purpose of professional development. The above data seems to confirm the idea that 'while participating in these online spaces may appear easy, creating a PLN is in fact a highly complex intellectual and emotional task' (Richardson and Mancabelli 2011: 19). It seems clear that besides a teacher's personal motivation to start using social media for professional development there is also a need for adequate training, not only in how social media may be used for such a purpose but also with the aim of convincing teachers as to why these tools should be used.

daniel.xerri@um.edu.mt

References

Nussbaum-Beach, S. and L. Ritter Hall. 2012. *The Connected Educator: Learning and Leading in a Digital Age.* Bloomington, Ind.: Solution Tree Press.

Richardson, W. and R. Mancabelli. 2011. *Personal Learning Networks: Using the Power of Connections to Transform Education.* Bloomington, Ind.: Solution Tree Press.

Schalger, M. S., U. Farooq, J. Fusco, P. Schank and N. Dwyer. 2009. 'Analyzing online teacher networks: Cyber networks require cyber research tools'. *Journal of Teacher Education* 60/1: 86–100.

12.10 CPD for young teachers: pedagogical internship in ELT

Ekaterina Shadrova *Vologda State Pedagogical University, Russia*

Background

The paper presents a scaffolding CPD scheme for novice teachers of English. Taking into account the difference between a novice teacher and an expert teacher (Richards and Farrell 2005), our university started a project, Pedagogical Internship, designed to help starting teachers to increase confidence and to encourage self-development.

Several problems have been identified in the regional education system. Firstly, language teachers are in great demand as, according to new Russian federal educational standards, schoolchildren now start to learn a foreign language in primary school while earlier they used to start in secondary school. Secondly, though our graduates are motivated to work at schools, about 82 per cent of them quit during their first months of being teachers. According to a survey, only 8 per cent were unsatisfied with their salaries, 48 per cent felt uncertain about teaching methods, and 87 per cent expressed the need for support. Though the terms 'teacher training' and 'teacher development' are often used with contrasting meanings, we rely on the idea of their integration (Ur 1998) and consider Pedagogical Internship to be a model which combines the best of both.

The project

Pedagogical Internship is a three-way partnership between our institution of higher education, an intern teacher and a school where an intern works. This collaborative form of CPD distinguishes Pedagogical Internship from PRESET or INSET programmes. Pedagogical Internship is flexible as novice teachers decide themselves whether they will take part in it. Thus it implies the responsibility of interns in their professional growth and presents the integration of training and development.

The main activities provided by Pedagogical Internship are as follows:

Seminars and workshops on ELT methodology

Starting teachers need to enhance their professional skills; they are given an opportunity to test some techniques during these workshops and discuss with their colleagues challenges they face in their classrooms. Basically, the topics are predetermined, but we plan them according to teachers' demands and requests provided in their feedback to our previous seminars.

Participation of novice teachers in conferences

At the beginning of their career novice teachers lack practical experience but they also seek theoretical information in order to reflect on what they do in the classroom. Many of them choose action research as a pathway for self-development which they may present at conferences. We organise an annual conference for foreign language teachers and familiarise our interns with other conferences as well.

Mentoring of novice teachers at school

Most novice teachers feel frustrated when observed by their colleagues from the same school. However, they stress that they would like to get constructive feedback from experienced teachers working in other educational institutions. We invite university lecturers and teachers from neighbouring schools to observe lessons and provide feedback to our interns.

A 'teaching club'

Socialising helps to build rapport among the interns, which influences their ability to establish positive relationships with their learners and teaching staff. Social meetings provide an opportunity to share ideas and opinions in a friendly and relaxed atmosphere. The most popular events are celebrating holidays, meetings with guests from English speaking countries, books and films discussions.

Training for taking part in professional competitions

Contests are regarded as a chance to demonstrate our interns' professional growth. In addition, novice teachers may get extra financial support in accordance with the conditions of contests. School mentors and university coordinators help to design a lesson plan and discuss how to conduct it efficiently during contests.

Support for novice teachers by means of Internet resources

Online materials are easy to find, which allows teachers to get most out of them. We supply teachers with materials on ELT on the university website and give coverage of the events organised by Pedagogical Internship. Social networks (for example, Facebook) are an effective way to inform our interns about forthcoming events.

Results

To evaluate the effectiveness of our project, we have analysed the results at the end of the school year. None of our interns has quit. One of our interns has won a municipal competition and has become 'The Best Teacher of the Year' among starting teachers. Our survey showed an overall increase in teacher confidence levels (up to 56 per cent). The number of participants uncertain about teaching methods has dropped to 14 per cent. All teachers who participated in this project expressed interest in it, and they wish to continue their professional development and participate in future internship programmes. We hope that our Pedagogical Internship can be a great starting point for professional and personal growth from a novice teacher into an advanced-level educator.

ekaterina-shadrova@yandex.ru

References

Richards, J. and T. Farrell. 2005. *Professional Development for Language Teachers: Strategies for Teacher Learning.* Cambridge: Cambridge University Press.

Ur, P. 1998. 'Teacher training, teacher development'. *English Teaching Professional* 8: 21.

12.11 *Leap Ahead in English*: a model for classroom-based CPD

Jane Cohen *British Council, Ramat Gan, Israel*

Background

It is generally accepted that confident, skilled and highly motivated teachers instil confidence and motivation in their learners, which leads to improved teaching and learning outcomes. However, too often teachers feel overwhelmed by the burdens of their chosen profession. Teachers are increasingly expected to participate in extracurricular INSETT to keep them up to date with the latest in pedagogy and to prepare them for the information age, and a world in which technology is the key player.

Such training is often regarded as burdensome, irrelevant and out of touch with their individual needs, and is not always implemented back in the classroom. It is with this in mind that the focus has shifted from INSETT to CPD (continuing professional development)—a career-long journey, which is generally regarded as the cornerstone for developing teachers' skills and competencies.

EFL teachers are in short supply in Israel, particularly in the socio-economic and geographical periphery; the gap continues to widen between the achievements of learners in the periphery and their peers in the centre. With this in mind *Leap Ahead in English* was developed in January 2011 by the British Council and The Association for Change in Education, through their Revadim initiative, to create a school-based professional development programme that includes mentoring, reflective practice, self-improvement, self-evaluation, peer evaluation and external monitoring, along with designated time within the school timetable for implementation. The programme, in its third year, is run in the south of Israel in seven Hebrew- and Arabic-speaking elementary schools. Teachers are provided with CPD training and learning both inside and outside their own classroom. Best practice in EFL teaching is modelled, and clear outcomes are set: classroom instructions are given in English; student talk is to exceed teacher talk; ICT is integrated; and pair/group work activities are the norm. The overarching aim is to assist the English teachers to move from traditional teacher-led and textbook-driven lessons to learner-centred lessons, where differentiated learning styles are catered for and English is the dominant language of instruction.

The programme

Leap Ahead in English is divided into two complementary components: the mentoring programme and the after-school programme, which are run once a week in each school. A British Council mentor is assigned to each school and meets weekly with the English teachers. In the morning mentoring programme, the mentor and English teachers set teaching and learning goals, plan lessons and reflect upon lessons delivered. A specially developed CPD tool is used to encourage the reflective and goal setting processes of the programme. Following the weekly meeting the mentor enters the classroom with the teacher and observes the English teacher lead a lesson using the ministry curriculum and approved textbooks. While in the classroom the mentor assists with the pair/group work activities and provides an extra pair of hands to assist pupils. Feedback is provided following the lesson.

The after-school programme caters for the more challenged language learners. The British Council mentor is the lead teacher, delivering lessons from the LearnEnglish Kids website and the TeachingEnglish website, while the school English teachers observe and team teach (peer observation), providing further opportunities to improve their classroom skills and proficiency. At the end of the year, pupils involved in the after-school programme put on a performance that is both a showcase and a platform for learning vocabulary and lexical chunks, both essential components of language acquisition. Increased confidence and motivation among the pupils has been the greatest outcome of the performances.

What next?

The journey of change commences with the acknowledgement that every child can succeed and that teachers are the drivers of change. Whether this process is facilitated or not depends on the school's willingness to accept the challenge of enabling every child to reach his or her full potential through a whole-school approach. As *Leap Ahead in English* nears the end of its third year it is clearly understood that teachers are the greatest resource that a school has, and that investment in their continuing professional development is essential for creating an optimal teaching and learning environment. Consequently *Leap Ahead in English* is about to move into Phase II, where the mentors will be school-based mentors, trained and supported by the British Council, with training, development and content that is of immediate and practical relevance.

Jane.cohen@britishcouncil.org.il

Epilogue

The final word in this volume belongs to plenary speaker Jun Liu, who sets the scene for IATEFL 2014 and conferences into the future by questioning which issues will be at the forefront of ELT discourse in years to come, and by predicting the competencies an ELT professional will need as we move forward in the 21st century.

Plenary: ELT tomorrow

Jun Liu *Georgia State University, Atlanta, Ga., USA*

Introduction

It is clear by now that globalisation and technological innovation are changing our world so quickly that it is difficult to track. How will the increasing global population, combined with technological innovation and globalisation, affect our everyday lives? Furthermore, how will it affect the future of English language teaching (ELT)?

These are questions that our field needs to consider carefully. As with any other discipline or profession, it is imperative that ELT reflects on the current state of affairs and responds proactively. Such an imperative can, in fact, be invigorating. Change can be celebrated as the welcome result of professional movements, of the advancement and accessibility of technology, and of the implementation of innovative approaches to problems new and old. ELT professionals today are quite different from their counterparts 50 years ago, and the same will undoubtedly be said of ELT professionals to come. This, inevitability, is indicative of the ongoing reflection, flexibility and innovation that characterise our field.

Before focusing specifically on ELT, let us first consider which current trends are most likely to drive the future of the world at large. One organisation, the Center for Strategic and International Studies (CSIS) is already attempting to do so. As part of its Seven Revolutions project, this bipartisan think-tank has proposed seven trends likely to influence the world through 2030. These include the following: population, resource management, technology, information and knowledge, economics, security and governance (CSIS 2013). Such indicators of future change have led other groups to re-consider what will constitute successful leadership skills in the future as well, for example, the Collaborative Leadership Network (CLN) and the Institute for the Future (Finlev 2009).

While the above deal with general predictions about the future of countries, companies, and global society, educators are undoubtedly curious about the future of education itself. Interestingly, some have argued that the greatest changes in education in the future will occur outside of the very institutions educators have traditionally relied upon in the past. KnowledgeWorks Foundation, a social enterprise organisation with a mission of better preparing students for both college and future careers, agrees: 'institutions face a critical dilemma: how to reconcile bottom-up developments in educational with the traditional top-down hierarchy that is currently in place' (KnowledgeWorks Foundation 2008: 2). Furthermore, KnowledgeWorks Foundation suggests that education will be challenged by a 'global learning economy' as 'geographic and digital migrations … facilitate the global movement of families, identity, values, educational resources, social capital, and innovations' (KnowledgeWorks Foundation 2008: 3). But where does all of this leave ELT specifically?

First, let me explain my use of the term 'ELT', which I intend to use to refer to ELT as a field of study, as associations, and as a profession, simultaneously (see Figure 1).

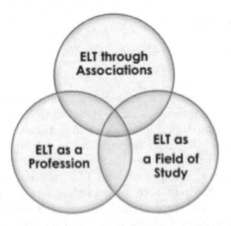

Figure 1: Three facets of ELT

ELT as a profession refers to the community of skilled practitioners who are actively involved in the teaching of English as a second or foreign language. This may include instructors, researchers, curriculum designers, materials developers, teacher trainers, administrators, tutors, test developers and policy specialists, among others. Essentially, ELT as a profession encompasses anyone who makes or influences (directly or indirectly) pedagogical choices in the English language classroom. ELT as an association may refer to professional organisations such as TESOL International Association, International Association of Teachers as a Foreign Language (IATFL), or The International Research Foundation (TIRF) for Language Education. Finally, ELT as a field of study includes any research, scholarship, publication, etc., which seeks to inform decisions regarding the teaching and learning of English as an additional language. As such, ELT as a field of study is multidisciplinary, encompassing education, applied linguistics, second language acquisition and learning, intercultural communication, language policy and planning, etc. All three facets of ELT—as a profession, as associations, and as a field of study—will be affected by globalisation in myriad ways. The goal of our research leading up to this plenary was to determine which trends are evident in past and current ELT research and to use them to predict the future of ELT as a whole.

Preliminary research

In a previous study, a graduate assistant and I conducted a thorough document analysis of *TESOL Quarterly*, arguably the flagship journal of ELT, both as a field of study and as a profession. First published in 1967, *TESOL Quarterly* (*TQ*) is a refereed, research-based academic journal that seeks to bridge theory and practice in ELT. As an international journal, *TQ* also welcomes submissions from around the world. As such, *TQ* serves as a venue for international perspectives and the application of a diverse body of research on language teaching and learning. Due to the lengthy publication history of this journal, in addition to the time-consuming nature of document analysis, we limited our study to *TQ* alone, though we certainly acknowledge that there are a plethora of quality academic journals in our field in addition to *TQ* and we did not intend to ignore their significant contributions to the field.

We began our analysis by collecting the titles and abstracts from each of the major articles published by *TQ* from 1967 to 2011. In doing so, we hoped to capture the most salient issues in the field of TESOL at the time of each volume's publication. We deliberately did not include reviews, reports, summaries, forums, reflections, editor's notes, etc., as we wanted to be consistent in our data collection by featuring only the main articles in each issue as the basis for analysis.

Once we had collected all 1,121 major article titles and abstracts published from 1967 to 2011, we applied open coding methods to conceptualise and categorise our data (Glaser and Straus 1967). Using key words from article titles as an initial indicator, we assigned labels to each article according to its most salient issue(s). At this point, the specificity of the label was primarily determined by the scope of the article, as we had not yet begun the comparative analysis of phenomena that would allow us to identify relationships and develop broader categories (Glaser 1978; Glaser and Strauss 1967; Goulding 2009). Thus, there was considerable overlap at this stage in the coding, and several articles were assigned multiple labels. When applicable, we also applied a parallel layer of coding which pertained to the level and context of language learning and/or teaching. For example, the article *Narrating America: Socializing Adult ESL Learners into Idealized Views of the United States during Citizenship Preparation Classes* (Griswold 2010) was coded as 'language context: ESL: North America'. Once we had amassed a considerable amount of preliminary data, we began the process of grouping concepts into broader categories, which might themselves contain other concepts or subcategories. From this process, several key categories began to emerge which both subsumed lesser categorisations and differentiated themselves from others.

Upon completion of our initial round of coding, we had assigned 243 different labels to the 1,121 major articles. After several more rounds of analyses, twelve issues-related categories and seven subcategories emerged. Of these, Figure 2 demonstrates the top ten issues-related categories, while Figures 3 and 4 demonstrate those issue-related categories which revealed upward and downward trending respectively.

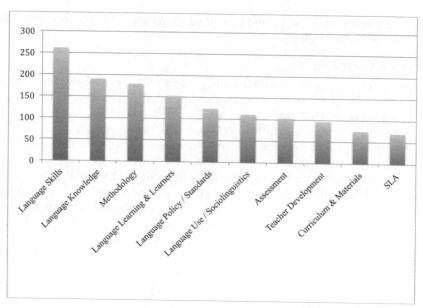

Figure 2: Top ten issues, TESOL Quarterly 1967–2011

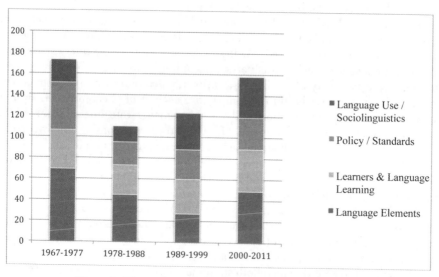

Figure 3: Upward trends, TESOL Quarterly, 1967–2011

For the purposes of our study, the sub-label 'language context' was used to refer to the described or anticipated environment in which an article's research, teaching and/ or learning takes place. For coding purposes, we recorded geographical region, as well as whether such an environment would be considered 'English as a second language' (ESL) or 'English as a foreign language' (EFL). While the distribution of articles involving ESL and EFL in TQ over the last 44 years was fairly even, Figure 5, which indicates language context in the journal by decade, reveals a gradual trend away from articles focusing on ESL and a substantial increase in EFL contexts, especially in the last 20 years. Figure 5 also suggests that the incidence of research and publication pertaining to ELF is more relevant today than it was several years ago. As this trend toward ELF itself challenges the manner in which EFL models have been traditionally defined for the last several decades, greater awareness of the expanding role of English and its resultant pedagogical implications may be partially responsible for the increase in articles written for/within an EFL context since the late 1980s as well.

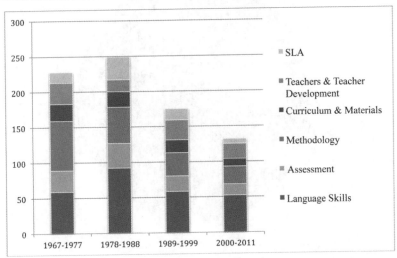

Figure 4: Downward trends TESOL Quarterly, 1967–2011

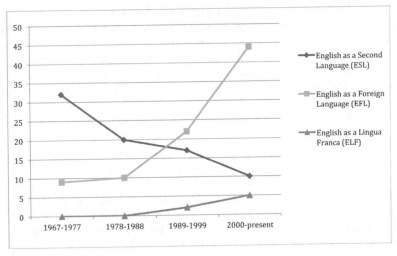

Figure 5: Language context by decade, TESOL Quarterly, 1967–2011

Of particular interest is Figure 6, which indicates that a majority of EFL articles incorporated an Asia/Asia-Pacific context. One potential reason for such a trend is the very high population of English language learners in Asia. Due to many complex factors, Asian learners are now being taught English at an earlier age and for an extensive amount of time, resulting in more and more focus on Asia/Asia-Pacific in TESOL research derived from and/or affecting this context.

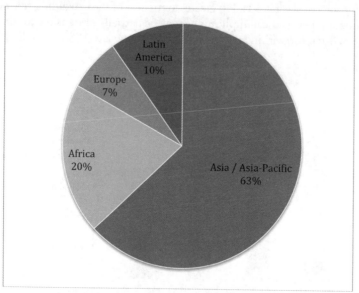

Figure 6: EFL contexts, TESOL Quarterly, 1967–2011

Although learners in tertiary-level education and EAP programmes have received the greatest focus from *TQ* researchers since its inception, a gradual rise in research addressing younger learners' needs is suggested by Figure 7, which indicates the distribution of language level in *TQ* per decade. In fact, the cumulative number of articles pertaining to young learners in the last 10 years is almost at the same level it was during *TQ*'s first decade of publication. While the majority of this early research took place within an ESL context and was likely fueled by interest in the critical approach and the so-called natural approach to language acquisition, the renewed scholarship we see pertaining to young learners today is predominately addressing EFL/ELF learning contexts. These findings are corroborated by the fact that evidence of students learning English at a much younger age can be found in the language policies in many Asian countries.

While our examination of *TQ* articles by language element from 1967 to 2011 revealed a principal focus on grammar overall, Figure 8 demonstrates greater initial disparity between language elements at the journal's inception, with grammar receiving by far the most attention. This is followed by a gradual decrease in overt research pertaining to language elements over the first three decades of *TQ*'s existence, and

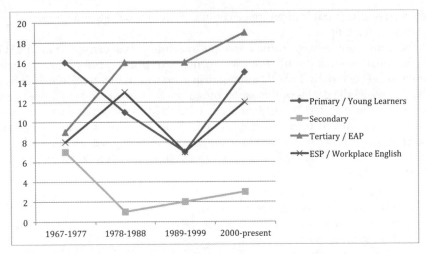

Figure 7: Distribution of language level by decade, TESOL Quarterly, 1967–2011

finally, a gradual pattern of increase with regard to all three elements, suggesting a potential convergence of the three. Though this convergence may be indicative of a move away from treating grammatical and lexical items as discrete, isolable units (Conrad 2000), another explanation can be found in a growing emphasis on overall communicative competence, diverging from the traditional focus on accuracy over fluency, and the expansion of communicative competence to include sociocultural and global competences (Liu 2007). As the role of English becomes more global, the acceptance of more varieties of English at the comprehensive level has also played a

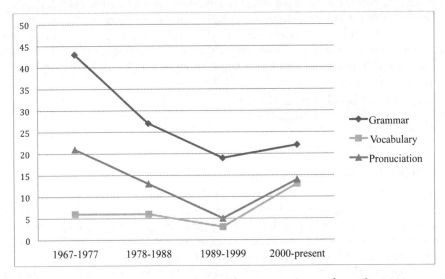

Figure 8: Language elements by decade, TESOL Quarterly, 1967–2011

role in reassessing what it means to be communicatively competent as an overall goal of language learning.

The above results were further triangulated using data derived from TESOL International Association position statements and from a survey questionnaire administered to various TESOL professionals representing the three dimensions of TESOL. While the details of this aspect of our research are beyond the scope of this plenary proceeding, data triangulation was conducted in order to verify our results and better capture all three dimensions of ELT discussed above. The triangulated results of our *TQ* analysis revealed four consistently recurring themes that we believe are currently upward trending and appear most likely to affect the future of ELT. These are as follows:

1 Language policy/standards
2 Language learners and learning
3 Curricula and teaching materials
4 Teacher learning and development

At this point, I would like to briefly consider the complexities of these four themes, as contextualised by current literature and trends in the field. Next, I will propose six abilities, borne out of reflection on these four themes, which are likely to characterise successful ELT professionals in the future.

Language policy/standards

Migration and globalisation have led to a redefinition of the role of English in the world, resulting in the legitimisation of nativised varieties of English, as well as a renewed focus on intelligibility and cross-cultural appropriateness over accuracy and/ or native-life proficiency. It is the case that the majority of interactions that occur between English speakers in the world today do not involve native English speakers (Graddol 2006). As more and more non-native English speakers use the language in contextually-specific and creative ways, English itself has changed, resulting in any number of the following re-conceptions of the English language, each of which will have vastly different implications for English language learners and pedagogy:

• English as an International Language (EIL)
• English as a World Language (EWL)
• English as a Global Language (EGL)
• English as a Lingual Franca (ELF)
• English as an Additional Language (EAL)

Language learners and learning

Two key issues that pertain to language learners and learning concern the very nature of language learning itself and the changing demographics of the learners whose needs influence our professional and pedagogical decision-making. First, there is a growing movement in ELT to treat language learners as language *users* (Cook 2002), thus encompassing anyone who uses a second language for real-life purposes and acknowledging the degree to which language users exploit the linguistic resources available to them regardless of their proficiency level (or access to education, for that matter). Furthermore, conceiving of language learners as *users* empowers L2 users and avoids attributing some sort of dependent status to the millions of non-native language users worldwide. Finally, the notion of language users subverts the long-held assumption of traditional SLA frameworks that learners that acquiring a system for later use and will never actually achieve full acquisition of the L2 to begin with (Cook 2002).

With regard to the second issue concerning language learners and learning, it has been estimated that by the year 2020, the number of children in the world will approach 3 billion (Canton 2007). At the same time, children across the world are beginning to learn English at a younger and younger age (Graddol 2006). These trends are relevant to our profession due to the very distinct qualities of young learners, especially in regard to language learning. Among other things, English for young learners (EYL) is likely to be characterised by a more holistic approach to language learning (versus a more analytic approach often taken by adult language learners), a great deal of imagination and movement (versus a need for real-world contextualisation), and a unique preference for digital learning as an interface with language.

Curricula and teaching materials

Three trends pertaining to curricula and teaching materials are likely to drive future innovation in ELT; these are a move toward digital learning, English as a medium of instruction, and English for specific purposes (ESP).

The term 'digital natives' has been used to refer to young people born in 1980 or earlier who have unique learning habits and preferences due to having been immersed in digital technologies their entire lives. Such learners are likely to have a penchant for multitasking, the tendency to express themselves and relate to others through digital technologies, and the ability to use technology to access information and create new knowledge (Palfrey and Gasser 2010). Furthermore, digital natives will have less tolerance for completing worksheets by hand or listening to lectures and a strong preference for 'customization, interaction, and user-control' (Collins and Halverson 2009: 4), resulting in a generation with little to no interest in pedagogical activities that do 'not match the average computer game's exciting presentation of information' (Beatty 2003: 55, as cited by Nunan 2011: 215).

It has been suggested that English learning is most successful when it is 'linked to the cognitive development of learners, rather than as something isolated from the rest of the curriculum' (McLean 2012: 32). It is not surprisingly, then, that English as a medium of instruction, often referred to as content-based instruction (CBI), is gradually gaining international popularity across a variety of academic contexts (Kaufman and Crandall 2005). CBI may also provide a more equitable balance with regard to multiple intelligences (Deller and Price 2007).

Finally, ELT professionals are growing increasingly aware that generic approaches to pedagogy, materials, and assessment no longer appropriate (Graddol 2006), resulting in a more 'situated view' of English use: 'tightly bound up with the community of practice in which the language is used' (Paltridge 2009: 292). English for specific purposes (ESP) practitioners have also begun to focus more on the integration of language with professional and cultural competence (Fitzpatrick and O'Dowd 2012).

New innovations in corpus linguistics have relieved instructors of the need to be experts in the genre in which their students need guidance, thanks to data-driven descriptions of domain- or register-specific language use much more accurate than native-speaker intuition has afforded in the past.

Teacher learning and development

As we consider the future of ELT, two traditional notions concerning teacher learning and development are likely to seem more and more outdated: the traditional native English speaking teacher (NEST) vs. non-native English speaking teacher (NNEST) dichotomy and one-dimensional definitions of communicative competence.

I would argue that the dichotomy between NESTs and NNESTs teachers is virtually irrelevant. The majority of English teachers in the world today are, in fact, NNES (Liu 1999). Furthermore, up to 80 per cent of all communication that occurs in English takes place between non-native-speakers (Prodromou 1997). The intuitive knowledge and supposedly 'native-like' pronunciation that NESTs are purported to possess are growing less and less valuable as World Englishes and nativised varieties of English continue to diverge from native norms. Graddol (2006: 114) has even suggested that NESTs 'may be seen as presenting an obstacle to the free development of global English'. Furthermore, every language user is a native speaker of a given language, in which case, there is no such thing as a non-native-speaking language teacher (English or otherwise). Thus, enlightened ELT professionals should seek to empower NNESTs through teacher development that focuses on language proficiency, content and cultural knowledge, a redefinition of the concept of research, and skills development.

Finally, our field's view of communicative competence should be one that is more appropriate for a global world, one in which neither grammatical accuracy nor pragmatic competence can guarantee social acceptability (Kramsch 2007). Instead, the challenges posed by globalisation, such as diverse speech communities, unpredictability, and a global 'communication culture', will require English language users to exhibit a high level of contextual awareness and the ability to adapt language use (Kramsch 2007). Thus, new pedagogical models of competence should help learners to cultivate culture-sensitive knowledge, mindful reflexivity and social identity negotiation skills. At the same time, the expansion of communicative competence will require greater instructional competence as ELT practitioners develop cognizance of students' insight into their own competencies, empathy toward learners' experiences and mindfulness of cross-cultural differences.

Six abilities of a competent English teacher in the future

Globalisation, migration and advances in technology and transportation continue to impact the field of ELT in myriad ways. Simultaneously, shifting learner demographics and a global context for learning and language use are redefining the role of English, triggering the emergence of nativised varieties of English, and sparking a shift from traditional to more communicative orientations. At the same time, there is the continuing potential for our field to achieve greater tolerance of pronunciation and language varieties, regard English learners as users, and broaden attitudes toward celebration of communication rather than penalising lack of accuracy. Moreover, it is nearly impossible to overestimate the role that computer technology will play in the future of ELT. Practitioners, administrators and researchers alike should also prepare for new modes of learning that will extend beyond the classroom.

As a result of such changes, ELT professionals should be prepared to acquire new knowledge, innovative pedagogical approaches, enlightened research perspectives and a fuller, more informed awareness of the very learners whose needs we profess to serve. In light of the need to innovate and evolve, I would like to propose the following six abilities that I believe will characterise competent and successful ELT professionals in the future. These include the following:

1 Make constant and effective changes
2 Learn and speak at least one other language
3 Teach less to maximise learning
4 Teach English in at least one subject area
5 Familiarise oneself with new learning and teaching modes
6 Ensure learning outside the classroom.

1. Make constant and effective changes

According to Fullan (1982b: 47), 'Trying new practices sometimes leads to questioning one's underlying beliefs', while 'examining one's beliefs can lead to attempting new behavior' (as cited in Markee 1997: 54). It is clear that innovation will drive the success of any enterprise in the 21st century. Because the qualities and skills that define a successful language professional today may be entirely different by 2020, ELT professionals should strive to cultivate adaptability and reflectiveness at the same time that they resist relying on practices or assumptions merely because they were acceptable in the past. Due to the themes and trends discussed above, English teachers will undoubtedly be challenged to adapt to their changing environment in unique ways. Such evolution may result in entirely new ways of defining one's own occupation, as Table 1 suggests.

Today	Tomorrow
EFL teacher....	ELF teacher
ESL teacher....	EIL teacher
ESP teacher....	EGL teacher
EAP teacher....	WE teacher

Table 1: English teachers today and tomorrow

2. Learn and speak at least one other language

It is easy to forget—or to fail to understand entirely—the complex and dynamic nature of learning to speak and understand a language other than the one a person grew up speaking. Learning to speak another language can provide ELT professionals with the opportunity to reflect on this experience of learning and, at the same time, cultivate greater empathy for their students. Experiencing the all-to-frequent anxieties and frustrations of language learning can also give instructors a more nuanced perspective on issues such as target-like objectives, intelligibility and acceptability.

3. Teach less to maximize learning

ELT professionals should tend toward more nondirective approaches in their English language classrooms, as students are far more likely to find learner-centred teaching intrinsically motivating than teacher-centered approaches (Brown 2007). This phenomenon of learning has been understood in our field for many years; however, only recently has technology and its resultant digital modes of learning truly made it possible for language learners (especially digital natives) to initiate their own learning process in such new and innovative ways.

4. Teach English in at least one subject area

As CBI gains traction worldwide, due in part to more integrative perspectives on the role of English in the classroom, ELT professionals are coming to realise that they are no longer 'just' language teachers. Increasingly, language instructors who are knowledgeable in at least one subject will be more competitive on the global job market. At the same time, ELT professionals should acknowledge the degree to which content teachers may need their support and guidance. Such support may take the form of language education, knowledge about language, language awareness and consideration of aspects of language learning that extend beyond the purely linguistic (e.g. cultural competence, pragmatic knowledge, etc.).

5. Familiarise yourself with new learning and teaching modes

How many ELT instructors today feel technologically prepared to work with digital natives? The question itself may provoke anxiety among 'digital settlers' (somewhat older digital users who grew up in an analogue world but who have learned to use new technologies in fairly sophisticated ways) and 'digital immigrants' (who have only learned to use email and very limited social technologies late in life) (Palfrey and Gasser 2010). Regardless, all ELT professionals have a responsibility to reimagine new ways of learning and teaching English made possible by digital technology, even in classrooms where 'technology' may be mean little more than a point-and-shoot digital camera or a single cell phone. Other language pedagogy forays into digital technology may include the following:

- handheld learning;
- e-learning;
- classroom technology;
- digital textbooks;
- digital English—extensive exposure to English input;
- net-based teaching; and
- digital teaching resources.

6. Ensure learning outside the classroom

As a result of the digital revolution, Collins and Halverson (2009) predict a break in educators' and policymakers' tendency to associate *learning* with *schooling*. They foresee a broadening of the ways in which we conceive of learning, suggesting that 'hybrid experiences' will originate in the classroom but quickly migrate into other contexts. Contexts beyond the classroom include the external world—either learners' personal world and/or the English speaking world—and experiences made possible by technology, such as online learning, self-paced learning, one-to-one learning, handheld learning, mobile learning, collaborative learning, time-shifted learning, synchronous/asynchronous learning and blended learning.

Conclusion

The future is here. Globalisation, migration, greater accessibility to technological breakthroughs and an increasing global population all suggest that ELT professionals cannot afford to hesitate any longer in preparing for the latter portion of the 21st century. As the global changes influence language use and ELT in nuanced and complex ways, the essence of a successful ELT professional will be adaptability, innovation, and a willingness to learn, each of which is reflected in the six abilities proposed above. In an ever-changing and increasingly connected world, the six abilities discussed above will characterise successful ELT practitioners *today*, as well as in the future.

junliu@gsu.edu

References

Brown, H. D. 2007. *Teaching by Principles: An Interactive Approach to Language Pedagogy.* White Plains, N.Y.: Pearson Education, Inc.

Canton, J. 2007. *The Extreme Future: The Top Trends that will Reshape the World in the Next 20 Years.* New York: Plume.

CLN—The Collaborative Leadership Network—Old vs. New Forms of Leadership. (Retrieved from http://www.leadershipskillsandvalues.com/clnontheweb-curriculum/old-vs-new-leadership)

Collins, A. and R. Halverson. 2009. *Rethinking Education in the Age of Technology: The Digital Revolution and Schooling in America.* New York: Teachers College Press.

Conrad, S. 2000. 'Will corpus linguistics revolutionize grammar teaching in the 21st century?'. *TESOL Quarterly* 34/3: 548–60.

Cook, V. 2002. 'Background to the L2 user' in V. Cook (ed.). *Portraits of the L2 User.* Clevedon, England: Multilingual Matters.

CSIS—Center for Strategic and International Studies. *The Seven Revolutions.* (Retrieved from http://csis.org/program/seven-revolutions)

Deller, S. and C. Price. 2007. *Teaching Other Subjects through English.* Oxford: Oxford University Press.

Finlev, T. 2009. '10 Workplace skills of the future'. *The IFTF Blog.* May. (Retrieved on 15 July 2013 from http://www.iftf.org/future-now/article-detail/10-workplace-skills-of-the-future-the-skills-workers-should-strive-to-have-and-the-skills-employers/)

Fitzpatrick, A and R. O'Dowd. 2012. *English at Work: An Analysis of Case Reports about English Language Training for the 21-Century Workforce.* The International Research Foundation for English Language Education (TIRF). (Retrieved from http://www.tirfonline.org/wpcontent/uploads/2012/04/TIRF_EnglishAtWork_OnePageSpread_2012.pdf)

Glaser, B. G. 1978. *Theoretical Sensitivity: Advances in the Methodology of Grounded Theory* (Volume 2). Mill Valley, Calif.: Sociology Press.

Glaser, B. G. and A. L. Strauss. 1967. *The Discovery of Grounded Theory: Strategies for Qualitative Research*. London: Wiedenfeld and Nicholson.

Goulding, C. 2009. 'Grounded theory perspectives in organizational research' in D. A. Buchanan and A. Bryman (eds.). *The SAGE Handbook of Organizational Research Methods*. London: SAGE Publications Ltd.

Graddol, D. 2006. *English Next* (Volime 62). London: British Council.

Griswold, O. 2010. 'Narrating America: socializing adult ESL learners into idealized views of the United States during citizenship preparation classes'. *TESOL Quarterly* 44/3: 488–516.

Kaufman, D. and J. Crandall. (eds.). 2005. *Content-Based Instruction in Primary and Secondary School Settings*. Alexandria, Va.: Teachers of English to Speakers of Other Languages, Inc.

KnowledgeWorks Foundation. 2008. *2020 Forecast: Creating the Future of Learning*. (Retrieved on 15 July 2013 from http://www.knowledgeworks.org/sites/default/files/2020-Forecast.pdf)

Kramsch, C. 2007. 'The uses of communicative competence in a global world' in J. Liu (ed.), *English Language Teaching in China: New Approaches, Perspectives, and Standards*. London: Continuum International Publishing Group.

Liu, J. 2007. 'Epilogue: Beyond communicative competence: A pedagogical perspective' in J. Liu (ed.). *English Language Teaching in China: New Approaches, Perspectives, and Standards*. London: Continuum International Publishing Group.

Liu, J. 1999. 'Nonnative-English-speaking professionals in TESOL'. *TESOL Quarterly* 33/1: 85-102.

Markee, N. 1997. *Managing Curricular Innovation*. Cambridge: Cambridge University Press.

McLean, A. C. 2012. 'Destroying the teacher: The need for learner-centered teaching'. *English teaching forum: 50 years exchanging ideas and experiences* 50/1: 32–5. (Reprinted from 1980. *English Teaching Forum* 18/30: 6–19.)

Nunan, D. 2011. *Teaching English to Young Learners*. Anaheim, Calif.: Anaheim University Press.

Palfrey, J. and U. Gasser. 2010. *Born Digital: Understanding the First Generation of Digital Natives*. New York: Basic Books.

Paltridge, B. 2009. 'Afterword: Where have we come from and where are we now?' in D. Belcher (ed.). *English for Specific Purposes in Theory and Practice*. Ann Arbor: University of Michigan Press.

Prodromou, L. 1997. 'Global English and its struggle against the octopus'. *IATEFL Newsletter* 137: 18–22.

Index of authors

Index of topics